DUNCAN PARK

EDWIN C. EPPS

Duncan Park

STORIES OF A CLASSIC AMERICAN BALLPARK

HUB CITY PRESS • 2023

Cover design: Meg Reid
Interior design: Bonnie Campbell
Copy editor: Melissa Walker
Proofreader: Laura Corbin

Printed in the United States of America

FRONTIS: *"The Duncan Park stadium grandstand today after restoration and renovation by Spartanburg County School District Seven"* (John Barron)

PHOTO CREDITS:
Austin Baker Photography
  From the collection of Marie Duncan: *p. 8*
  From the collection of Luther Norman: *p. 31, 32, 33, 36, 37*
  From the collection of Susan Wood Pope: *p. 56, 104, 105, 106, 107*
Gerry Pate: *p. 100, 101, 109* (from the collection of John Barron)
Spartanburg County Public Library: *p. 34* (from the collection of Luther Norman)

Hub City Press gratefully acknowledges support from the National Endowment for the Arts, the Amazon Literary Partnership, the Chapman Cultural Center and the South Carolina Arts Commission.

Manufactured in the United States of America
First Edition

HUB CITY PRESS
200 Ezell Street
Spartanburg, SC 29306
864.577.9349 | www.hubcity.org

For Carol, Cat, and William, who love baseball
and whose biggest fan I am.

DONORS

The Hub City Writers Project thanks our friends who made contributions in support of this book and other Hub City programs.

Susan Bridges
Bea Bruce
John and Kirsten Cribb
ExxonMobil Foundation
Katherine and Charles Frazier
Susu and George Dean Johnson
Sara and Paul H. Lehner
Deborah F. McAbee
  and J. Byron Morris
Maggie Miller
Stephen Milliken
Weston Milliken
Milliken & Co. Charitable
  Foundation
Carlin and Sander Morrison
Alane and Rex Russell
Stone Family Foundation
Betsy Teter and John Lane

C. Mack and Patty Amick
Marjorie and Kofi Appiah
Lisa and Greg Atkins
Paula and Stan Baker
Bill and Valerie Barnet
Christi and Charles Bebko
Lynne and Mark Blackman
Julia Burnett
Judy and Brant Bynum
Sister Simone Campbell
Camilla and Jeff Cantrell
Kathleen M. Cates
Beth Cecil and Isabel Forbes
Mary Ann Claud and
  Olin Sansbury
Victoria T. Colebank
Stephen Colyer
Michele and Halsey Cook
Bernadette Davis
Megan DeMoss
Magruder H. Dent
Gail Ebert
Coleman Edmunds
Edwin and Carol Epps
Abby Fowler

Elaine and Barney Gosnell
Susan Hamilton
Elisabeth E. Hayes
Laura Beeson Henthorn
Nancy Kenney
Dorothy Josey
Cathryn Judice
Stacy and John McBride
Nan and Thomas McDaniel
Harriet McDougal
Marguerite McGee
Karen and Bob Mitchell
Brelan Montgomery
Hannah Palmer
Dwight Patterson
Ron and Ann Rash
Julian and Beverly Reed
The Rose Montgomery Johnston
 Family Foundation
Kim Rostan and Matt Johnston
Pamela Smith
Diane Smock and Brad Wyche
Chris Smutzer
Betty Snow
Sally and Warwick Spencer
Melissa Walker and Chuck Reback
Susan Webb
William and Teresa Webster
Alanna and Don Wildman
Ana Maria and Dennis Wiseman

Betsy Adams
Heather and Winthrop Allen
Vic and Lynn Bailey
Susan Baker
Georgianna and Harold L. Ballenger
Joan and Tom Barnet
Cyndi and David Beacham
Elizabeth D. Bernardin
Mary Nell and George Brandt
Katherine K. and William W. Burns
Lynne and Bill Burton
Lori and Fritz Butehorn
Jan and Toni Caldwell
Kathy and Marvin Cann
Renee and Jay Cariveau
Sally and Randall Chambers
DB Childress
Janeen and Robert Cochran
Sally and Jerry Cogan
Molly and Gregory Colbath
Douglas Congdon
Sue and Rick Conner
Haidee B. and Gardner Courson
Betsy Cox
Chris and Garrow Crowley
Mary Crowley
Martha Cruz
Rachel and Kenneth Deems
Susan and Rick Dent
Jean Dunbar
Susan Dunlap
Alice Eberhardt
Anne Elliott
Angelina Eschauzier
Lynn Ezell

Manning Fairey

James Farmer

Betsy Fleming

Delie Fort

Carroll Foster

Julia Franks

Williams Gee

GM Industrial Inc

Andrew Green

Susan Griswold and John Morton

Marianna and Roger Habisreutinger

Jo Hackl

Mary Halphen

Anita and Al Hammerbeck

Greg Hancock

Tracy and Tom Hannah

Carolyn C. Harbison

Frances Hardy

Darryl Harmon

Lou Ann and John Harrill

Michele and Peyton Harvey

Nancy Hearon

James Hendrick

Patricia Hevener

Ed Hicks

Erin and Yogi Hiremath

Charlie Hodge

Marilyn and Doug Hubbell

Eliza and Max Hyde

Silke and Nick Jager

Geordy and Carter Johnson

Melissa and Steve Johnson

Ann Mullins and Stewart Johnson

Wallace Johnson

Betsy and Charlie Jones

Vivian and Daniel Kahrs

Lynn and James Karegeannes

Jeanette Keepers

Ruth and Bert Knight

Beverly Knight

Sharon and Mark Koenig

Lily Kohler

Barbara Latham

Kay and Jack Lawrence

Janice and Wood Lay

Ruth and Joe Lesesne

Frances and George Loudon

Elizabeth Lowndes

Julie and Brownlee Lowry

Suzan Mabry

Gayle Magruder

Nancy Mandlove

Judy McCravy

Diana D. McGraw

Larry E. Milan

Mary and Don Miles

Deborah Minot

Laura and Scott Montgomery

Lynda and Bert Moore

Paula Morgan

Lawrence Moser

Susan Myers

Pamela Nienhuis

Liz Newall

Margaret and George Nixon

Susan and Walter Novak

Nancy Pemberton

Janice Piazza

Mary and Andrew Poliakoff

Jan and Sara Lynn Postma

Mary Frances Price

Norman and Jo Pulliam

Eileen Rampey

John Ratterree

Elizabeth Refshauge

Meg Reid

Hub City Writers Project is a literary nonprofit organization located in Spartanburg, South Carolina. Comprised of an acclaimed book publisher, an independent bookshop, and a literary programmer focused on education and outreach, our mission is cultivating readers and nurturing writers in both the Spartanburg community and throughout the South to foster an inclusive literary arts culture.

Tax-deductible donations support: the publication of extraordinary new and unsung writers from the American South; book prizes that support early career writers; workshops, scholarships and conferences aimed at fostering literary community in Upstate South Carolina and beyond; residencies and internships that support creative writers from across the nation, as well as local students, enabling them to learn about the business of publishing without requiring the traditional outlay of their own resources; access initiatives such as Growing Great Readers, Books at the Bus Stop and Books as Mirrors.

CONTENTS

· ·

Introduction: A Fan Is Born *1*

1. Pregame: Why Duncan Park? *7*

2. "Play Ball!" The Spartans Step Up to the Plate *13*

3. The Spartanburg Sluggers: Black Semipro Baseball in the Hub City During the Jim Crow Era *25*

4. A Peach of a Team *51*

5. Heart of the Lineup: Thirty Years of the Phillies *65*

6. Love of Country and Baseball: American Legion Post 28 *99*

7. Seventh Inning Stretch: Gotta Keep 'Em Coming *115*

8. Later Innings: Newcomers and a Revolving Carousel of Players *126*

9. The Sun Rises on a Whole New Ballgame *137*

   Appendix I: Spartanburg Sluggers Games, 1911-1961 *153*

   Appendix II: The Spartanburg Peaches Residency *184*

   Appendix III: Spartanburg Peaches Who Made The Show *185*

   Appendix IV: A Timeline of the Spartanburg Phillies, 1963-1994 *188*

   Appendix V: Ninety Years of American Legion Baseball *197*

   Appendix VI: Recipients of the American Legion Post 28 Brian Peahuff Scholarship *203*

   Appendix VII: Teams at Duncan Park stadium, 1995-2021 *205*

   Acknowledgments *207*

   Notes *213*

   Bibliography *225*

MAY • 59

The author in his Civitans uniform

INTRODUCTION

- -

A Fan Is Born

I FIRST BECAME A baseball fan when I was growing up in Columbia, South Carolina, in the 1950s. In those days baseball was still "the national pastime," a claim that today is hard to defend. In the early twenty-first century there is too much competition. The National Football League plays on television now, not just all day Sunday and Sunday night but on Monday and Thursday nights as well. Football bills itself as "America's Game" these days, and we export "our" game to England as well, subjecting the British to annual contests in Wembley Stadium and elsewhere featuring two NFL teams for fans of rugby, cricket, and the real football to puzzle over while they munch their crisps and fish and chips and swill their pints of bitter. Every home this century has monster screen televisions offering dozens of channels of all kinds of so-called entertainment, and if we are absent our home screens we have laptops and tablets and even telephones that offer up endless movies, game shows, and reality series to substitute for the actual realities in our deficient lives. VRBO and AirBnB offer alternative escapes, and rare is even the modest sized community without a skate park, roller rink, climbing wall, and sixteen-screen movie megaplex. These days one rarely thinks of actually attending a ballgame given the wealth of other experiences available to us from the cradle to the grave. One has to work hard to be a baseball fan today.

In the 1950s, however, baseball was king. I stopped at Powell's Grocery on the corner across the street from Schneider School in Columbia every Monday afternoon to spend my allowance on jawbreakers and Mary Janes and, mostly, baseball cards—not the team sets and individual specialized cards with fragments of "game used" balls and uniform jerseys that Topps and Upper Deck and Donruss market so energetically today, but individual gum packs containing five cards of mostly second and third tier players with occasionally a Whitey Ford or Elston Howard emerging from the dross. Yes, the Yankees were my team back then. I never saw them play of course. We could never have afforded a trip to New York City, and there was no Major League team anywhere in the South until the former Milwaukee Braves, late of Boston, moved to Atlanta when I was a college freshman. And my father, a salesman who peddled Jell-O gelatin, Swans Down cake mixes, Log Cabin syrup, and Post cereals to grocery store managers across the Palmetto State, never had enough vacation time for us to travel to Florida for spring training games.

Spartanburg native, teacher, and songwriter Randy Foster had a similar childhood relationship with America's Pastime. He, too, collected baseball cards, and by the time he was nearing the end of his youth he had amassed a Hefty garbage bag full of cards. He knew this was the amount because that's what he filled up when his mother told him he finally had to get rid of his collection. Ever a resourceful soul, Foster plunged a hand into the pile before the top was sealed and withdrew a single fistful of about forty cards. Recently, when he researched the value online, he discovered that those forty salvaged cards had a current retail value of about $700.00. *Sic transit gloria mundi.*

Baseball was definitely king in the 1950s, and I loved the ABC Game of the Week on television, begun in 1953 and watched on seventy-five percent of home TV sets that year. By 1960, when I was twelve, Pee Wee Reese had joined Dizzy Dean in the ABC broadcast booth, and I watched as many games as I could, singing along with Dizzy whenever he launched into his inimitable version of "The Wabash Cannonball." I loved the Yankees better than all other teams. I loved the legacy of Babe Ruth, Joe DiMaggio, and Lou Gehrig. I loved the sports cathedral that was Yankee Stadium. I loved Mickey Mantle and Roger Maris and their pursuit of the Babe's all-time single-season home run record in 1961. I loved that Sumter, South Carolina's own Bobby Richardson played second base for the Yankees. And I loved the Yankees' names: Moose Skowron, Tony Kubek, Joe Pepitone, Yogi Berra, Cletis Boyer, and Tom Tresh could *only* have *ever* played together as New York Yankees, and God, I loved those guys.

So did my pal Edward Caughman. As youngsters Edward and I knew individual position players' batting averages and pitchers' win/loss records, and like most little boys at the time if we weren't shooting marbles in the dirt in the backyard we traded baseball cards. We also spent lots of afternoons playing mechanical baseball games. Was it the old Parker Brothers Game of

Peg Baseball or the Gotham Push Button Baseball? I honestly don't remember, but those were the days, and baseball was my game. I played "Columbia Little Boys Baseball" on the Civitans team in Columbia, where I was a poor hitting outfielder and where I remember the itchy wool uniforms during the Midlands summer heat and an end-of-season banquet that featured ex-MLB players Albie Pearson, Billy O'Dell, and James "Ripper" Collins as our honored guests. I wasn't much good as a baseball player, but I was a first-rate fan. In Spartanburg at about the same time Randy Foster was also less than an All-Star, but he too loved the game and remembers now how he used to walk down to the Duncan Park stadium infield after his youth league games were over and stand at the home plate while belting one ball after another over the outfield walls—Randy *was* coordinated and had a good sense of timing as a kid—in a one-person home run derby.

Twenty-five years later when my wife, Carol, and I moved to Spartanburg, South Carolina, from Staunton, Virginia, I was still a fan, and one of the joys of our relocation was my discovery that not only was Spartanburg home to a Class A affiliate of the Philadelphia Phillies but also that the local Phillies played in a vintage wooden-grandstand stadium built in 1926. The sign at the entrance to the public park where the stadium was located proclaimed "Beautiful Duncan Park," and I was sure at first sight that this name embodied the stadium as much as if not more than the park itself.

We started going to games at Duncan Park soon after our move, and we spent many happy hours drinking cheap beer, eating cheap ballpark hot dogs, and listening to the dulcet tones of announcer Ed Dickerson as he signaled the approach of Wally Hernandez or Ryne Sandberg or Scott Rolen to the plate. The Phillies' glory days were already more than a dozen years behind them, but there were still nights when the fans' cars almost filled the lower parking lot, and painted signs advertising local businesses covered most of the leaning concrete outfield wall that even then looked like it might one evening collapse upon an unlucky right or center fielder. We went to occasional American Legion games, too, especially after our children were born, and later, after the Phillies had departed for the greener pastures of Kannapolis, North Carolina, we watched the Crickets and the Stingers of the Coastal Plain League, and Spartanburg High School teams.

Early on we began to learn bits and pieces of Duncan Park history. In 1927 the whole city of Spartanburg had shut down to go to Duncan Park to celebrate the arrival of Charles Lindbergh, who had just recently completed his epic flight across the Atlantic Ocean. Spartanburg American Legion Post 28 had won the 1936 American Legion World Series at Duncan Park. The New York Yankees had played an exhibition game at Duncan Park in 1937 on their way back to the Big Apple from Spring training in Florida. Cleveland Indians fan favorite Rocky Colavito had played outfield for the 1952 Spartanburg Peaches and had roomed in the basement of a modest cottage nearby. In the 1960s future Orlando Magic vice president and legendary motivational author and speaker Pat Williams had gotten his start in sports management when he was offered the general manager's job in Spartanburg by a neighbor in Philadelphia who was a family friend. During his tenure in Sparkle City Williams was named Minor League Executive of the Year, and the Spartanburg Phillies set attendance records. Phillies and St. Louis Cardinals Hall of Fame third baseman Scott Rolen played a year in Spartanburg, and future Atlanta Braves stars such as Tom Glavine, Dale Murphy, Ryan Klesko, and Mark Lemke played games in Spartanburg on their journeys to the Show with teams in Greenville or Greenwood or Macon.

And then it almost came to an end. Facing the same declining fan attendance experienced by many Minor League teams in old ballparks in the 1990s, the Phillies left Spartanburg in 1994. For a while fans in the city hoped—some even believed—that Duncan Park would be able to attract another Minor League franchise, but as time went on it became clear that the old stadium would never be able to compete with the broad concourses, updated food concessions, expanded fan experiences, and nifty architecture featured in more modern stadiums like Greenville's Fluor Field, where the Red Sox affiliate the Greenville Drive played, and Columbia's Spirit Communications Park, where Heisman Trophy winner Tim Tebow played for the Mets affiliate the Columbia Fireflies in 2017. College wooden bat league teams the Crickets and the Stingers did play at Duncan Park, but attendance was disappointing and the future seemed dim when the old stadium could only attract teams whose players had to be housed with volunteering local families.

In 2005 The Friends of Duncan Park was founded in hopes of helping to promote, maintain, preserve, and restore Duncan Park stadium, but in spite of some promising publicity and leadership consisting of Wofford College's Associate Athletic Director Lenny Mathis, local attorney Terry Haselden, and others, little came of the effort to bring another Minor League team to the area. The local American Legion Post, whose headquarters is at Duncan Park and which has sponsored a Legion baseball team at the stadium for ninety years, is an enthusiastic promoter of the ballpark, but its funds are limited and spread thin across many Legion projects. The City of Spartanburg has sponsored events, including summer music concerts and holiday celebrations, at the park off and on over the years, but a succession of mayors and city councils have been unwilling to provide the funds necessary to fully upgrade, restore, and expand the facility without a guarantee that events at the ballpark would be able to fund it. Recently a partnership between the City and Spartanburg County School District Seven has stabilized the condition of the physical plant and the field and gives some hope for the future, but there are no long-term guarantees.

In the end, it seemed to me that there was a need for a history of Duncan Park stadium to preserve some of the details of that history before they were lost forever. To be sure, team and player statistics can be found at the websites of SABR, seamheads.com, and baseball-reference.com, and there are occasional stories in the local newspaper, *The Herald-Journal,* but many of the old players whose cleats bit the red dirt of the infield are now gone, and more memorabilia from the glory days of the stadium disappears every year. Who knows anymore that there was once a semipro Black team called the Sluggers who played at Duncan Park? Who today remembers the antics of Max Patkin, the Clown Prince of Baseball, who appeared a number of times at Duncan Park? Who today saw Eddie Feigner, "The King," and his *three* teammates (his "Court"), who took on all nine-member softball teams that dared challenge them during epic battles at Duncan Park? Who today remembers the smell of gasoline and smoke from the time when the grass in the ballpark was burnt before being re-seeded at the beginning of a new season? Not many people, for sure, but these are essential chapters in the history of the stadium. I have been digging up that history, poking around, and interviewing former players, batboys, managers, scorekeepers, fans, and others for some thirty years now and am getting long in the tooth myself. It's time to share the story before even I lose it.

The Duncan Park stadium grandstand today after restoration and renovation by Spartanburg County School District Seven

CHAPTER ONE

Pregame: Why Duncan Park?

THE REASON WHY the public park on the south side of Union Street is named *Duncan* Park has to do with history, entrepreneurship, and philanthropy. The city of Spartanburg has a long and important tradition of philanthropy to which some of its most successful private citizens have contributed generously to enrich the lives of its residents. The generosity of Jimmy Gibbs, for example, George Dean Johnson, Jerry Richardson, and local families the Millikens, Chapmans, Montgomerys, Barnets, and others has transformed the city of Spartanburg in many ways. The list could be expanded to a length exceptional for such a modest-sized Southern town as Spartanburg, and it would be difficult to prioritize the contributions of the various donors because so many have had such important impacts.

THE MAJOR. Among the precursors of Spartanburg's contemporary philanthropists is an earlier civic leader whose history is closely connected to that of both the city of Spartanburg and Duncan Park: Major David R. Duncan. Major Duncan's success story, like that of many of his entrepreneurial colleagues, owes much to railroads and the coming of the textile industry to Piedmont South Carolina in the late nineteenth and early twentieth centuries.

The Major's father, born in rugged County Donegal in northwestern Ireland, graduated from Glasgow University early in the nineteenth century—he was a student in the "Junior Mathematical Class" in April 1809—came to America in 1817, and served as principal of Norfolk Academy, a "flourishing classical

Major David Duncan's father, Professor of Ancient Languages at Wofford College

school" in Virginia then and a prosperous school even today, from 1817 until 1835, when he became Professor of Ancient Languages at Randolph-Macon College. While his father was at Randolph-Macon, David Duncan was born on September 27, 1836. He attended Randolph-Macon himself, graduating in 1854 and moving to Spartanburg in 1855, where he became the first teacher hired by Odd Fellows' High School. Apparently the academic life was not for young David Duncan, though, so he studied law and was admitted to the bar in 1857, practicing until the outbreak of the Civil War in 1861.

By then David's father had become Professor of Ancient Languages at Wofford College in Spartanburg, where he served from 1854 until 1881, and the younger Duncan was commissioned as 1st lieutenant of the Forest Guard, Company C, Thirteenth South Carolina Volunteers, a contingent of Stonewall Jackson's Corps. As did many young officers because of the appalling number of casualties during the Civil War, Lieutenant Duncan received a succession of battlefield commissions and advanced to the rank of major by 1864. He saw substantial action in some of the bloodiest battles of the war, including Cold Harbor, the Wilderness, and Petersburg. At the conclusion of the war, Duncan returned to Spartanburg and established a successful law practice.

Duncan was popular and respected by his fellow citizens, who elected him to the South Carolina General Assembly in 1865 and 1870 and to the State

Senate in 1872. In 1880 he was elected solicitor of the 7th Judicial Circuit and was re-elected to this position in 1884. Meanwhile he was expanding his business interests as well, in 1875 becoming president of the Spartanburg and Asheville Railroad Company, the first railroad across the Blue Ridge. He was also assistant division counselor to the Richmond and Danville Railroad, and by the time of his death he had become a director of Spartan Mills, one of the preeminent textile companies in the region, and of the Iron District Fire Insurance Company. He died on January 28, 1902.

THE HEIRS' GIFT. It is with the death of Major Duncan that the story of the park which bears his name really begins. The Major had married Virginia Nelson of Mecklenburg County, Virginia, on July 9, 1856. Virginia and the Major had four children—Mary Elizabeth Duncan Garlington, Martha Nelson Duncan Wannamaker, William Nelson Duncan, and Carrie Virginia Duncan—who inherited the family property, which included 300 acres of land next to "Union Road" and a large manor house, now known as "The Duncan Estate," constructed in the 1890s. In the fall of 1922 these heirs wrote a letter to the City of Spartanburg, announcing their intention to donate most of the family property except that on which the house was located to the city to be developed as "the culmination of the desire of David Robinson Duncan." A contingency of the gift was that the property "would be developed for park purposes" with the stipulation that athletic, recreational, and other equipment "of worldly nature, more or less, could not be used on Sunday."

The city proceeded cautiously. Although it decided to accept the donation of around 100 acres on February 6, 1923, that action was complicated by the passing of a bill to abolish the City Park Commission, which awaited the governor's signature. This particular bill and opposition to it apparently reflected political differences within the city. The county delegation supported the repeal of the 1920 creation of the Park Commission, which was not accountable to city government although its members were appointed by City Council. A 1921 amendment to the bill creating the commission had expanded its powers, and the commission subsequently had authorized widening both Church and Union streets, a policy which would cost the city some $2,000,000 according to Senator William Simpson Rogers. Members of the Park Commission and the secretary of the Spartanburg Chamber of Commerce opposed the abolition of the commission and appealed to the governor to veto the legislation, but Governor Thomas McLeod, citing substantial "division among the people," refused and signed the bill on February 15, 1923.

Responsibility for the City of Spartanburg's parks therefore returned to City Council, but the County Delegation's refusal to grant a request for a 5.33 mill

The Duncan Estate, a popular event location today, just off south Union Street not far from Duncan Park stadium; this home was built by one of Major Duncan's daughters and her husband.

increase in local property taxes, one mill of which was to be dedicated to the development of parks, meant that the city could *not* develop the new Duncan Park right away; the city then returned the deed to the Duncan heirs. This decision proved unpopular, of course, the *Spartanburg Herald* even declaring it "something of an emergency." Urgent conversations must have ensued among members of the County Delegation and City Council, likely also within the local business and civic communities, because although the papers again reported on March eleventh that the one mill tax increase for parks had been denied, ten days later the *The Spartanburg Journal and Carolina Spartan* reported that the city had accepted the park property and "development of this property south of the city will be undertaken as soon as funds are available." The same day City Council officially accepted the gift of the Duncan heirs, and the deal was sealed when the City water works department agreed to lay the pipes necessary for work to proceed.

The legislative and budgetary obstacles were overcome presumably because of the size and attractiveness of the property, which included a natural amphitheater (remnants of which can still be found in tangled undergrowth not far from the entrance to Duncan Park today) and numerous brooks "that could be developed probably into a series of small pools and natural waterfalls or cascades." City planner Dr. John Nolen was assigned the task of developing landscaping plans, and the project was underway.

Title to the property was conveyed by the heirs to the city for the nominal price of one dollar in a deed dated February 28, 1923. Among the provisions were requirements that the property was "to be used and developed by the said City for Park purposes;" that the park "shall be officially and permanently named and called 'DUNCAN PARK' in memory of the father of the Grantors, the late David R. Duncan;" that the city provide sewerage, water, and public roads; and that "the Sabbath Day shall be respected within the Park in keeping with the Christian spirit of the age." In keeping with another "spirit of the age," there was also a provision that on the slightly elevated area known as University Hill there could be constructed "public buildings and school buildings *for White people, only,*" [emphasis added].

The deed transfer specified that "the development of the donated area for park purposes" should commence "without unnecessary delay," but it was three years before construction on the stadium began. Design was by the local firm of Collins & Simpson Architects, but the plans and architectural drawings for the stadium do not survive. J. Frank Collins instructed his family to destroy his drawings upon his death, and they obeyed his wishes. Apparently there are also no Sanborn fire insurance maps, a common and invaluable source of the architectural history and development of a community, showing the location of the stadium, its materials, and the original dimensions. A search of existing maps turned up no images of the ballpark, and even an examination of the online records of the Library of Congress archives was unsuccessful.

Work toward the stadium began slowly. Roadways within the park donation were completed within a year, but it was not until December of 1925 that City Council voted to build the ballpark. Sealed bids for the removal of 7,000 cubic yards of dirt in preparation for the athletic fields at Duncan Park were received in early January 1926, and the contract for the $38,000, 2,500-seat stadium itself was awarded to C. M. Guest and Son of Anderson later in the month, with work to begin as soon as the site preparation was completed. A stadium envisioned to be "one of the best in the southeast" was promised, and in January the stadium already had been leased to the Spartans, a semipro team in the South Atlantic League, for four years. The outfield fence was financed by Spartanburg advertising companies who would pay for it by selling advertising to local patrons and "keep it up for five years." The *Spartanburg Herald* writer reporting on the construction of the stadium and its lease to the

PLAYERS WHO GAVE SPARTANBURG FIRST CHAMPIONSHIP IN SOUTH ATLANTIC LEAGUE

The 1925 Spartanburg Spartans, Champions of the South Atlantic League and future tenants of Duncan Park stadium

Spartans announced that it would meet "a long-felt need" and go a long way towards developing future interest in the park. In a concurrent development, sealed bids were also solicited for a bandstand at the park.

CHAPTER TWO

. . . .

"Play Ball!" The Spartans Step Up to the Plate

THE STADIUM IS BUILT. As optimistic as the City of Spartanburg had been when it let the contract for construction of Duncan Park stadium—ultimately for a bid of $30,946 from C. M. Guest and Son of Anderson, South Carolina—in January 1926, by the end of the month it already looked like rain and cold weather would prevent the stadium from being completed before the opening of the Spartans' season in the spring. No less an authority than architect Frank Collins opined that if the city were to receive its usual rainfall in the first two weeks of February, the opening would have to be delayed.

The city hoped Collins was wrong and eagerly anticipated the start of the season. The citizens of Spartanburg hoped the stadium lived up to its hype. The grandstand "covering," that is, its roof, was to be finished first in order to protect the ground underneath for the laying of the concrete foundation. There would be only one row of iron supports likely to obstruct fans' views of the field "in any way," apparently a real accomplishment for a stadium built in 1926. There were to be 475 reserved seats "with out-door opera chairs" and "comfortable benches with backs and plenty of knee room" in the rest of the grandstand. An eight-foot-wide walkway would serve as a concourse at the rear.

The city purchased seats for the stadium in February 1926. Council ordered 350 "wooden chairs" at $1.42 each for the reserved seats, 460 "seats" for the bleachers at $2.60 each, and additional seating in concrete tiers for a total grandstand seating capacity of 2,500. In the end, though, not only was the stadium *not* ready for occupancy by the city's Spartans by the time their season opened in April, but it was not *finally* ready for play until the eighth of *July*. On that date Coach Mike Kelly's team opened against the Macon Peaches; the local nine lost by a score of 5-1 before a crowd of 2,500.

The stadium itself was a notable success, however. The mayor of Macon, Georgia, was in attendance to inspect the ballpark to see which of its features might be incorporated into the stadium *his* city was about to build. The correspondent for *The Spartanburg Journal and Carolina Spartan* newspaper waxed positively ebullient in extolling the virtues of the structure. "[F]or general symmetry and beauty," he wrote, fans "have never seen the equal of the local stadium, though there are many larger." The $40,000 stadium, he observed, "planned to seat 4,000 with perfect comfort, is regarded as one of the most perfect at the disposal of any minor league team in the country." Although constructed to blend with its natural surroundings, which at the time included wooded areas beyond the outfield fence and a gently hilly site, the planning had been so considerate of those expected to attend games that "the sun will be on the grandstand spectators at no time during the game." The paper's overall estimation was that the construction of the stadium "signals what is probable [*sic*] one of the most progressive steps ever taken to forward outdoor [s]ports in the city of Spartanburg."

Some confusion exists over the precise seating capacity of the new Duncan Park stadium. The earliest announcement stated that the stadium would accommodate 2,500 fans, but the newspaper story reported a capacity of 4,000. Elsewhere it was stated that there would be 2,500 seats in the grandstand with another 500 in the bleachers. It might be that an additional 1,000 could be accommodated on the grassy berm beyond the bleachers.

THE COMMISSIONER COMES TO TOWN. The City of Spartanburg was so eager to celebrate the construction of the new ballpark that it even held a special luncheon in honor of the occasion on Wednesday, July 28, at the downtown Cleveland Hotel. Attended by 200 citizens, the luncheon featured guests of honor Judge Kenesaw Mountain Landis, who had been appointed the first commissioner of Major League Baseball in 1920, and M. H. Sexton, president of the National Association of Professional Baseball Leagues. Persuading judge Landis to come to Spartanburg was a major accomplishment, and the local papers made the most of it. The *The Spartanburg Journal and the Carolina Spartan,* for example, called the judge, a figure widely credited with saving Major League Baseball after the fiasco of the 1919 Black Sox scandal, "the greatest figure in league baseball" and reported that "[l]ocal fans are enthused and aroused over the prospect of an official visit from the big mogul of baseball." J. Wirron Willson, the secretary of the home team Spartanburg Spartans, had met judge Landis in Asheville a year and a half earlier, when the Judge had mentioned the possibility of coming to the Hub City "some time." The "time" now seemed ripe, and the judge in fact had responded positively to the invitation.

For his part Landis *was* suitably impressed by the stadium, calling it somewhat lugubriously "the completest park in minor leaguedom." The judge also praised the park's wooded setting and size, noting the suitability of outfield dimensions for inside the park homers. Hosts of the event additionally lauded Ollie Anderson, the dean of Sally League umpires, for the advice that he had given during the planning for the stadium.

PREDECESSORS. Fans waited expectantly for the opening of the new stadium during the early part of the 1926 season. After all, professional baseball had existed in the city for years before Duncan Park stadium was built and officially opened in July, and others would come after they left. The predecessor teams had been these:

- *The Spartanburg Pioneers* (South Atlantic League Class C, 1919-1920); a Pioneers player named **George Dueward Foss** played four games for the Washington Senators in 1921 after playing 19 games for the Pioneers in 1919. Another, **Doc Bass**, played two games for the Boston Braves in 1918; he was a Pioneer in 1920 and also played an unknown number of games here in 1919.

- *The Spartanburg Pioneers* (South Atlantic League, Class B, 1921); two members of this team played in MLB: **Stanley W. "Rabbit" Benton,** who played six games for the Philadelphia Phillies in 1922, and **Will Konigsmark**, who pitched one game for the St. Louis Cardinals.

- *The Spartanburg Spartans* (South Atlantic League, Class B, 1922-1925); the Class B Spartans produced 9 MLB players during these years: **Jesse "Pete" Fowler,** who played for the Cardinals in 1924; **Joe Wagner** (Reds, 1915); **Harry Kelley** (Senators, 1925-26 and 1938-39, Philadelphia Athletics, 1935-36 and 1938); **Jack Berly** (Cardinals, 1924, and Phillies, 1932-33); **Ike Eichrodt** (Indians, 1925-27, and White Sox, 1931); **Bob Fisher** (Dodgers, 1912-13, Cubs, 1914-1915,

Reds, 1916, Cardinals, 1918); **Skipper Friday** (Senators, 1923); **Dutch Holland** (Boston Braves, 1932-33, Indians, 1934-35); and **John Jones** (Athletics, 1923, 1932). **Mike Kelley**, who managed the Spartans for nine years total, managed the team for five years before Duncan Park was built.

THE SPARTANS (1926-1940). The first professional team for which Duncan Park served as its home field was the Spartans, the Class B Sally (South Atlantic) League ball club who were an affiliate of the Cleveland Indians in 1938-1939 but were otherwise one of many independent teams in the often helter-skelter, frequently changeable minor and semipro leagues of American baseball. Minor league baseball at this time was largely composed of teams that were *not* affiliated with or owned by Major League Baseball clubs, a fact that characterized the Spartans until near the end of their existence. Except for an extended hiatus during the Depression the team played at Duncan Park from its opening in 1926 until 1940, when it moved to Charleston and became the Rebels. Gaps in the Spartans' residency, notably 1930 and 1932-1937, were caused by the economic uncertainty and hard times occasioned by the Great Depression during this period.

The earliest semipro/independent/minor league team to play in Spartanburg before the construction of Duncan Park was the team called the Spartans, which played in the short-lived, six-team *Class D South Carolina League* only in 1907. The other five teams in that league were the Sumter Gamecocks, the Orangeburg Edistoes, the Darlington/Florence Fiddlers, the Anderson Electricians, and the Greenville Mountaineers. The immediate predecessors of the Spartans who played at Duncan Park as members of the South Atlantic League were the team first called the Spartanburg Pioneers, active members of the Sally League in 1919–1929 and 1938—1940; the name changed to the Spartans in 1922.

The classification levels of Minor League Baseball are sometimes difficult to understand and follow. Today there are actually five distinct levels, with one being further subdivided. In descending order below the Major Leagues, these levels are AAA; AA; High-A (formerly A-Advanced, including some first-round draftees and experienced college players); Single-A (the lowest level to play a full season); and Rookie (formerly Class A-Short Season, featuring per-haps slightly younger players with less experience as professionals and playing a shorter season). There are also a few independent teams not affiliated with MLB teams and collegiate wooden bat league summer teams who are considered amateurs and not professionals. As a point of reference for readers who may be familiar with some teams nearby to Spartanburg and Duncan Park today, the Gwinnett Braves are a AAA affiliate of the Atlanta Braves; the Greenville Drive are a High-A affiliate of the Boston Red Sox; the Charlotte Knights are a AAA affiliate of the Chicago White Sox; and the Asheville Tourists are a High-A affiliate of the Houston Astros. The Spartanburgers of the Atlantic Coast League, who played at Duncan Park during the summer of 2021, were a collegiate wooden bat league team.

The minor league classification system during the time of the Pioneers and the Spartans at Duncan Park was a little different. During most of the Pioneers/Spartans' existence there were also five minor league levels: AA, A, B, C, and D. Players in level D had no experience or were less proficient than those at higher levels. During 1919-1920, the first two years of the Pioneers' existence, the Sally League was a Class C league; from 1921 and during the entirety of their time in residence at Duncan Park stadium, the Pioneers/Spartans were a Class B team.

THE MANAGER. The longest serving manager of the Spartans was the ever-popular **Mike Kelly**, who became the team's leader in 1922, four years before the move to Duncan Park, and managed through 1929, when he left Spartanburg to become a coach for the Chicago White Sox. During his tenure the Spartans compiled a modest overall record of 566-539 but were league champions in 1925, when they won 31 more games than they lost. Even with Kelly at the helm, though, the Spartans usually placed fourth or below in an eight-team league, and in the years after Kelly moved on to Chicago they never again had a winning season.

Kelly was a man of many abilities, and in addition to managing the Spartans he also played on the field, usually at first base, while compiling a .309 batting average at Duncan Park. During the years before the move to Duncan Park, Kelly also served as a player-manager, his best year being 1925, when he had a .365 average playing 129 games at first. Kelly's last year as a frontline player was 1928, when he batted .305 in 73 games; in 1929 he played in only 33 games and batted .268, but he still managed the team.

Kelly was also one tough cookie. One summer while playing against the Asheville Tourists he was brushed back from the plate by a tight inside ball from the opposing pitcher. Not one to back down from a challenge, Kelly stood his ground on the next pitch and was downed by a hard-thrown beanball. That was the end of his season and very nearly the end of his baseball career as well. His right arm became paralyzed, and only serious exercise and rehabilitation during the winter allowed him to play again. Such tenacity and dedication to the game, as well as Spartanburg's first league pennant during the 1925 season, made Kelly

Popular and accomplished Spartans Manager Mike Kelly

a fan favorite. As *The Spartanburg Journal and Carolina Spartan* observed, "… in Spartanburg—well, they'd elect Mike mayor or dog-catcher or anything anytime he wanted to run for office."

THE PLAYERS. Although the Spartanburg Spartans were a lower tier minor league team and never matched the later success of the Spartanburg Phillies, and although during their existence they must have had to compete pretty strenuously with Spartanburg City and County Textile League teams for players, they were regarded both fondly and seriously by their fans and even sent a number of players on to The Show. The ex-Spartans who had the most success in Major League Baseball were **Hal Wagner**, born in 1915, who played for twelve years for the Philadelphia Athletics and the Phillies and the Detroit Tigers, and was a two-time All-Star; **Debs Garms**, born in 1907, who also played for twelve years for four teams; **Eddie Moore**, born in 1899, who played for eight different teams during a 10-year career in the Majors; **George Murray**, born in 1898, who played for six years at the Major Leagues level; and **Tommy O'Brien**, born in 1918, who played for five years. Not all Spartans who graduated to MLB were stars, of course, or even journeymen players, some being called up long enough for only the traditional cup of coffee. **Joe Price, Ren Kelly, Dick Hahn, Mike Palagyi, Leo Moon,** and **Al Williamson** played in just one game each in the Majors. Price played in the outfield for one game for the New York Giants in 1928, but batted over .300 in four separate years in the Minors and stroked the ball well enough to acquire the nickname "Lumber."

All told, more than 40 former Spartans played Major League Baseball. Their tenure in the Bigs ranged from a single game for a few to a dozen years. Most of those who graduated to the Major Leagues played for the Spartans when they were affiliated with the Cleveland Indians, although 1929 was also a good year, seven members of that Spartanburg team also moving up to the Majors.

Among the Spartans deserving a more extended commemoration of their Major League careers was **Hal Wagner,** twice an MLB All-Star. Wagner was born in East Riverton, New Jersey, in 1915, and played baseball at both East Riverton and Palmyra high schools. He and his high school teammates also watched the nearby Philadelphia Athletics play, and after a neighbor invited Wagner to Shibe Park, he was noticed by Connie Mack, who encouraged him to play college ball at Duke. This the young outfielder did, playing for Duke, semipro Tarheel teams, and the Athletics in the late 1930s. In the process he also was converted into a catcher, and it was as a catcher that Wagner played for the Spartans in 1938, appearing in 63 games and batting .326 in 215 plate appearances. In August he was called up by the A's, and although he was sent back down again in 1939, thereafter he played mostly Major League ball. In all, during the 12 years from 1937 to 1949 Wagner played for the Athletics, the Red Sox, the Tigers, and the Phillies. His batting average was a journeyman-like .248, but his true value to MLB teams seems to have been his fielding skills. During three seasons he was in the top 10 in putouts as a catcher; in 1942 he was fifth in assists and fourth in double plays as a catcher; and for three seasons he was in the top 10 for fielding percentage as a catcher. Wagner was also on the field on the last day of the season in 1941 when Philadelphia played Boston and Ted Williams upped his average to .406 for the year, the last time a Major League player batted over .400 for a season.

A second Spartan who made The Show was **George Murray,** worthy of note among other reasons because his first-rate baseball nicknames, in addition to "Tarheel," included "Smiler" and "the Clark Gable of Dallas." Born in Charlotte in 1898, Murray played high school ball in Charlotte, then played football and baseball at North Carolina State University, from which he graduated in 1921 with a degree in textile engineering. He signed with the Yankees in the summer of the same year, beginning a peripatetic six-year Major League career that saw him pitch for the Yankees, Red Sox, Senators, and White Sox from 1922 to 1927 and 1933. During this same time and later into 1939 he also played for nearly a dozen Minor League teams from Minneapolis to St. Louis and points west and south. He played in 110 Major League games, compiling a record of 19-26 and a 5.38 ERA; he never won more than seven games or lost more than 11 in a year. Murray was more successful in the Minors, winning 20 games for the Dallas Steers of the Class A Texas League in 1931 and 24 games in 1932; in 1932 also, his ERA was a more than respectable 2.86. He played professional baseball until he was 40 years old in 1939, in which year he was 8-15 playing for Savannah, Spartanburg, and Winston-Salem.

Les Sweetland, another Spartan alum with a five-year Major League so-journ with the Phillies and Cubs, had what one biographer has called "the dubious achievement of having posted the highest earned-run average in a major-league season." This was 7.71, accomplished during 1930 when Sweetland pitched for a Philadelphia Phillies team that lost twice as many games as it won. A native of St. Ignace, Michigan, Sweetland had performed acceptably during six years in the Minors, compiling a 59-43 record for the Orlando Bulldogs, the Jacksonville Indians, the Charlotte Hornets, and the 1926 and 1927 Spartans. Even as a Minor League pitcher, though, Sweetland's ERA had tended toward the upper end, usually above 4.0, even though in 1924 he achieved a 2.92 with the Hornets. Plagued throughout his career by inconsistency and frequent wildness, and unable to get along with manager Rogers Hornsby at the end of his career while a Chicago Cub, Sweetland never quite lived up to what occasionally seemed real promise and finished his Major League career with a 33-58 record and 6.10 ERA. He was a decent hitter, however, especially for a pitcher, compiling a .272 batting average and in 1927 batting .316 in 25 games with the Phillies.

In 1940 when he was 33 years old **Debs Garms** won the National League batting title with an average of .355, incidentally also besting American League batting champion Joe Dimaggio by three points. Eleven years earlier he had played part of the 1929 season with the Spartanburg Spartans, spending the rest of the season with the Augusta Tygers. Garms spent 19 years all together in professional baseball, 12 years in the Majors, playing mostly in the outfield and compiling a Major League batting average of .293. He played against Babe Ruth, Jimmy Foxx, Dixie Walker, and Joe Nuxhall, and played for managers Rogers Hornsby, Casey Stengel, Pie Traynor, Frankie Frisch, and Pepper Martin, among others. Never a power hitter, Garms played with heart and hustle and was also known for his speed on the bases; at one time he held the Major Leagues record for most consecutive pinch hits (7). An interesting side fact about Garms is that when he was born on June 26, 1907, he was named after American Socialist leader and perennial presidential candidate Eugene V. Debs. After leaving professional baseball, Garms became a successful cattle rancher in Texas.

A few other Spartans deserve mention as Major Leaguers. One, **Tommy O'Brien**, was barely a Spartan, having played only 20 games at third base in 1940, batting only .230 for the team that was to be superseded in July by the Charleston Sally League team. O'Brien owed much of his Major League career to World War II, having played as a backup for the Pirates during the mid-1940s while more able players were away on the battlefield. Other former Spartans had much shorter stays in the Majors.

Debs Garms, 1940
National League
Batting Champ

Eddie Moore, who had a 10-year career in Major League Baseball, playing for five different teams in both leagues, played part of the 1938 season with the Spartans. At this point his Major Leagues career was already four years behind him, but he contributed a .255 batting average in 52 plate appearances to the Spartanburg team's disappointing record of 54 wins and 82 defeats. Moore also managed in Spartanburg and in addition spent part of the year with the Syracuse Chiefs of the International League. His Major League batting average was a respectable .285, but he was not a memorable fielder, at least for his *positive* accomplishments: in 1925 he committed 36 errors at second base, the most in the National League, and in 1928 he committed the third highest total errors in left field.

The Spartans also produced players worth noting who were standouts locally but never made it to the Bigs. Among these were perennial player/manager Mike Kelly, noted above as a fan favorite, seasoned first baseman, and competent batsman who in 1926 batted .377 and whose cumulative batting average while playing at Duncan Park with the Spartans was a respectable .309. Kelly also managed respectably: his Spartan teams compiled an overall record of 287-297 in the years when they played at Duncan Park. After leaving Spartanburg,

Kelly went on to manage and coach for a number of Major League teams.

There were other Spartan players who performed well during their time at Duncan Park if not in the Majors. Among them were the following:

Joe Guyon, one of the more interesting former Spartans, was born on November 26, 1892, on the White Earth Indian Reservation in Minnesota and played baseball and football at the same high school attended by Jim Thorpe, with whom he later played in the NFL. Guyon was also a two-sports star at Georgia Tech, where he became a football All-American in 1918. In 1920 he began his professional baseball career, playing for Atlanta and Little Rock in the Southern Association and Augusta in the South Atlantic League. From 1921 through 1928 Guyon played for Atlanta in the Southern Association and Louisville in the AA American Association. Beginning in 1919 Guyon also played professional football, the high point coming in 1927 when he was a running back for the NFL Champion New York Giants. An injury ended Guyon's football career in 1928, and he became coach of the Clemson University baseball team from 1928 to 1931. In 1931 Guyon became player-manager of the Anderson Electrics/Spartanburg Spartans and batted .315 in 38 games; he was player-manager of the Asheville Tourists in 1932 and of the Fieldale Towlers in 1936. Although he played professional baseball for 12 years, Guyon never played in the Majors and is better known for his football prowess: he was inducted into the Pro Football Hall of Fame in 1966 and the College Football Hall of Fame in 1971.

Hoss Chestnut, beloved for his name if for no other reason, played in the infield, mostly second base, for the Spartans from 1923 to 1929 as well as for two other teams. His overall batting average in Class B was .285, and he played second base with a .941 fielding percentage.

John Walker pitched for the Spartans in 1926 and 1927, compiling records of 17-18 and 21-16. His Minor League totals were 89 wins and 63 losses over five years.

Walter Hunter batted .330 while playing catcher for the Spartans in 1927. After that year, though, his career was effectively over; he played only some 20 additional games for five different teams during the next three years and disappeared thereafter.

Milton Hodge pitched well for the Spartans in 1927, wining 16 and losing only five, but played for three teams the next year and then apparently left professional baseball.

In 1927 **John Buvid** won 21 and lost only 11 for the Spartans while posting a 3.44 ERA. Unfortunately there are no records of his having played again in the Minor Leagues. That same year **James Scott** went 15-13 with a 3.45 ERA but also disappeared from the record books thereafter.

Bill Good, a perennial Minor Leaguer, played for the Spartans in 1939 (139 games) and 1940 (27 games) during a career which saw him play for 11 teams over the course of 10 seasons, 1936-1949, excluding the war years of 1942-1945. Although the Spartans were a Cleveland Indians affiliate when Good played for them, he never made The Show. His best years were 1936, when he batted .319 in 103 games for Johnstown of the Middle Atlantic League; 1946, when he batted .328 in 129 games for Leesburg of the Florida State League; and 1948, when he batted .316 in 114 games for Fitzgerald of the Georgia State League. In Spartanburg in 1939 he batted just .265.

In 1940, a year which saw the Spartanburg team move during the season to Charleston, where they played as the Rebels, **Garrett McBryde**, another career Minor Leaguer, batted .324 in 151 games while playing in the outfield. In nine years McBryde played for 12 teams; his year in Spartanburg/Charleston was his best at the plate except for 1944, when he batted .348 while playing in only 36 games for two teams in the Southern Association.

The Spartans failed to field a team in 1930, but they returned in 1931, playing only 22 games (record: 4-18) under three managers (Joe Guyon, Ken McNeill, and Frank Walker) in the Palmetto League. In the same summer the team was superseded by the Anderson Electrics (record: 14-40), who relocated to Spartanburg on June 29. There was no local team again from 1932 through 1937. From 1938 through 1940 a Spartan Sally League team returned, managed by Eddie Moore and Chick Galloway in 1938, by Leon Pettit in 1939, and by Cecil Rhodes in 1940. In 1938 and 1939 the team was affiliated with the Cleveland Indians, who were to re-affiliate with Spartanburg when the Peaches were organized near the end of the decade of the 1940s.

The best source for information about the Spartans as a team and their standing in the Sally League is *The South Atlantic League, 1904-1963: A Year-by-Year Statistical History* by Marshall D. Wright (Jefferson, NC & London: McFarland & Company, Inc., Publishers, 2009). Here the inquisitive fan will find League standings year-by-year, as well as team rosters, players' batting averages and pitchers' records, facts about multiteam players, and occasional anecdotes about special events, players experiencing outstanding years, etc. While generally reliable, even this excellent book's data sometimes contain lacunae (some players' first names are missing, for example, because they weren't included in the newspaper stories which form the basis of these records); and there are also lapses, such as the failure to note that the "Bernard" Kelly listed as first baseman on the 1929 Spartans is the same player as the "Mike" Kelly who was player-manager in previous seasons.

Three other highly useful sources of information are worth mentioning. First is the online database of Baseball-Reference.com, the aim of which "is to answer our users' questions with the easiest-to-use, fastest, and most complete sports statistics anywhere." At this site can be found annual team and player records, both for Minor League and Major League Baseball teams, past and present, and a serious fan can easily lose him- or herself for hours after initiating what seems to be a casual search for a single piece of information. Another indispensable site is that of SABR (sabr.org), the legendary Society of American Baseball Research, whose "SABR Baseball Biography Project" provides surprisingly comprehensive biographies of often obscure and forgotten players penned by careful and thorough researchers. SABR sponsors regional chapters, groups and special interest committees such as Ballparks, Negro Leagues, and Baseball and the Arts, also Baseball Cards and even Concessions and Latino Baseball. Hall of Fame broadcaster Ernie Harwell called SABR "the Phi Beta Kappa of baseball." Finally, the most complete records available, also the most frustrating because they are often hard to find and difficult to slog through, are the daily stories and box scores to be found in local newspapers. For the Spartans I have used *The Spartanburg Daily Herald* and *The Spartanburg Journal and Carolina Spartan,* and in other chapters of this book I also have looked into the periodicals in newspapers.com and files of *The Atlanta Daily World* and *The Palmetto Leader* (Columbia, South Carolina), both sources for hard-to-find information about Black semipro leagues of the early 20th century

CHAPTER THREE

. . . .

The Spartanburg Sluggers:
Black Semipro Baseball in the
Hub City During the Jim Crow Era

HOW I GOT HERE. This is an almost accidental chapter. When I began my
research, I knew a lot about the tenure of the Spartanburg Phillies at the old
stadium from the 1960s through the early 1990s and a little bit more about that
of the Spartanburg Peaches, originally the Browns, an affiliate of the Cleveland
Indians in the 1940s and '50s. As I proceeded, I encountered a surprisingly
rich trove of information about other teams: the old semipro Spartanburg
Spartans early in the 20th century and, later on, the residencies of the Wofford,
University of South Carolina Upstate, Spartanburg High School, independent,
and wooden bat league teams of the later 20th century. What truly surprised
me as I sifted through books, articles, and online databases, though, was the existence of an independent semipro Black baseball team called the Spartanburg
Sluggers, previously unknown to me and still largely unknown today to most
residents of the Hub City.

I first saw the name of the Sluggers in an occasional side reference in articles about other teams or games at Duncan Park stadium, and then I stumbled across a couple of articles by Linda Conley for the *Herald-Journal* newspaper. One was a profile of "Lefty" Bob Branson, a standout pitcher for the

Sluggers in the 1940s; another was a story about Newt and Vi's, a restaurant in Spartanburg's old Black business district on Short Wofford Street. Newton "Little Newt" Whitmire, the owner of Newt and Vi's Place, also was identified as the owner of the Spartanburg Sluggers, and his father, "Big Newt," also had been the owner of the team and was its founder.

I was hooked and began a deeper dive into the available sources. At first I could find nothing. None of the standard works on Negro Leagues Baseball contained any information at all about the Sluggers, and there was also next to nothing at any of the online database sites. Then I happened to find two unexpected sources of information about the Sluggers. One was provided by Brad Steinecke, the assistant director of local history in the Kennedy Room at the Spartanburg County Public Libraries. Steinecke, a former student of mine, responded to my online query that the library held the only three extant copies of *The Hub City Observer,* a defunct local Black newspaper from the 1920s; moreover, two of the three issues contained brief accounts of Sluggers games. The other source was Luther Norman, who showed up in the audience of a Lunch and Learn presentation I made at the Spartanburg County Historical Association. Luther, it turned out, was the son-in-law of Little Newt Whitmire, a local archivist, an unofficial historian of the Black community, and a big baseball fan who had been a player himself. Norman had an archive of photographs, memorabilia, and print documents about the Sluggers; he also knew former players, and of course, had a wealth of personal information about the Whitmires and their team. Norman and I met, we talked, and we became friends. Since then we have worked together on a number of projects. In the process I accumulated more information and more images of the Spartanburg Sluggers.

THE CONTEXT. Who were the Spartanburg Sluggers? On many levels it's difficult to say. Basically they were an independent semipro Black baseball team that played, often in Duncan Park, often sporadically, from the 1920s— and possibly from as early as 1911—until the early 1950s. Even this sentence requires qualification, however. The so-called Negro Leagues themselves are a slippery slope for researchers, ephemeral and shape-shifting, relentlessly relocating and roster-redefining over time, documented by an almost insanely dedicated corps of baseball historians but inevitably imperfectly fixed on the pages of the many books and articles devoted to them.

Here's an example of how bedeviling it can be to dip into the pool of Negro Leagues data. The Negro Leagues Database, part of seamheads.com hosted by The Baseball Gauge, lists 10 main ("major league") teams in its dropdown

"Teams" menu, but there is also an appended category of "Other Teams" at the end of this list. Clicking on this category takes one to another dropdown list, this one containing a maddening table of no fewer than 170—yes, *one hundred and seventy*—"All-Time" teams, most short-lived and many in existence for only a single season, stretching back into the 1880s. Needless to say, this is a problematic listing since, as the website points out, "One of the biggest issues with Negro Leagues statistics is that they are incomplete. We don't have box scores for every game and we currently do not have data for every season and league." As a result, many—most?—Negro League players, especially those who played on the Minor League, independent, semipro, and barnstorming teams that were the mainstay of Black American baseball for most of its existence, form a little known cadre of "enigmatic specters still hidden in the sundown shadows of baseball history," according to pioneering Negro Leagues researcher James A, Riley.

There are many reasons for the incomplete status of data about the Negro Leagues. Many of these teams played in out-of-the-way or unfamiliar places like Buxton, Iowa; West Baden Springs, Indiana; French Lick, Indiana; Darby, Pennsylvania; Algona, Iowa; and Spartanburg, South Carolina. Some were Cuban teams. Many played during the segregation era in communities that had no local Black newspaper and were not covered by the White media. In too many instances team archives have simply not survived the ravages of time. As Gary Ashwill, one of the stalwarts of the Black baseball research community, observes, "Numerous small (and usually short-lived) [B]lack baseball circuits were scattered around the country that went virtually unnoticed in the national (and even local) press at the time, and have been almost completely forgotten since."

Nevertheless I turned hopefully to The Negro Leagues Database early on in my research for *Beautiful Duncan Park*, but I quickly came up against the first of many walls I encountered: The Spartanburg Sluggers were *not* among the 170 teams listed in The Negro Leagues Database. Nor were any of the few Sluggers players whose names I knew listed as players in the database either. So naturally I turned to the website of SABR, the Society for American Baseball Research, the venerable source of all statistical sources for all things baseball. Nothing there either. Hope dwindling fast, I searched baseball-reference.com with similar results. My project was rapidly becoming daunting indeed.

I did find, surprisingly, that there have been two books written about the history of baseball in Asheville, North Carolina, and the Upstate of South Carolina, and this fact rekindled a small gleam of hope. Inevitably, though,

I was disappointed by both volumes. The Asheville book contains only three paragraphs about Black teams in Asheville in its 126 pages, and while I was to find that three of the teams mentioned—the Royal Giants, the Black Tourists, and the Blues—had played against the Spartanburg Sluggers, there was nothing about the Sluggers in the book and precious little about the Asheville teams themselves. *Baseball in Greenville and Spartanburg* was, if anything, even less helpful. While it does contain mention and photographs of a couple of Negro Textile League teams and also acknowledges Black high school baseball during the segregation era, it contains nothing at all about the Sluggers or even the Greenville Black Spinners. I was back to square one.

Then I talked with Steinecke, who shared with me the Spartanburg County Public Libraries's three issues of *The Hub City Observer,* which contained two reports of Sluggers games. The first report, from June 22, 1929, was of a game played at Duncan Park stadium the previous Monday in which the Sluggers defeated the Anderson Hard Hitters at Duncan Park by a score of 1-0. The newspaper account includes neither line nor box scores and mentions only two players and these only by their last names: Wilburn, the Sluggers pitcher, and Williams, the Hard Hitters ace. The game, described as "an interesting tilt," was a whirlwind affair, lasting only an hour and 15 minutes and "without a squabble." Nevertheless, the Anderson team still managed four hits and Spartanburg six. The only score occurred in the first inning. The reporter recorded no other details whatsoever.

The second game report from the *Observer* is a little more detailed. On the Fourth of July in 1929 the Sluggers played the Asheville Black Tourists, another long-lived Black team, "walloping" them by a score of 7-3 in the morning game of a double header in which they also "slammed" the Charlotte Hard Hitters by a score of 5-2 in the afternoon. Here the details begin to become murkier. In the second game the Charlotte pitcher, identified only as "Blake," gave up 11 hits, three of them to the Sluggers first baseman, "Rosebud." Other hits were registered by Mains (two), Wiggins (two), Fuller (one), Whitmire (one), Teague (one), and Talley (one). Whitmire, Rosebud, Mains, Teague, and Talley each scored once; the pitchers for the Sluggers were McSwain and Tucker. Again, as in the account of the game played in June, there is no line or box score, and no players are identified by their first names. Interestingly, though, the crowd in attendance is identified as "the largest ever assembled here at a ball game." Frustratingly, the actual number of fans is not reported. And disappointingly for fans of Duncan Park, *these* two rare reports of Sluggers in action record games played on the holiday at *Wofford Park,* a frequent venue hosting the Sluggers, not the classic 1926 stadium.

SPORTS

The Spartanburg Sluggers had quite an interesting tilt with the Anderson Hard Hitters at Duncan Park last Monday afternoon. The game proved to be a "pitchers' battle," and was hard fought throughout the 8½ frames. Only one score was registered, and that by the Sluggers in the first inning, after which the pitchers "settled down" and the books were closed. Wilburn, pitching for the local club, proved himself a master of the art in extricating himself from apparently impossible holes. Williams, with the visiting club, also comes in for much praise for falling off the mound. The game was played in one hour and fifteen minutes, and without a squabble. The line-up follows:

Summary

Anderson	Spartanburg
Hits, 4; Scores, 0.	Hits, 6; Scores, 1.

Elaborate plans are under way for the big Fourth of July celebration, which will be conducted at Wofford Park. Word has just been received that about half of the people on the big excursion from Winston-Salem, going to Greenville on that day, will unload here for the morning game at Wofford Park. The morning game will begin at 10:30. The afternoon game will begin at 4:00. Preparations for entertaining the largest crowd ever assembled in an outdoor entertainment are under way.

A VISIT TO FAIRWOLD

While in the city of Columbia attending the State Bible Convention, held at Benedict College, last week the citizens made it pleasant for the

FOUR-H CLUB ACTIVITIES

The Four-H Clubs are now planning ways and means to go to the State short course to be held in Orangeburg, July 22, 23, 24. This course is given every year around the same time. Last year, fifteen members represented the county. This year we are expecting to have at last thirty members to represent the county. The party will leave from Spartanburg, Sunday, July 21st, at 11 o'clock A. M.

Each club is planning and raising its own funds by giving entertainments, concerts, selling refreshments and garden products.

The Shady Grove Club has had two socials in the interest of their club. The net profit of their first social was $2.50 under adverse circumstances. They had another social Saturday evening, which has not been reported yet. This whole club (fifteen members) is planning to go. This is the oldest club in the county, and they have learned to realize the good of the Four-H Club work.

Roebuck met last week and made all plans for a full program from now until time for the short course. I am sure that all the active members of the club will be able to attend. They have started full of pep and strength to put over their program. There will be an entertainment Saturday, June 22nd, at the school house.

Prospect Club met last week with a regular club meeting. The business to arrange to raise funds to send a girl to the short course was taken up. They are having an entertainment on Saturday, July 6th. The Four-H boys and girls of Fairmont had a joint meeting Saturday evening. An exceptional crowd was present. Total members present, 38. They have also planned for their entertainments and socials to raise their funds. The active members of this club will surely be

June 22, 1929, issue of The Hub City Observer, one of two issues containing stories of Sluggers games

The Spartanburg library's third issue of *The Hub City Observer* contains no information about the Sluggers. Fortunately other newspapers do, and some of their accounts record games at Duncan Park as well as away games in the cities that are home to the other periodicals. As I delved into the pages of these newspapers, a clearer picture of the Sluggers began to emerge.

Luther Norman helped me fill in the record. Norman introduced himself to me at the conclusion of my program on the history of the old Duncan Park stadium during a lunchtime meeting of the Spartanburg Historical Association. Beginning in March 2018 and continuing through the duration of my research, Norman and I talked on the phone and met together frequently to discuss the history of the Spartanburg Sluggers and Negro Leagues Baseball. We became good friends and members of the steering committee that brought the Negro Leagues documentary film *The Other Boys of Summer* to Spartanburg in February 2020, just before the onslaught of the novel coronavirus.

What was especially fortuitous about my meeting Luther Norman is that he had married Lorraine Whitmire, whose father Newt and mother Viola had operated a hotel and a restaurant called Newt and Vi's Place on Short Wofford Street in the Black business district of Spartanburg. Newt was also an entertainment promoter who brought artists such as Duke Ellington, Ruth Brown, Count Basie, Ella Fitzgerald, and others who performed on the southern "chitlin' circuit" to Spartanburg during the early and mid-20th century when they were unable to perform in venues reserved for Whites. Even more fortunate for me was the fact that "Little" Newt Whitmire had been the owner of the Spartanburg Sluggers; moreover Norman possessed a trove of photographs, documents, clippings, equipment, and other memorabilia of the Sluggers, much of which has never been seen before in public, that he was more than generous in sharing with me. Norman also knew a lot of family history and oral history and had relationships with a number of surviving Negro League players. His cooperation in my research has been integral to the development of this history.

THE WHITMIRES. The larger story of the Whitmire family itself is instructive regarding the history of the Spartanburg Sluggers, their support in the Spartanburg community, and their legacy both to later baseball fans and to a more comprehensive understanding of Black history in the city. Originally, the Whitmire family came from the small town of the same name, the "Pearl of the Piedmont," located alongside the Enoree River about 45 minutes southeast of Spartanburg. The town of Whitmire was named for a family that moved to the area in the decade before the Civil War. The family owned a tavern, which became the site of the area's first post office. The town's economic prosperity, such as it was, was later tied to that of the Georgia-Carolina and Northern Railroad and to the success of the Glenn-Lowery Mill.

The original Whitmires of the small community in Newberry County were White. The family of Newton Whitmire and his descendants were Black and acquired their surname as enslaved people belonging to the White Whitmires. Following the Civil War and the end of slavery, Ella, Newton Whitmire's formerly enslaved mother, moved from Whitmire to Spartanburg. Her son, "Big Newt," became a railroad porter and lived behind Wofford College. He started Octavia's Restaurant (known to later residents as The Eatery), which he subsequently expanded into a hotel that became a well-known stop on the Black "chitlin' circuit," which featured venues where prominent Black artists performed for Black audiences in the Jim Crow South. Newton Whitmire Jr., "Little Newt," moved back to Spartanburg from New York City in 1946 to care for "Big Newt" and take over the business. He opened Newt & Vi's in the historic Black business district.

*Newt Whitmire Sr.,
posing downtown
on Evins Street near
Wofford College*

The "chitlin' circuit" hosted many Black musicians who were also favorites of White America but whose Black fans could not attend performances in the segregated halls, which was the rule before the Supreme Court opened public accommodations to all citizens. Among these were such familiar names as Cab Calloway, Ella Fitzgerald, Duke Ellington, Lionel Hampton, and Moms Mabley. Most stayed at the Whitmires' hotel, even after Black and White audiences were able to attend the same shows at Spartanburg Memorial Auditorium, where during segregation Black patrons danced on the floor of the arena while Whites sat watching in the balcony above. (Such scenes were common throughout the South. When I was a high school senior in Columbia in the mid-1960s I sat with other White spectators in the balcony of Township Auditorium watching Black patrons dancing below while James Brown and The Famous Flames, Bobby "Blue" Bland, and Cab Calloway performed on stage.) During World War II

Ella Whitmire, the mother of 'Big Newt' Whitmire, the founding owner of the Spartanburg Sluggers

the presence of many Black soldiers training at Camp Croft swelled the local Black population and increased the number of audience members at dances and concerts by popular "chitlin' circuit" performers.

Newt, Viola, and the Whitmire family had genuine relationships with many of the performers who ate or lodged with them. Viola made preserves for Duke Ellington and owned Christmas cards sent to the family from the Duke. It was not uncommon for Newt and Vi to hear a knock on the door of the restaurant late at night and to find Ellington waiting there after closing his gig for the evening. The Whitmires always opened the kitchen and prepared the musician a sandwich or snack. In return they were treated to an informal private performance that might last for hours.

Black business owners in many cities had the necessary capital to finance a baseball team, and both Big Newt and Little Newt Whitmire fit this mold. Big Newt founded the Spartanburg Sluggers and passed the team down to his son, who was himself a player and team manager. In addition, his other business ventures—the restaurant and hotel—were natural places for promoting the Sluggers. (Newt's uncle, Claude Whitmire, was also a local businessman; he

*Little Newt Whitmire
and one of the Sluggers
pitching aces, "Lefty"
Bob Branson, who also
worked at the
Whitmires' restaurant*

brought Yellow Deluxe Cab to Spartanburg, where future entrepreneur and owner of Atchison Transportation Charles Atchison was one of his drivers.)

Little Newt created a now rare poster, the only known copy of which was restored for an exhibition at the Spartanburg County Public Libraries, featuring the team, and there were calendars and announcements on a local Black radio station. He also promoted exhibition games between prominent members of the senior Black baseball circuit, including a Duncan Park clash between the Negro American League Indianapolis Clowns and Kansas City Monarchs in September 1951. The game, attended by 2,000 fans, was won 12-5 by the Monarchs. Jackie Robinson's barnstorming All-Stars played in Spartanburg, too, and Whitmire also promoted a Spartanburg appearance by United States Olympic champion and track and field legend Jesse Owens. Owens, a national hero, participated in "an exhibition race with members of the Spartanburg Sluggers" on Thursday, July 17, 1941. Although Owens's appearance did stimulate some interest in a potential "track and field meet for interested Camp Croft soldiers," it seems not to have had much lasting impact. Boxer Sugar Ray Robinson was also brought to Spartanburg by the Sluggers owner, and

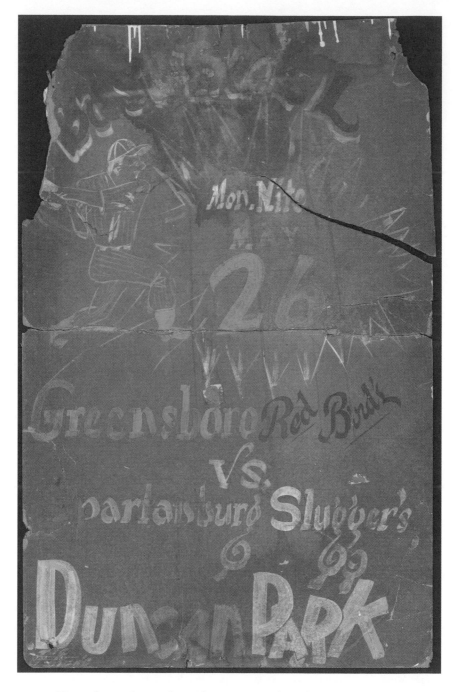

Uniquely rare Spartanburg Sluggers poster, the only surviving example

on August 30, 1926, Whitmire actually promoted a boxing match at Duncan Park between "local colored lightweight" Kid Jones and Asheville's "Battling Brown;" the Kid won in the third round of a scheduled 10-rounder in the "Field Day" event.

The Whitmires were familiar figures in Spartanburg in both the Black *and* White communities. Jim Harbison, whose family owned a furniture store in the mid-1940s across the alley from Newt & Vi's place in downtown Spartanburg, recalled that "Mr. Whitmire was a highly respected man. All of them [sic] people looked up to Mr. Whitmire." As a teenager Harbison hung out with Sluggers ballplayers in the alley behind his family's store and worked with Willy Smith, who was an umpire for the Sluggers and a 40-year employee of the furniture store. He got to know Newt Whitmire well, and the owner would let young Harbison sit in the owner's box when he went to Duncan Park to watch Sluggers games.

"Little Newt's" daughter, Lorraine (1951-2013), married local businessman and community activist and historian Luther Norman, who today continues the family's involvement in and promotion of Black baseball and its legacy. Norman played baseball himself at South Carolina State University and North Carolina A&T University and as a member of the Pittsburgh Pirates Minor League organization. He is also a youth sports coach and supporter of central city youth programs through his Youth Sports Bureau. He sponsors youth baseball clinics and tournaments and works hard to publicize the contributions of Negro Leagues Baseball to life in America, notably through introducing old Negro Leagues players to Black youth in the Carolinas and beyond and through participating in Negro Leagues conferences and reunions. In February 2020 Norman was a founding member of an ad hoc committee that brought the documentary film *The Other Boys of Summer* to Spartanburg to facilitate discussions of both Negro Leagues Baseball and of diversity, racism, and building bridges across communities.

THE TEAM. One of the most surprising facts about the Sluggers was their longevity. Not only was there a team called the Spartanburg Sluggers included in the lineup of the Blue Ridge Colored Baseball League in a brief notice in *The Charlotte Observer* in March 1921, but I also discovered actual game reports at Wofford Park or the Fairgrounds going back as far as August 1911. As was often the case in early games, the 1911 contest was part of a larger celebration involving a special excursion train, speakers, and carnival rides. The Sluggers were sometimes members of other organized Black baseball leagues but not always. On June 17, 1946, a legal notice in *The Daily Herald* announced that the

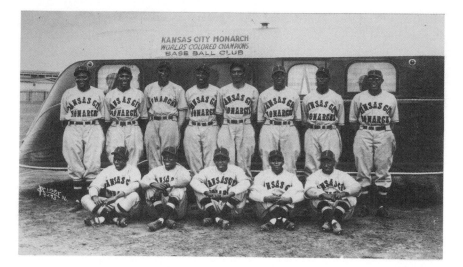

ABOVE: *Legendary Negro Leagues team the Kansas City Monarchs, who played an exhibition game at Duncan Park stadium*
RIGHT: *Hall of Famer Jackie Robinson, whose All-Stars barnstorming team played at Duncan Park*

team had been formally organized as a corporation with the following "corporators": N.H. Whitmire, Charles Whitmire (Big Newt's son), Stacy Whitmire (a daughter), and Earle Whitmire (another son). In January 1948 the Sluggers were under consideration for membership in the Negro American Baseball Association, but in the following summer they actually played in the Southern Negro Baseball League. During most years it seems that the Sluggers were an independent semipro and/or barnstorming team, as were most of their competitors and contemporaries in Black baseball.

I have been able to document more than 360 total games played by the Sluggers through 1961, admittedly an average of only seven or eight games per year during the period of their existence, but this number is actually higher than the traceable number of games for many Negro Leagues teams. Due to the infrequency and undependability of White media coverage of Black teams, the number of games actually played was likely a good bit higher than the ones I have been able to reliably document. In addition, there are two years—1937 and 1951—for which I have been unable to discover any games whatsoever played by the Sluggers. This does not mean that there might not have been Sluggers games during those years; there is a real possibility that there were, in fact, games, but they were not covered in any newspaper accounts. There is

also another plausible possibility: since these years include one during the time of the Great Depression, it could very well be that local economic conditions did not allow owners to profitably operate teams or players to be able to afford to play for the amount of pay that could have been offered during this period.

The number of Sluggers games actually documented varies widely from year to year of their existence. It should be remembered that Duncan Park, their favorite and most frequent home venue, was not constructed until 1926 and that the late 1920s and 1930s were the time of the Great Depression, not an era of much disposable income for non-essential entertainments like baseball. The early 1940s saw some recovery, perhaps because of the large numbers of soldiers, both Black and White, being trained just beyond the city limits of Spartanburg at Camp Croft, but the number of games seems to have drastically declined in 1944 and 1945, presumably because most men of active baseball-playing age were actually fighting abroad during this time. After the end of World War II in 1945, the number of recorded contests rebounded in 1946 and 1947 and spiked notably in 1948, as attendance did nationwide in the post-war recovery of Major League Baseball, and then declined again in 1949-1952. It is tempting to correlate these numbers with the integration of Major League Baseball in 1947 and the subsequent drafting of many former Negro Leagues players into formerly White baseball after 1947, as well as with the fact that opportunities for Black men were beginning to expand beyond sports after the end of the war, but it would be difficult to prove any real cause-effect relationship between these historical facts and Sluggers games. Also it is worth noting that Newt Whitmire Sr. died at midnight on March 20, 1949, and the transition to Little Newt as the new general manager and Lefty Bob Branson as the manager on the field could not have been without impact on the team.

The spotty, imprecise record left by the Spartanburg Sluggers over the course of their history is typical of most Black semipro and independent teams, even those from larger cities. As Dr. Layton Revel, the founder of The Center for Negro League Baseball Research, has observed, "There is so much conflicting information…. There's a lot of misinformation out there." Other researchers agree. Patrick Sauer, writing for *Smithsonian Magazine,* reports "so much of the history vanished like a ball crushed over the Green Monster." The main reason for this, of course, is the fact that Black teams and baseball leagues received spotty coverage at best from White newspapers and other media. Even John Hammond Moore's *South Carolina Newspapers* includes the notation "NFK" for "No Files Known to Exist" for virtually all of the Black newspapers identified in Spartanburg County. The task for a researcher is, therefore, challenging at the least and involves hours of work in online databases and library microfilm reels. Such digging, though, can pay unusually rewarding dividends.

There remain pitfalls, of course. When a Negro Leagues team did belong to a league that scheduled games well in advance and then released those schedules publicly, there was no guarantee that all such scheduled games were actually played. Sometimes a game was rained out and then rescheduled, but neither the new date nor the outcome of the new game was reported in a newspaper. Occasionally a scheduled game did not occur because the out-of-town opponent simply did not show up and was not ever rescheduled. Sometimes a game was tied in late or extra innings, and the game was called because there were no electric lights and the game could not be continued in the dark. At other times a game disappeared from all public records even though it is clear that it was, in fact, played. Finally, the same game was sometimes reported on different dates or in contradictory locations, and there is no way to determine what the actual case was. In the games chart that is included at the end of this book, therefore, although there has been every conscientious effort to be comprehensive and to report accurately, there will inevitably be lacunae and unknown errors.

The usual venue for Spartanburg Sluggers home games was Duncan Park stadium. The irony of this fact is inescapable since David R. Duncan, the original owner of the property, was an officer in the army of the Confederate States of America, and the Spartanburg Sluggers, one of the first teams to be based there, played during the Jim Crow era, when Blacks were discriminated against in many different ways and when, in fact, Black fans even had to sit in a restricted area for Blacks when they attended games played by White teams such as the Spartanburg Spartans or Spartanburg Peaches. Black players could not eat in White restaurants, ride in the front seats of public transportation, or stay in downtown hotels, and their station in society was legally and socially inferior to that of White citizens.

Still, the construction of the Duncan Park stadium was an occasion of some importance locally. The ballpark was regarded as "one of the best in the southeast," and six months before construction was complete it had been leased for four years to the Spartanburg Spartans, a semipro team in the South Atlantic League.

Most Spartanburg Sluggers home games were played at Duncan Park, but some also were played at Wofford Park, the same field where in 1913 MLB Hall of Famer Ty Cobb had a verbal disagreement with a Wofford College player that led to a later confrontation in his room in the Ottaray Hotel in Greenville, during which Cobb gave the young man a considerable beating. The advantage of playing at Wofford Park for the Sluggers was that this field was on the edge of downtown and thus relatively more convenient for Black fans than some other venues.

I have been unable to locate any photographs of the Sluggers playing at Wofford Park or even contemporaneous pictures of the field, but there is a campus map from circa 1912, drawn by a student, that includes the baseball field. Current residents of Spartanburg and Wofford students will recognize the location as the site of the current Snyder Field at the college. The Sluggers played also locally at the Spartanburg Fairgrounds, and many other games took place in the home ballparks of opponents and were recorded in the newspapers of the towns in which these fields were located.

Most of the Sluggers' opponents were nearby. The most frequent of these were the Greenville, South Carolina, Black Spinners and the Black Sox; and the Asheville, North Carolina, Black Tourists and Royal Giants and the Asheville Blues. Also in close proximity were the Gaffney, South Carolina, Black Tigers a little way east on U.S. Highway 29; the Anderson, South Carolina, Hard Hitters just beyond Greenville; the Orangeburg, South Carolina, Tigers; and the York, South Carolina, Grays. Farther north across the state line were the Charlotte Hard Hitters, the Raleigh Tigers, and the Greensboro Red Birds

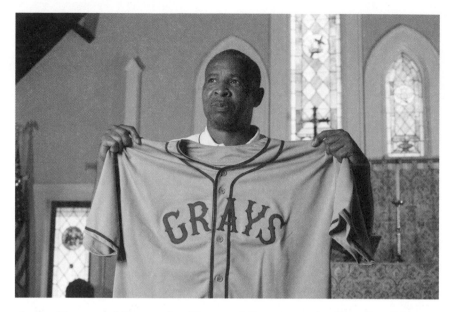

Luther Norman holding a replica Homestead Grays jersey; the Grays played the Sluggers at Duncan Park in April 1948

(sometimes called the Red Wings; there was also a Greensboro Red Sox team.). The Sluggers even played exhibition games against the legendary Negro League teams the Homestead Grays (losing 4-9 at Duncan Park on April 2, 1948) and the Ethiopian Clowns (again at Duncan Park on April 30, 1941, score unknown).

On August 20, 1944, **James Dunn**, the Sluggers' second baseman, was a member of a South All-Star team that played a Negro U.S. Marines team in Greensboro, North Carolina. The next month in 1944, on Sunday, September 24, the Sluggers' **Al Cunningham**, position unknown, played even farther afield for a team of South Carolina All-Stars in Yankee Stadium against the Philadelphia Stars on "Carolina Day." This game was the second game of a double-header, the first game of which featured a *North* Carolina All-Star team playing the New York Black Yankees. The sponsor of this special day of baseball was the Negro National League, and the New York newspaper reported that "one of the season's greatest crowds is anticipated to sit in and see the Tarheels and Palmettos [*sic*] give those stuck-up Northerners a thorough shellacking."

The Sluggers participated in other special and notable events. On July 4, 1929, they played the Charlotte Hard Hitters before the largest crowd of fans

Black patrons attending games at Duncan Park stadium purchased their tickets at a separate ticket box from that used by White fans.

who had ever viewed a game at Wofford Park up to that time. On August 5, 1941, they played the Asheville Black Tourists in the first game played between Black teams at McCormick Field, another classic ballpark constructed in 1924 two years before Duncan Park and used as one of the settings in the film *Bull Durham;* the next year, on July 6, the Sluggers played the same team in the Black Tourists' first ever night game. Five years later the "first annual semipro baseball tournament open to all colored teams in South Carolina and sanctioned by the National Baseball Congress" was held over a four-day period at four different sites across the state; the Sluggers participated, playing the York Grays in Rock Hill Stadium. Back at home in early April 1948 the Sluggers played what must have been a memorable game against the Homestead Grays, that year's victors in the Negro League World Series; the Grays roster in 1948 included such well-known players as **Louis Marques**, **Bob Boston**, and their fabled first baseman, **Buck Leonard**. During the final years of their existence the Sluggers played a noteworthy game on August 9, 1953, against the Columbia Red Caps at Capital City Park in Columbia, in which they included in their lineup an unnamed "girl first-baseman," no doubt in an attempt to bolster what by then must have been flagging attendance.

THE PLAYERS. A key question regarding the Sluggers, as with all other Negro Leagues teams, is who played for the team? Here the answers are incomplete at best, often frustrating in the recording of players' last names only, and even occasionally maddening in the listing of a player by merely an intriguing nickname. In many instances when players' names are known, the positions they played are not.

A surprisingly perceptive source of background information about semipro Black baseball teams is Bijan Bayne, whose "Early Black Baseball in North Carolina" appeared in 2011 in *Tar Heel Junior Historian* of all places. Bayne's comments are especially apropos since they are based upon his research in neighboring North Carolina, a state whose Black baseball history is much like that of South Carolina. Bayne characterizes the experience of Black players in the early 20th century as follows:

> Most of these semipro players earned very little from baseball, making a living through other jobs. Games often were scheduled quickly or on short notice—even while a team was on the road, in large touring cars packed with players. Sometimes fans passed a hat around the stands to collect money to support teams. Owners took about 70 percent of team earnings for operating expenses that included travel, uniforms, promotion, and umpire pay. The rest was divided among 12 to 16 or 17 players, counting substitutes and pitchers. The teams played on weeknights, usually Thursday, the traditional day off for many African Americans working as domestic employees.

Bayne also observes that "[m]ost team owners were well-to-do preachers, owners of segregated funeral parlors or taxi companies, or African American men in other businesses who loved baseball," a description that fits Big and Little Newt Whitmire.

The best known Slugger whose name I have been able to discover is that of left-handed hurler **Bob Branson**, the subject of two feature stories in Spartanburg newspapers. A familiar face on the local baseball scene, Branson had played regimental ball during World War II and was encouraged to try out for the professional Negro Leagues after his discharge in 1946. Nothing came of this effort, but Branson pitched for the Sluggers in at least 10 years—mostly in the 1940s—and was invariably singled out as a star attraction in newspaper announcements of upcoming games. Usually identified as "Lefty Bob Branson," he also was called "one of the best left-handers in the South" and "the league's outstanding pitcher," had the adjective "sensational" attached to his name in at least three different newspaper accounts, and once was described as interestingly "colorful." On July 7, 1948, Branson pitched against the Orangeburg Tigers in a 2-1 Sluggers victory that lasted 12 innings and in which he struck out the remarkable total of no fewer than 21 opponents but also gave up seven hits. Three weeks earlier he had struck out 10 Tigers in a 4-1 win, which was the first time the Tigers had lost to another Sandlapper team that year. Branson pitched many times against the Tigers, against whom he seems to have usually been victorious, and also appears to have been a regular starter against the Asheville Blues; a frequent mound rival was the Tigers' Jafers Parler.

A telling fact about the coverage that Branson received is that his name was often misspelled in press accounts. I have discovered his surname spelled variously as *Brinson, Bronson,* and *Brunson* in addition to the correct *Branson.* The appearance of these errors likely testifies not only to the unfamiliarity of the reporters with the player himself but also to the infrequency with which local papers assigned coverage of games between Black teams. The fact that in-house copy editors also failed to catch and correct the errors merely underscores the inequity of Jim Crow-era treatment of Black Americans in general.

Other Sluggers players receive mention, occasionally several times, in newspaper accounts, among them Branson's fellow pitchers "**Austin**," "**Chambers**," "**Wilburn**," "**Winford**," "**Garner**," "**Smith**," "**Grady**," "**Humphrey**," "**Evans**," "**Crausby**," "**Glenn**," "**Foster**," the intriguingly nicknamed "**Crossfire Crosby**" (A submariner? The same player as the possibly misspelled "Crausby"?), and "**S. Whitmire**" (perhaps a relation of team owner Newt Whitmire). Among the few position player whose name I have discovered are centerfielder **"Ghost" Kelly**, a speedster base stealer identified by the *Atlanta Daily World* as "the fastest man in baseball;" power hitter **Buster "Blue" Glenn**; **Johnnie James**; and **"Tracy"** (singled out because of two hits against the Asheville Blues on March 30, 1947), although in an era when players often played more than one position any or all of the aforementioned pitchers also might have played elsewhere on the field. The Sluggers also fielded an unnamed "girl first-baseman" in a game against the Columbia Red Caps on August 9, 1953, the last game I have discovered any published account of. Anecdotal testimony suggests that the girl who played in the August 1953 game played in at least two other games for the Sluggers.

Other than "Lefty" Bob Branson there are other Sluggers players and players who were Sluggers opponents who are known today simply because they survived into the 21st century and are remembered by contemporary residents of Spartanburg. These include **George Wanamaker** (or "Wannamaker" with two *n's*), **Clifford Layton**, and **Ken Free**; and Spartanburg native **Ted Alexander**, who played for four teams in the Negro Major Leagues, including the Kansas City Monarchs and Homestead Grays, and is buried in nearby Chesnee, South Carolina.

George Wanamaker might be the surviving Sluggers player most familiar to Hub City residents today. A third baseman and outfielder, Wanamaker played with Clifford Layton, a North Carolina Negro Leagues veteran, as a member of the Indianapolis Clowns in 1954-1955 and was also a teammate of Hank Aaron when he played with the Clowns. The Clowns were a legendary team composed of many individual legendary players, whose names are known today. Among these were Buster Haywood, "Big Daddy" Wooton, Harlem Globetrotter "Goose" Tatum, Paul Casanova, and "Choo-Choo" Coleman. Wanamaker also had played in the U.S. Army when stationed at Fort Knox, Kentucky, in the early 1950s, and in February 1955 he was signed by the Milwaukee Braves and assigned to their Jacksonville Braves affiliate in the South Atlantic League. At spring training his hitting was inadequate, though, and he was sent back to the Clowns for additional seasoning. He does not appear to have returned to MiLB.

Clifford Layton, formerly a pastor at First Baptist Church in Fayetteville, North Carolina, was a pitcher in the 1940s. A native of Harnett County, North Carolina, he moved to New Jersey and then New York City, where he attracted the attention of the Indianapolis Clowns while playing in Central Park. He played for the Clowns, the New York Black Yankees, and the Raleigh Tigers, and in 1951 he was given the opportunity to try out for the Brooklyn Dodgers, a chance he missed because of shoulder trouble. During his time with the Clowns, Layton was paid $250 a month. Layton's career can be traced in the following timeline:

1947-1948:   New York Metros (Central Park Community League)

1948:   Dunn Hornet Blues (Independent)

1949:   Raleigh Tigers (Semi-Pro)

1950:   New York Metros (Central Park Community League)

1951-1954:   Indianapolis Clowns (Negro American League)

1954:   Baltimore Elite Giants
              New York Black Yankees (Independent)

1955-1965:   East Orange Browns (Essex County League)

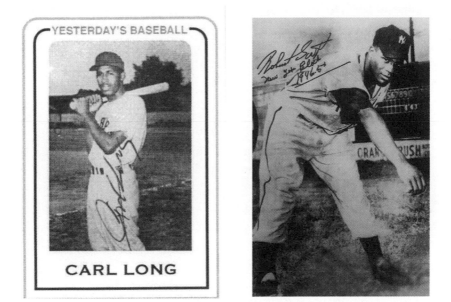

LEFT: *Birmingham Black Barons player and Rock Hill native Carl Long*
RIGHT: *Macon, Georgia, native Bob Scott, featured in the documentary film* The Other Boys of Summer, *played for the New York Black Yankees and the Memphis Red Sox. Scott fondly remembered playing at Duncan Park but passed away as the manuscript of this book was being written.*

Another Negro Leagues veteran from the Carolinas is Rock Hill, South Carolina, native **Carl Long**, a star hitter for the Birmingham Black Barons, who in retirement made appearances with Clifford Layton and Luther Norman to keep alive the flame of Negro Leagues history. After playing with the Barons, Long signed with the Pittsburgh Pirates in 1954 and played in their Minor League franchise in Quebec. He also played in the Pioneer League for the Montana Mustangs and, in 1956-57, for the Kinston Eagles in the Carolina League. His career is as follows:

1951:	Nashville Cubs (Negro Southern League)
1952:	Philadelphia Stars (Negro American League)
1952-1953:	Birmingham Black Barons (Negro American League; also Barnstorming vs. Jackie Robinson's All-Stars in the winter)
1954:	St. Johns (Quebec)
	Minot Mallards (Mandak League tryout, Leeds, ND)
	Birmingham Black Barons (Barnstorming vs. Jackie Robinson's All-Stars)
1955:	Billings, MT (Pioneer League)
	Waco, TX (Big State League)
1956:	Kinston, NC, Eagles (Carolina League)
1957:	Mexico City Tigers (Mexican League)
	Beaumont (Texas League)
1958:	Lincoln, NE (Western League)
1958-1961:	Kinston Grays (Independent)

Long still holds the Carolina League record for RBIs with 111 in 1956 and played against future MLB Hall of Famers Willie McCovey and Curt Flood in the Carolinas. It is likely that he played against the Spartanburg Sluggers at some point during the early or later 1950s.

Kenneth Allen "Ken" or "Kenny" Free is another Carolinian with time in the Negro Leagues and a presence today on the Old Timers memorial circuits. Free was born in Greensboro, North Carolina, in 1939, played as an infielder with Satchel Paige, and appeared in the last Negro League All-Star Game. He also played Minor League Baseball for four integrated teams in four different leagues, including the Western Carolinas and Carolina Leagues in the early 1960s. His chronology is the following:

1953-1955:	Greensboro Red Wings (Independent)
1955-1958:	Service in the military
1958:	Lexington Indians (South Atlantic League)
1959:	Raleigh Tigers (Negro American League)
1960:	Winston-Salem Giants (Independent)
	Satchel Paige All-Stars (Barnstorming/Independent)
	Cuban Giants (Independent)
	Hickory (Western Carolina League)
1961:	Raleigh Caps (Carolina League)
1962:	Quincy
1963-1964:	Salinas (California League)

Free played on the Negro League All-Star Team in 1959. It is probable that he played against the Sluggers and perhaps *with* former Sluggers players as well.

Ted "Red" Alexander never played for the Spartanburg Sluggers, but he was born in Spartanburg on September 15, 1912, and is buried nearby in the Brooklyn C.M.E. Church cemetery in Chesnee. During a 10-year stretch from 1938 through 1948, Alexander played for four different teams in both the Negro American League and the Negro National League: the Indianapolis ABC's, the Chicago American Giants, the Kansas City Monarchs, and the Homestead Grays. He also played for three teams at a lower level, including Satchel Paige's All-Stars, and while stationed at Camp Breckinridge, Kentucky, during World War II, he encouraged Lieutenant Jackie Robinson to write to the Kansas City Monarchs, who needed players. Alexander twice played in the Negro Leagues World Series, appearing with Monte Irvin and fellow South Carolina native Larry Doby in 1946 and giving up the winning base hit to a young Willie Mays in Game Three of the Series in 1947. Alexander continued playing until 1952, and although I cannot document that he ever played at Duncan Park, his Spartanburg County gravesite today is a silent memorial to many former Negro Leagues players like him who are but dimly remembered by contemporary baseball fans.

LEGACY. In spite of the relative paucity of information about specific Sluggers games and players' performances, there is still evidence that indicates that the Sluggers were a popular and successful organization. On August 29, 1911, for example, the Sluggers played at the Spartanburg Fairgrounds against a "Columbia Railroad [?]" team as part of what the newspaper identified as the "negroes' Emancipation day celebration;" on that occasion there was a $50 purse to be awarded the winners. On August 17, 1922, the Sluggers won a game against the Greenwood Giants by a score of 3-1; this day was particularly celebratory since a railway excursion brought 500 fans from Greenwood to Spartanburg, and in the Hub City the festivities included "the Kid Thomas Review Company, featuring the Creole Jazz Band." Excursions were apparently highly successful occasions: on May 21, 1923, an excursion train took a group of Spartanburg fans to Greenville, where the Greenville Black Spinners defeated the Sluggers 12-7 at League Park on Perry Avenue. On July 4, 1947, the Sluggers beat the Orangeburg Tigers 4-0 in a night game at Duncan Park after traveling to Spartanburg immediately following a 2 o'clock game at the Tigers' home field.

The Sluggers were a featured attraction on other special occasions. On July 4, 1929, the Sluggers defeated the Charlotte Hard Hitters at Wofford Park before the largest crowd to view a baseball game on that field until that date. On Labor Day 1935 the Sluggers played the Tryon Giants at the Baptist Assembly Grounds in East Flat Rock, North Carolina, on a day that also featured the Southern Railway and Pullman Porters Band, spiritual quartets, bicycle and foot races, and an address by Dr. C.F. Gandy. A different kind of excitement was offered at Duncan Park on April 30, 1941, when the Sluggers played the Ethiopian Clowns, whose slapstick-and-pantomime style presented celebrities like "Showboat" Thomas, one of the first two Black players to try out for a Major League team and later a scout for the Brooklyn Dodgers. Other players for the Clowns in Spartanburg were Albert "Khora" Heywood, who batted and ran the bases in his catching gear, and "Peanut" Nyasses, a standout pitcher and comedian.

The Sluggers also played opponents who are today better known than the Spartanburg club. In addition to the Greenville (Black Spinners, Stars, Black Sox, and Giants) and Asheville (Black Tourists, Blues, Stars, and Royal Giants) teams, the Sluggers as a team or individual All-Star Sluggers played against the legendary Ethiopian Clowns (April 30, 1941); a U.S. Marine Corps nine (August 20, 1944); the Philadelphia Stars (September 24, 1944); the Homestead Grays (including Buck Leonard, Louis Marques, and Bob Boston on April 2, 1948); the Charlotte Red Sox (three times in 1918 and 1919); the Columbia Red Caps (August 9,1953); and the Orangeburg Tigers (at least 18 games games in 1946-1949). Without a doubt there were other opponents as well in games whose records have not survived.

One final additional fact about the Sluggers that deserves mention is that they, like most Black ball clubs, had a substantial number of White fans during the Jim Crow era. Game announcements invariably contain phrases like "special reservations for White people," "large crowd of White people expected,"

*Ball autographed by Negro
Leagues star Buck Leonard,
who played in an exhibition
game at Duncan Park*

"large numbers of White and colored fans are expected," "reserved seat section for White spectators," "a grandstand section will be reserved for White people," "special section for White spectators," and "reserve section for White spectators." The popularity of the team among White fans is particularly sad and ironic at a time when local White media did not cover the Sluggers always or even regularly and when the Sluggers owner opened his kitchen at night to make sandwiches for Black entertainers who could not find after-hours service in White-owned establishments. The popularity of the team among Whites also attests to the talent of the players and the enthusiasm with which they played the game.

The Spartanburg Sluggers, then, had a long history, lasting in some incarnation from 1911 until 1961 and maybe later. They played in various leagues, including the Blue Ridge and, perhaps, the Negro Southern League and Negro American Association. Best described as a "semipro" and/or "exhibition" team, they were not affiliated with either Major League Baseball or—with just a couple of irregular exceptions—professional Negro Major Leagues teams, and they produced no national stars like Satchel Paige, Buck Leonard, or Jackie Robinson and Willie Mays early in their careers. Yet they had a dedicated local following and provided skilled and accomplished entertainment for thousands of Black and White fans. They played in familiar ballparks, mostly in Spartanburg and Greenville, but also elsewhere. Today their story is unknown to many, but their history is an essential part of the larger fabric of the history of Spartanburg's Black communities.

Appendix I at the conclusion of this volume contains a record of every Sluggers game I have been able to document.

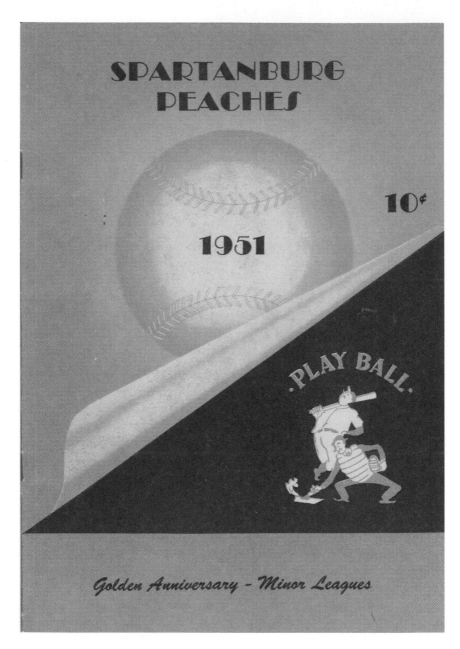

Vintage 1951 Spartanburg Peaches program

CHAPTER FOUR

. . . .

A Peach of a Team

SUNRISE ON A HAPPIER ERA. As the summer of 1946 approached, things were looking up in Spartanburg as in the rest of the United States. World War II was over, as was the Great Depression at last, and America was about to embark on a period of prosperity that would define the 1950s as the decade that established the middle class and which was the basis for future generations' nostalgia for the "good ol' days." Internationally the Marshall Plan was rebuilding a devastated Europe, and the emerging United Nations (1945) seemed a harbinger to a new era of peaceful coexistence, while the North Atlantic Treaty Organization (1949) would guard against mischief and codified our wartime alliances to protect freedom.

At Duncan Park things also were looking up. It had been half a decade since the Spartans had left town, and although the Sluggers continued to play only irregularly, Post 28 still played under the wooden roof, and there was talk of a new professional team coming to establish residence in the stadium as well. This turned out to be the Spartanburg Peaches, a Class B Minor League affiliate of, first, the St. Louis Browns (1946), and then the Cleveland Indians (1947-1955).

As was the case with most minor league franchises, the founding fathers of the Peaches were successful, civic-minded local businessmen who hoped to make a buck while providing a public service. In Spartanburg the leaders in the process were **G. Leo Hughes** and **R.E. Littlejohn Jr**. Hughes and Littlejohn were the highly successful owners of an oil transport business in Spartanburg.

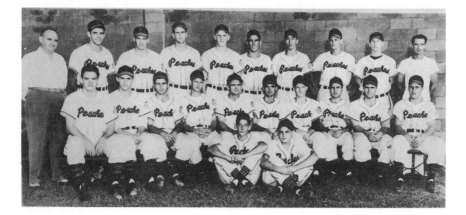

Undated team photo of the Spartanburg Peaches circa early 1950s

They would own the Peaches for their entire tenure in Spartanburg, and later on they also would become early owners of the Spartanburg Phillies. Hughes eventually became "tired" of baseball and relinquished his presidency of the team to Littlejohn. The latter was to have a huge influence on the young Pat Williams when he came to Spartanburg as the general manager of the Phillies in the mid-1960s, setting the 24-year-old on the sports administrative path that took him to the Philadelphia 76ers, the Chicago Bulls, and ultimately the Orlando Magic, where he served as executive vice president and where today he continues to be an imposing presence in publishing, public media, and promotional speaking. That story, though, will be told in the next chapter.

With the Peaches the Hughes-Littlejohn partnership presided over 10 years during which the team had more wins than losses most years and was an official affiliate of MLB teams, a fact that had not been true of the Spartans except at the very end of their 20-year presence in four different leagues. The Peaches were firmly embedded in the old Tri-State League for the entirety of their existence, but three aspects of their story are primarily notable today. One is the fact that MLB mainstay and fan favorite **Rocky Colavito** played here in 1952. Another is the fact that local hero **Ty Wood**—the bat boy of the World Champion Spartanburg Post 28 American Legion team in 1936, a player on the same team in 1938, and a central figure in local Textile League baseball—also played for the Peaches. The third is a racial incident that took place in 1954 when Peaches opponent the Knoxville Smokies fielded a Black third baseman.

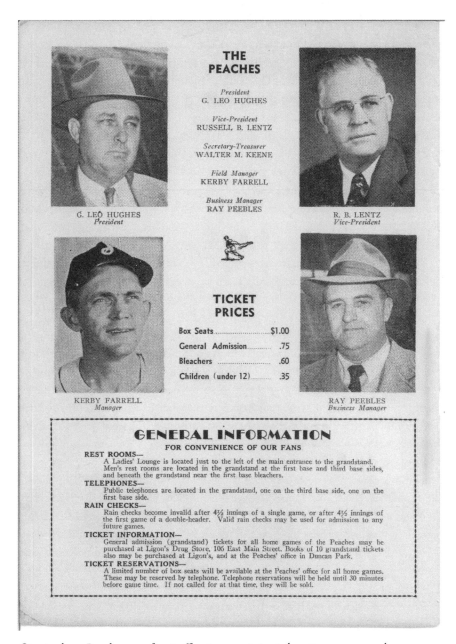

THE PEACHES

President
G. LEO HUGHES

Vice-President
RUSSELL B. LENTZ

Secretary-Treasurer
WALTER M. KEENE

Field Manager
KERBY FARRELL

Business Manager
RAY PEEBLES

G. LEO HUGHES
President

R. B. LENTZ
Vice-President

TICKET PRICES

Box Seats $1.00

General Admission .... .75

Bleachers .... .60

Children (under 12) .... .35

KERBY FARRELL
Manager

RAY PEEBLES
Business Manager

GENERAL INFORMATION
FOR CONVENIENCE OF OUR FANS

REST ROOMS—
A Ladies' Lounge is located just to the left of the main entrance to the grandstand. Men's rest rooms are located in the grandstand at the first base and third base sides, and beneath the grandstand near the first base bleachers.

TELEPHONES—
Public telephones are located in the grandstand, one on the third base side, one on the first base side.

RAIN CHECKS—
Rain checks become invalid after 4½ innings of a single game, or after 4½ innings of the first game of a double-header. Valid rain checks may be used for admission to any future games.

TICKET INFORMATION—
General admission (grandstand) tickets for all home games of the Peaches may be purchased at Ligon's Drug Store, 106 East Main Street. Books of 10 grandstand tickets also may be purchased at Ligon's, and at the Peaches' office in Duncan Park.

TICKET RESERVATIONS—
A limited number of box seats will be available at the Peaches' office for all home games. These may be reserved by telephone. Telephone reservations will be held until 30 minutes before game time. If not called for at that time, they will be sold.

Spartanburg Peaches 1950 front office team; missing is longtime owner and Spartanburg city father R.E. Littlejohn.

PEACHES HISTORY. During 1946, the Peaches' first year in Spartanburg, the team was one of 11 Minor League affiliates of the now defunct St. Louis Browns of the American League. They played in the Class B Tri-State League against five other teams from three states, including South Carolina, North Carolina, and Tennessee: the Anderson A's, Asheville Tourists, Charlotte Hornets, Shelby Cubs, and Knoxville Smokies. The inaugural campaign was not auspicious, as the Peaches compiled a dismal record of 52-87, a woeful *41 games behind the first place Hornets.* Four players from this team—catcher **Jerry Lynn**, outfielders **Frankie Pack** and **Ken Wood**, and pitcher **Ted Petoskey**— all eventually made it to The Show, but as a group in Spartanburg they were not much good. Lynn batted .312, but Pack hit only .135, Petoskey just .200, and Wood .230. Petoskey pitched only eight innings in three games and compiled a record of 0-1.

Petoskey, a Michigan native who played football and basketball in addition to baseball and had been an All-American as a running back at the University of Michigan, was an outstanding athlete who had a long career as a coach in three separate sports at two South Carolina colleges. At Wofford College he coached football (1942 and 1946), basketball (1942-46), and baseball (1945-47); and at the University of South Carolina he coached basketball (1935-40) and baseball (1940-42 and 1948-1956). He also scouted for the New York Yankees and went to Columbia in 1959 to get Capital City Park ready for Yankees spring training. In that same year he was a member of the board of directors of Columbia Little Boys Baseball when the author of this book played for the Civitans team.

Local residents hoped that 1947 would be a better year. For one thing, the Peaches were now a farm team of the Cleveland Indians; for another, Bill Veeck, the renowned president of the parent ball club, brought in **Kerby Farrell** as manager *and* player. Farrell still had his mojo apparently. He played first base, batted .295 in 491 at-bats, and even pitched in seven games, compiling a 2-1 record and a 1.93 ERA, the lowest on the team. The Peaches also won about as many games in 1947 (88) as they had lost in 1946 and finished first in the Tri-State League.

A large measure of the team's turnaround must be attributed to Farrell, who was to remain at the helm through 1950. By the time he came to Spartanburg in 1947, the native Tennesseean had played and managed for 17 years in professional baseball, including two years in MLB (1943 with the Boston Braves and 1945 with the Chicago White Sox), and he was to play two more years after leaving the Peaches. In 1957 he managed the Cleveland team, compiling

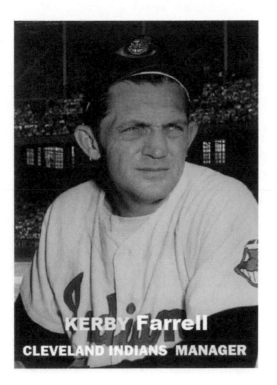

*Peaches Manager Kerby
Farrell*

a 76-77 record and placing sixth in the American League. He can best be described as a veteran Minor Leaguer with substantial skills acquired through years of experience in 11 different leagues in the South, the Midwest, the Pacific Northwest, and the Mid-Atlantic. His overall record as a Minor League manager was 1710-1456, and in addition to his first place finish in 1947, his Peaches teams also finished second in 1949 and 3rd in 1950. His Peaches record was 317-251.

Another member of the 1947 Peaches also became a Major Leaguer: **William James "Pete" Milne,** an outfielder from Alabama, who batted .326 the year Farrell became manager. Milne played a dozen years in professional baseball, including three different stints with the New York Giants in 1948 (12 games), 1949 (31 games), and 1950 (four games). His best Minor League season was the one he spent in Spartanburg.

On July 11, 1947, Milne also took part in a unique event in the Peaches' history. The score was 7-7 against the Knoxville Smokies in Duncan Park stadium in the bottom of the ninth inning, and Milne came to bat with one out and the bases loaded. He stroked the ball cleanly through the infield, streaked

Future Spartanburg Peach Ty Wood when he played for Post 28 in the 1938 American Legion Little World Series.

toward first base, and the runner on third headed home with the winning run. That was when the stadium lights went out. They remained off for a minute or so. Eddie Hearn, the umpire, called the play a hit and the outcome a win for the Peaches. The Smokies protested over the cheers of the 2,000+ fans in the grandstand, and Hearn called C.M. Llewellyn, the president of the Tri-State League, who ordered a replay of Milne's at-bat. By then the fans and the official scorer had gone home, so the scorer had to be called back to the ballpark from his home, and Milne stepped back up to the plate. This time the outfielder grounded out, the game went into the 10th inning, and the Smokies won the game 13-7 after scoring six more runs in the top of the inning, once again proving that in baseball anything can and eventually will happen.

Local baseball icon **Ty Wood**, a founder of the annual Textile League reunions that took place annually for years in Spartanburg, also played for the Peaches. Wood had grown up in Spartanburg, and baseball was in his blood. He was the bat boy for the Spartanburg Post 28 American Legion team in 1936, the year the team won the Legion Little World Series, and in 1938 he was

*Ball signed by the
1947 Spartanburg
Peaches*

team captain and played third base on the team that was runner-up. During
1939-1943 he played baseball for Spartanburg Methodist College and then
Wofford; and he also played Textile League ball, ultimately joining former
players Powerhouse Hawkins, Manning Bagwell, Pete Brown, Pete Kleitches,
Ox Taylor, and Red Ellison, and local radio legend Bill Drake in the 1970s to
organize the August Textile League commemorative celebrations that often
drew 400 participants.

After service in the Coast Guard during World War II, Wood also played
for the Spartanburg Peaches, in 1946 and maybe 1947, although he is not listed
in the team rosters for those years at baseball-reference.com. He played shortstop and second base and is mentioned in several newspaper clippings in the
possession of his daughter, Susan Pope. An endearing story told by Pope is that
on the day that she was born her father was scheduled to practice with the Post
28 American Legion team, which he was coaching at the time. While waiting
on his daughter's birth, Wood asked the nurse in charge "if he could leave the
hospital for a while to go to the practice." The nurse replied, "You aren't going
anywhere!"—and he didn't.

Another unique piece of Spartanburg Peaches 1947 history is the signed
baseball found by author and Hub City Writers Project Board Chairman **John
Cribb** when he and his family moved into their new home in Converse Heights.
The house previously had been owned by former Spartanburg mayor **Neville
Holcombe**, and the ball apparently had been presented to Holcombe by the

LEFT: *Al Aber, 1948-49 Spartanburg Peach.* MIDDLE: *George Zuverink, 1948 Spartanburg Peach.* RIGHT: *"Big Jim" Fridley, 1949 Spartanburg Peach who played 14 years in MLB.*

team. Holcombe would have known team owners and officers Leo Hughes and R.E. Littlejohn, and he surely also appreciated the Peaches' contributions to the local economy.

The remainder of the Spartanburg Peaches' time at Duncan Park was typical of that of many other ball clubs except for one matter discussed in greater detail below. During their tenure in Spartanburg, the Peaches racked up a respectable record, with wins exceeding losses in seven out of the 10 years they were here. More complete details can be found in **Appendix II: The Spartanburg Peaches Residency and Appendix III: Spartanburg Peaches Who Made The Show.**

Of all the Spartanburg Peaches who played in Duncan Park, the best remembered today is **Rocky Colavito**. Colavito was born on August 10, 1933, in the Bronx and attended Theodore Roosevelt High School, which he left after his sophomore year to play baseball. He impressed Mike McNally, a scout for Cleveland, during a tryout at Yankee Stadium, and McNally wanted to sign him, but the rule was that a young player could not sign a professional contract until his high school class graduated. It took an appeal to MLB Commissioner Happy Chandler for Colavito to be allowed to sign with the Indians.

Success came early for Colavito in the Minor Leagues. In 1951 he played for the Daytona Beach Islanders in the Class D Florida State League, where he hit a respectable .275 as a 17-year-old. By 1952, when he was still only 18 years old, he had been promoted to the Class B Spartanburg Peaches, with whom he had continued success, hitting .252 in 66 games while knocking 11 home runs and 14 doubles.

All-time great Peach Rocky Colavito, who led the AL in home runs in 1955 and played all of 1965 for the Indians without an error in the outfield. Colavito is shown here with South Carolina native and MLB HOFer Larry Doby and Negro Leagues great Minnie Miñoso.

In Spartanburg Colavito rented a room on South Converse Street in the home of future Reverend Kirk Neely's grandmother, Belle Hudson. As do many fans who saw Colavito play, Neely recalls the power in his bat that made him a formidable home run hitter, as well as the power in his arm, which allowed him to fire a strike to the plate from center field during a contest held at the 1952 Tri-State League All-Star game. When challenged by the public address announcer to surpass that feat, the right fielder unleashed another throw that sailed over the stadium *and* the parking lot toward the former Morningside Baptist Church beyond.

Colavito's prowess on the baseball diamond 70 years ago is still celebrated in Spartanburg today. The power of his throwing arm was known far and wide, and he threw the ball from home plate over the centerfield fence in more than one Minor League ballpark just for fun and to impress his fans. In 1956, when he played 35 games for the Cleveland affiliate in San Diego, he threw such a ball 435 feet 10 inches over the outfield wall from home plate, just seven feet short of the longest throw ever recorded in professional baseball. His power as a hitter was also impressive. He once lofted a ball over the centerfield fence in Duncan Park and then over the grove of trees beyond the fence and *then* onto the youth baseball field beyond that. In 1956 his batting average in San Diego in the nearly Major Pacific Coast League was an impressive .368; clearly he was ready to return to Cleveland.

Colavito left Spartanburg in 1952 to play for the Cedar Rapids Indians of the Illinois-Indiana-Iowa League. A year later he was with the Reading Indians in the Class A Eastern League, and the year after that he was at the pinnacle of the Minors, playing for the AAA Indianapolis Indians in the American Association. In 1955 he made the Majors, where he played, with two interludes, until 1968, first with Cleveland, then the Detroit Tigers, the Kansas City Athletics, the Chicago White Sox, the New York Yankees, and the Los Angeles Dodgers. His Major League career was notable for a number of reasons. He was a six-time American League All-Star, and he led the league in home runs (42) in 1959 and in RBIs (108) in 1965; he hit 40 home runs in three seasons, 30 home runs in seven, and 20 home runs in 11. His Major League total of 374 homers during his career places him just ahead of Gil Hodges and Ralph Kiner, and his overall stats on measures of standard Hall of Fame criteria place him in a class with Frank Howard, Boog Powell, and Norm Cash. He is not a member of the MLB Hall of Fame, but his record is as good as those of some who are, and he is cherished in the hearts of Indians fans everywhere.

A DARKER TIME. Colavito, then, is perhaps the brightest star in the Spartanburg Peaches cosmos, but there are also starless nights in the Peaches universe. One involves a series scheduled between the Peaches and their Tri-State League rivals the Knoxville Smokies in August of 1954. The Peaches had been members of the Tri-State League since their inception, and although the number of teams in the league varied a little from time to time, in 1954 there were six teams, including those from the nearby towns of Asheville, Rock Hill, Greenville, and Anderson, as well as more distant Knoxville.

Times were changing in baseball as in the larger American society in 1954. Both the National League and the American League had been integrated for seven years, in the National League by Jackie Robinson and in the American League by South Carolinian **Larry Doby**, who had been born in Camden in 1923. Doby had played for the Newark Eagles in the Negro National League and, like Colavito, played several years with the Cleveland Indians, where in 1948 with Satchel Paige he became one of the first two Black players to win a World Series. Still, change was coming slowly to the Jim Crow South. The Supreme Court's decision in Brown vs. the Board of Education was rendered in only 1954, and it was prelude to several decades of resistance, violence, and backlash, including the murders of NAACP official Medgar Evers in his own driveway; of student organizers Michael Shwerner, James Chaney, and Andrew Goodwin on a dirt road in rural Mississippi; and of young girls Addie Mae Collins, Cynthia Wesley, Carole Robertson, and Carol Denise McNair at a choir rehearsal in the 16th Street Baptist Church bombing in Birmingham.

In Spartanburg things seemed calm on the surface. Governor James F. Byrnes, nearing the end of his four-year term in 1955, actively opposed integration, as did most White citizens of South Carolina, but overtly active opposition largely took the form of promoting "separate but equal" schools for Black students so, at least theoretically, there would be no need for integration to equalize the opportunities of minority students. There eventually would be lunch counter demonstrations against White-only seating at the downtown Woolworth's, but those would not occur until the summer of 1960.

Meanwhile other forces were at work in the Hub City to help make integration, when it did come, at least palatable to all. Among these were leaders in the White community. Textile magnate Roger Milliken, for example, whose parents had moved south from the industrial northeast and were influential in the integration of the Spartanburg Cub Scouts and youth sports, was instrumental in the integration of Wofford College and the foundation of a second country club in the city so that his employees, especially executives who were Black or Jewish and were therefore barred from membership in the existing country club, might join a club that welcomed them.

City school superintendent McCracken shepherded Spartanburg County School District Seven through a largely successful and peaceful merger between all-White Spartanburg High School and all-Black Carver High School. The two schools were not to be merged into a single integrated secondary school until 1970, but when the schools did merge, there were no marches, no demonstrations, and no attacks against school buses transporting Black students to formerly all-White schools like there were to be even in Boston and other cities beyond the Mason-Dixon line. Local students, teachers, and administrators of both races facilitated this process and contributed much to its success.

The work of Milliken, J. G. McCracken, and others was influential and important, but it must be noted that their efforts occurred mostly in the 1960s and subsequent decades. In 1954, racism was alive and well in American sports, even in professional sports and especially in the American South. Despite increasingly frequent and better and more widely accepted opportunities for Black ballplayers, discrimination and hatred still reared their ugly heads from time to time. A case in point is the four-game series scheduled between the Spartanburg Peaches and the Knoxville Smokies in August 1954.

The first game in the series was played on Monday, August 2. This was the opener of the final Tri-State League series in Knoxville in 1954, and the article in *The Knoxville Journal* announcing the series opener promised nothing out of the ordinary. Things went well apparently until the fourth inning. Then, **Aldo Salvent**, the Black Smokies third baseman, either came to bat for the first time in the game, or he was inserted into the lineup as a pinch hitter. The latter possibility is most likely as Salvent played both third base and shortstop and had two at-bats, and two other players also played third base and short and had at bats in the game. Salvent had a double in one of his at-bats, and the Smokies won the game 5-1.

R.E. Littlejohn, the Peaches club president, was furious. The Spartanburg City Council had passed an ordinance that prohibited local teams from playing at Duncan Park against visiting teams that had Black players. This wasn't an issue in the August second game because it was played on the Smokies' home field, not at Duncan Park. Littlejohn, however, maintained that he also had a "gentleman's agreement" with the other five teams in the Tri-State League, according to which they had all agreed not to field any Black players whenever the Peaches traveled to their home cities for an away game. The Smokies had violated this agreement when they brought Salvent onto the field. Moreover— and more to the point—Littlejohn had "promised Spartanburg citizens the team would not play against Negroes."

Littlejohn's ire and its repercussions are hard to believe today. He immediately got on the phone and told Bobby Hipps, the Tri-State League president, that the Peaches would not play the remaining three games in the series with the Smokies, that Spartanburg would withdraw from the league, and that all of the Peaches players would be sent to other Cleveland Indians affiliates, thereby bringing an end to professional baseball in Spartanburg. According to his statement to *The Brownsville Herald,* the circumstances were "beyond my control." What happened next is not entirely clear at a distance of 69 years, but the phone lines connecting the Tri-State owners surely sizzled for most of that night and the next day. In the end, the Smokies must have apologized and Littlejohn relented. Salvent, who had only joined the Smokies 11 days before the game against the Peaches, was reassigned to another team in "another league of B classification," and the Tri-State League, whose schedule and perhaps mere existence were threatened by the Peaches' near withdrawal, was saved. The Peaches remained members of the Tri-State League, and none of the players had to pack their bags.

It is important to note that the Peaches at this relatively late date chose to protest the on-field presence of a Black player from another team rather than to integrate their own team and acknowledge that times were changing. Minor League Baseball had integrated eight years earlier, and in 1954 there were Black players in both the National League and the American League in Major League Baseball. It is significant, too, perhaps, that it was team president Littlejohn, responsive to the citizenry of Spartanburg, instead of manager **Jimmy Bloodworth**, a seasoned baseball professional, who issued the order not to play. Change came slowly in the South.

The narrative of Littlejohn and the Peaches' opposition to the presence on the field of a Black player was reported across the nation. Stories appeared in newspapers in North and South Carolina, Texas, Tennessee, Alabama, California, Washington state, Connecticut, Delaware, Pennsylvania, Georgia, New Jersey, Iowa, New York State, New Jersey, Louisiana, Florida, Utah, Kentucky, Ohio, and Montana, and perhaps elsewhere. *The Hartford (CT) Courant* quoted Littlejohn's statement, "This is the worst kick in the teeth I ever had," and went on to observe that two years earlier a fate similar to Salvent's had been met by Black player **James Mobley** when Tri-State League teams objected to his presence in a game in Rock Hill, South Carolina. It was also true that Salvent had been withheld from playing in a Smokies game a week earlier against the team in Anderson, a city that had a similar local ordinance.

Many southern White owners and fans—and likely more than a few White players as well—supported the dismissal of Salvent and the reinstatement of Spartanburg into the Tri-State League. A final word, though, was that expressed by Marion E. Jackson, the *Atlanta Daily World's* sports editor, in his "Sports of the World" column on August 12. Jackson, a widely read and respected Black journalist, first quoted Luther Thigpen, the White sports editor of *The Macon News* who had himself been a ballplayer at Mercer University and was to become a free speech champion as executive editor of the *Asheville Citizen-Times* during the 1970s, who had written:

> It is almost incredible that such a thing could come about now. Three or four years ago, it would have been understandable.

> But frankly it seems old fashioned now for a baseball club or its followers even in the Deep South to get upset because of a Negro player in the lineup.

Jackson agreed, commenting, "Thigpen's viewpoint is indicative of the New South and we reprinted it to show that not all Southerners are steeped in hate and prejudice...."

In the end, the Peaches front office decided to hang on for one more year, but their heart was no longer in it. Former club President G. Leo Hughes had resigned in June of 1952 and handed over the reins to his partner, Littlejohn, telling friends that he was "just tired of baseball." One of the things that he was likely "tired of" was the poor attendance at Duncan Park. *The Greenville News* reported in June 1952 that attendance was so low that year that the team might not be able to finish the season unless it picked up. Things were not to get much better. In 1954 the team lost $11,000, and a new ownership committee called Citizens Baseball Inc. and including Mayor Neville Holcombe was organized for 1955. The year after the controversy over Aldo Salvent was difficult for the team: losses increased to $15,000, and the Peaches finally threw in the towel. There was to be no Minor League team again in Spartanburg until the coming of the Phillies in 1963. In one last irony, however, the Black Spartanburg Sluggers remained and were to play their brand of enthusiastic baseball at Duncan Park and elsewhere until 1961.

CHAPTER FIVE

. . . .

Heart of the Lineup:
Thirty Years of the Phillies

THIS CHAPTER OF THE HISTORY of Duncan Park stadium should have been the easiest to write, but it was also in some ways the hardest. The Spartanburg Phillies came to Duncan Park in 1963 and left in 1994, a period of three decades of Minor League ball. Although the team's success naturally varied considerably over time, the mere fact that the Phillies spent 30 years in the Hub City is notable in itself since their time here was two to three times as long as the other Minor League teams that called Spartanburg home. The Sluggers played longer, but their tenure was always intermittent and optimistic at best, and they never were officially affiliated with any Major League Baseball or, for the most part, major Negro Leagues team.

So there is a wealth of material and statistical data surrounding the Phillies' residency at Duncan Park. This fact is both a blessing and a curse of course. It is a blessing because a wonderfully talented group of guys played and managed and coached here. The Spartans might have had future MLB stalwart Debs Garms and the Peaches Rocky Colavito, but the Phillies had **Scott Rolen** and **Ron Allen** and **Denny Doyle** and **Ozzie Virgil, Greg Walker, Ryne Sandberg,** and many others. Mike Kelly might have been a fan favorite when he managed the Spartans and Kerby Farrell when he managed the Peaches, but the Phillies had **Pat Williams** *and* **Bob Wellman** *and* **Rosie Putnam** *and* **Mel Roberts** in the office and on the field. The Spartans and the Sluggers might have played for much of their residencies at the Fairgrounds and Wofford Park, but the Phillies played in a stadium that had lights, a broadcast booth and

Scott Rolen, one of the best third basemen in baseball, was a Spartanburg Phillie in 1994.

public address system, and a legitimate concessions stand (even at times including waitress delivery to the box seats). Promotions early on in the history of Spartanburg baseball might have been limited to greased pigs and flagpoles, but under the Phillies, especially when Pat Williams was general manager, fans saw the **Phillie Phanatic**, the **Famous Chicken**, softball phenom **The King and His Court**, **Morganna the Wild One**, a donkey diving into a shallow pool of water from an elevated platform, the NBA's **Oscar Robertson,** and even legendary quarterback **Johnny Unitas.**

You get the picture, I think. The wealth of talent and promotions and facilities—plus the abundant documentation of all of these riches—is also a curse for anyone writing about the Phillies when they were at home at Duncan Park. The reality is that there is *so much* information about the Phillies that any chronicler must of necessity be selective. Indeed, it would be possible to write a hefty book about the Phillies alone at Duncan Park, and perhaps someday someone will; even that endeavor would be daunting. So what follows is inevitably a matter of choices made, and, of course, those choices are mine and mine alone. I am to blame if your favorite player does not get a paragraph of his own. I am to blame if your favorite stat from Scott Rolen is omitted. I am to blame if your favorite Atlanta Brave is not mentioned even though he played seven or eight games here when he competed for Greenwood or Greenville or Augusta before graduating to The Show. I promise that I will do my best to paint a reliably characteristic portrait of the Phillies when they took the field in the shadow of Morningside Baptist Church just off Union Street, but I fear I will inevitably fall short of your expectations. If so, I apologize—and I will be happy to let you borrow any of my unused primary materials if you would like to finish the job.

The origins of the Phillies' move to Spartanburg is a pretty good story in itself. The official vote by City Council setting things in motion took place on Thursday, January 10, 1963. On that date, largely at the instigation of Spartanburg Mayor Robert L. Stoddard, council agreed to lend a "citizen's baseball committee" headed by R.E. Littlejohn and Leo Hughes, the former principals in the organization of the Spartanburg Peaches, funds for the repair of Duncan Park stadium. On that same date the Philadelphia Phillies also came to "a full working agreement" with the same group. The arrangement was that the City of Spartanburg would lend the citizens group between $18,000 and $20,000 for repairs to the stands and that the ownership group would repay the loan over a five-year period. The loan would be interest free, and

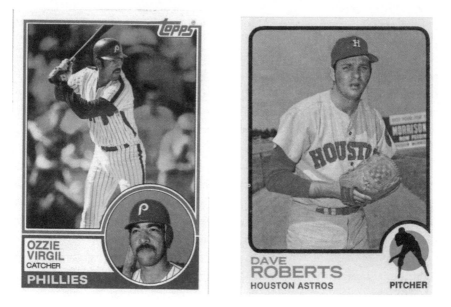

LEFT: *Ozzie Virgil, a stellar catcher in Spartanburg in 1977 and later in Philadelphia, Atlanta, and Toronto.* RIGHT: *Dave Roberts, a journeyman lefty, played on the Phillies first team in Spartanburg in 1963.*

if the team became unable to repay the funds, Littlejohn and Hughes would personally guarantee repayment. Going forward, the city would rent the stadium to the nonprofit citizens group for the nominal sum of $1 a year and pay the cost of lighting, and the team would maintain the upkeep of the stadium and grounds. Wes Livengood, a Philadelphia scout who negotiated on behalf of the big Phillies, agreed that the Major League team would supply players and a manager and pay their salaries, while the local team would absorb the operational expenses. The team would become a member of the eight-team Class A Western Carolinas League (later the reconstituted South Atlantic or Sally League), a pro forma step according to the League President John Moss. The ensuing favorable vote by City Council was unanimous, and the Phillies, too, were apparently well satisfied: "We (the Phillies) are well aware of the baseball reputation of Mr. Littlejohn and Mr. Hughes and we are exceedingly happy to have a working agreement with the Spartanburg club," the Phillies' Livengood said. Mayor Stoddard was rewarded for his part in bringing the team to the city by being chosen to throw out the first pitch in the first game. (In a sad irony, Stoddard also was chosen to throw out the ceremonial first pitch in the Phillies' *last* game at Duncan Park 31 years later as well.) Stoddard's son, Robert, recalls that "My energetic father often told me one of his happiest accomplishments during his 12 years as mayor of Spartanburg was his role in bringing the Phillies to play in Duncan Park."

The Phillies were to remain in Spartanburg until 1994, but their beginnings at Duncan Park were inauspicious. **Lou Kahn**, a Minor Leagues catcher with 17 years' service, mostly in the Cleveland and St. Louis organizations, was named manager for 1963, and under him the team finished 66-58, good enough for third place during the regular season in the eight-team Western Carolina League. The 1963 Spartanburg Phillies did have four players who made the Majors: **Jackie Brown**, who pitched for seven years and compiled a record of 47-53; **Dave Roberts**, who pitched for eight teams during 13 years in MLB; **Gene Stone**, a first baseman who played part of one year with Philadelphia; and **Dick Thoenen**, who pitched in one inning for the National League Phillies in 1967, giving up two hits and a run. The next year the Class A Phillies fared worse, finishing 47-80 and dead last under Manager **Dick Teed**, who had played in the Minors but struck out the only time he ever came to the plate in the Majors in 1953; Teed had played 17 years in the Minors, however, and was to return to manage the Phillies in Spartanburg in 1967. The '64 Spartanburg team had only one player who made the Majors, a pitcher named **Mike Jackson**, who compiled a 2-3 record and a 5.80 ERA playing parts of four seasons for the Phillies, the Cardinals, the Royals, and the Indians.

THE *WUNDERKIND* AND HIS TEAM. The 1965 season brought General Manager **Pat Williams** to Spartanburg, where he was to begin a stellar career in professional sports administration. Williams had played baseball himself, first at Tower Hill School in Wilmington, Delaware, under his own father and with his pal, Ruly Carpenter, son of Philadelphia Phillies owner and his father's friend Bob Carpenter. The two boys spent a lot of time in the Phillies clubhouse and dugout and got to know stars of that era like Ruben Amaro, Tony Gonzalez, Robin Roberts, Richie Ashburn, Stan Lopata, Curt Simmons, and future manager Sparky Anderson. Williams was a good enough high school catcher that he went on to play at Wake Forest University for four years and was then offered a contract with the Miami Marlins, at that time a Class D Minor League team in the Florida State League, by family friend Bob Carpenter.

In Miami, Williams had a pretty good first year, batting .295 and walking 10 times in 61 at bats—but he also had only three extra base hits—in 1962. The next year was not so good; in 1963 he averaged only .204, although he apparently had a pretty good eye since almost 30 percent of his at bats resulted

Pat Williams, the legendary general manager of the Spartanburg Phillies in 1965-1968, became a National Basketball Association executive after leaving Spartanburg.

in walks. He was also a hard worker and enthusiastic, but it was clear that Williams would never make his mark in Major League ball. What next for him then? Interestingly, Phillies scout Wes Livengood, the same individual who negotiated the Phillies arrangement with the City of Spartanburg in 1963, although he recognized that Williams did not have the skills to make it in the Majors, did have enough vision to note of the young catcher that he "[ha]s a bright future in a front office."

Marlins GM Bill Durney apparently agreed with Livengood and hired Williams after his playing career ended as the Marlins' business manager from 1962 to 1964. In this role Williams proved successful, kept his nose to the grindstone, and also studied during his time off to earn a master's degree in physical education from Indiana University. In addition he was given an introduction to Major League owner, innovator, and promoter extraordinaire **Bill Veeck** by Durney. The result of that introduction, a meeting in Veeck's retirement home on the Chesapeake Bay in September 1963, was a friendship of more than two decades and some good advice, among which were "Know somebody" and "Learn to type." Williams listened, learned, and as a result was offered the job as Spartanburg Phillies general manager in 1965. In a move that would set him on his lifelong path toward the senior vice presidency of the National Basketball Association Orlando Magic, he accepted the offer.

Williams proved to be a natural promotional son of Veeck and a wunderkind of managerial expertise. Andre Thornton, who met Williams in 1968 and then played first base for Spartanburg in 1969, later playing for the Chicago Cubs, Montreal Expos, and Cleveland Indians, recalls Williams's enthusiasm and hard-working energy: "Pat was all over the stadium." Thornton and Williams became lifelong friends.

Williams's legendary promotions on the field at Duncan Park and elsewhere are discussed in Chapter Seven below; here we will consider the other sides of his acumen as GM in Spartanburg. During his first year in the Hub City, the Phillies compiled a record of 54 wins but 68 losses, finishing seventh out of eight teams under Manager **Moose Johnson**. The next two years, however, were much better. The team finished first both years, in 1966 under **Bob Wellman**, an experienced Minor League manager, who managed for 25 years and had an overall record of 1,663 wins and 1,470 losses; and in 1967 under former Manager **Dick Teed**. The 1966 Phillies were later ranked 78th out of the top 100 minor league teams of all time. The team won 91 of its 126 games, including 25 wins in a row from mid-July through mid-August; among the 25 wins were 20 complete games and only 17.1 innings pitched by relievers. In 1968 the Phillies did well also under Manager **Bobby Malkmus**, finishing second but losing in the League Playoffs.

By the end of 1966, Williams had begun to accumulate the first of the many awards he was to receive during his long career as a professional sports executive. He had been named Outstanding Young Man of the Year by the Spartanburg Jaycees and had twice won the Western Carolina League Manager of the Year Award. The year 1968 was to be Pat Williams's last year in Spartanburg, but by then there was little that he had left undone. As a result he was named Minor League Executive of the Year in 1967, partly because of attendance at Phillies games, for which the team set a Class A attendance record in 1966.

Williams made many friends in Spartanburg, but the most important was R.E. Littlejohn, the Phillies owner and a businessman who owned a hugely successful petroleum transportation business, which expanded into petroleum equipment, trailer sales, and a real estate holding company which possessed assets in Atlanta, Blacksburg, and Woodruff, some of the successors of which were still active in Spartanburg at the time this history was being written. People who met Littlejohn were impressed with him. When Williams knocked

*Baseball signed by
Pat Williams and
other Spartanburg
Phillies*

on his door on Glendalyn Place in Spartanburg to introduce himself, he was met by the businessman's wife, who told him in no uncertain terms, "No matter how long you're in baseball, you'll never meet another man like my husband."

Mrs. Littlejohn's statement was true. Littlejohn was one of the best known, most widely respected, and most impactful citizens of the Spartanburg of his day. He became young Williams's friend as well as his boss and mentor, and through him Williams found a comfortable spiritual home at First Baptist Church, the beginning of a lifelong journey of devout Christian discipleship which has defined his personal and business relationships ever since his time in the Hub City. In his memoir *Ahead of the Game,* in corporate and civic presentations around the country, and in many conversations with others, Williams has called Littlejohn a father figure, just the guide he needed as a young man unsure of his path in life. "Mr. Littlejohn had a rare quality called wisdom," the retired NBA executive recalled. "I think about him every day."

Among Williams's achievements with the Phillies was the fact that he had brought broadcaster **John Gordon** to Spartanburg with him in 1965. The two had met in Indiana, and when Williams came to the Hub City as the new 24-year-old general manager of the Phillies, he invited his friend Gordon, who was then living in Michigan, to come to Spartanburg, where the team had a contract with WORD radio but no broadcaster. At WORD Gordon was "a big part of what we did," according to Williams, but then in the winter of 1965-1966 a new manager, Bob Brown, was hired by the station. Brown, variously described as "outspoken" and "aggressive," had "big plans for WORD," but his plans did *not* include John Gordon. Brown intended to fire Gordon, and the result was an angry meeting in team owner Littlejohn's office. Williams

Pat Williams's first Spartanburg Phillies team, 1965; Field Manager Moose Johnson is at the center of the front row.

remembers the meeting as the only time that he either saw the businessman visibly angry or heard him utter a four-letter-word. The outcome was that the team "fired" radio station WORD and signed on with the better, more powerful WSPA, which then re-hired Gordon. Williams and Gordon lived together for the four years that they worked together for the Phillies; along with his and Williams's young friend Bobby Pinson, Gordon also helped build the Duncan Park press box. Littlejohn's confidence in Gordon was publicly vindicated, too, when the broadcaster was named South Carolina Sportscaster of the Year for 1968. Characteristically, also, Gordon did not learn about what Littlejohn had done on his behalf until more than 50 years later; the team owner never was one to promote his benevolence toward others in a public way.

Gordon's time in Spartanburg, where he and Williams were popular enough to be called the town's most eligible bachelors, provided him with personal as well as professional benefits for a lifetime. Here he met his wife, Nancy Razor, who was working as a county agent for the Clemson University Home Economics Department, and he and his wife were both active members of the

First Baptist Church community, where they were married by Dr. Alastair Walker. After Gordon had worked in Spartanburg for five years, he then moved on to more prestigious jobs with the Baltimore Orioles, the University of Virginia, the Columbus (Ohio) Clippers and Ohio State University, the New York Yankees, and finally the Minnesota Twins, where he ultimately retired after working in the booth from 1986 through 2011. Years later, though, he still remembered his time in the Hub City fondly, recalling that "I always referred to Duncan Park as 'Beautiful Duncan Park.' It was always the most beautiful ballpark in the league."

Things were good for Williams, too, and important people beyond Spartanburg had noticed him as well. He was considered the leading candidate for the job of general manager at the Phillies Class AA team in Reading, Pennsylvania, a position he ultimately declined on the advice of Littlejohn. He had been interviewed by both National Radio Hall of Fame broadcaster Bill Stern and journalist/commentator Walter Winchell, and Sandy Grady profiled him for the *Philadelphia Daily News.* In the baseball offseason he was broadcasting football and basketball games himself for Wake Forest, Clemson, Duke, Davidson, and Georgia Tech. More importantly, he had met his own future wife, **Sandy Johnson,** and became a devout Christian, a decision that changed his life in many ways.

To top off his year, Williams received a phone call on July 8, 1968, from Jack Ramsay, the coach of professional basketball's Philadelphia 76ers, a real surprise because Williams had been working in baseball. As surprised as he was by the call, he was more than gratified by Ramsay's offer to become the business manager of the 76ers. Ramsay told him that many people in Philadelphia had noticed his success in Spartanburg, and he offered him $20,000 a year to come to the City of Brotherly Love. Williams could not say no.

Pat Williams left Spartanburg after the 1968 season, but there would be no more popular figure associated with the team in the 31 years of their tenure at Duncan Park. **Rosie Putnam**, a Montanan who became a later general manager of the team and was the wife of Spartanburg's postmaster, was also popular and a familiar face among fans in the grandstand; and **Mel Roberts**, an established coach well liked by both players and fans, served the team as field manager for four years in the late 1980s and early 1990s, but neither he nor Putnam surpassed Williams in the hearts of local fans, and neither is remembered as fondly today. Still, the Phillies continued to play at Duncan Park for another 26 years.

Included at the end of this narrative as **Appendix IV: A Timeline of the**

Rosie Putnam, Phillies GM who was a familiar presence in the Duncan Park grandstand and brought team mascot "Rookie," who did double duty as night watchdog after the gates were locked, to the stadium.

Spartanburg Phillies, 1963-1994 is a table that records an historical overview of the Phillies in Spartanburg, but, of course, it cannot give anything like a complete picture of the teams that represented the city on behalf of the Philadelphia parent club. For that one must turn to www.baseball-research. com, to MLB, to SABR, and to a double handful of other websites and print sources that can help fill in the blanks and flesh out the picture. Here the most that can be presented is the briefest of overviews, primarily in some stories that follow. It is, after all, the stories that are the *best* thing about baseball.

One of the best player stories from the Phillies years at Duncan Park is that of young **Jerry Martin**, who played there in 1972. Martin had grown up in Columbia, where his family lived in the historic Olympia Mills community and where his father, Barney, and his uncle, Buddy, had played Textile League baseball. Martin played baseball at Spartanburg Junior College for two years and then finished at Furman University, where he starred in both basketball and baseball. Not big or powerful enough for professional basketball, he responded to the call of the Phillies, signing as an amateur free agent, with the result that he played Major League ball for 11 years and then had a long and satisfying coaching career as well.

Martin describes his year in Spartanburg as his best in baseball. He batted .316, hit 12 home runs, had 112 RBIs, and was named MVP of the Western Carolinas League. "I hit fourth," Martin says, "and every time I came up to bat it seemed like there were guys on base, and luckily I drove in a lot of 'em." In addition Bob Wellman was "a good manager," and "another good guy, Mel Roberts, he was the coach;" Roberts later managed the Phillies and also coached in Philadelphia.

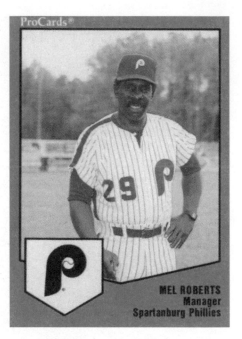

Mel Roberts, probably the Spartanburg Phillies all-time most popular manager

In a doubleheader in Charlotte one day Martin went 0 for 8 at the plate, but the next day he was 8 for 9. Unsurprisingly, "That kinda sticks in my head," Martin says today.

In many ways Martin was living the dream in 1972 in Spartanburg. In addition to his conspicuous success on the field, he had friends in town. One, Bob Martin, a barber he had known at the junior college, had a "fishin' hole" and "I loved to fish," Martin says. "Bob was a good guy, and I'd go over there to his house, and we'd catch bream at his fishin' hole." Martin also enjoyed the perk of free meals at the local steakhouse whenever he hit a home run. He would wait until he had hit two home runs, and then he and his wife would go eat a free steak dinner—"That was a big deal." Another bit of unexpected good fortune was seeing textile magnate Roger Milliken at the barber shop. "Mr. Milliken would walk from his house in Converse Heights to the barber shop," Martin says. Milliken's fellow mill owner Walter Montgomery used to drive "an old car" to the same barber shop.

Examining the records of talented players like Martin on the roster of the Spartanburg Phillies from 1963 through 1994 reveals some surprising facts and an unexpected number of players who made significant marks in Major League

Baseball after departing the Hub City. In the 1993 commemorative program celebrating the Phillies' 30th year in Spartanburg—and the year before the Phillies were to *leave* Spartanburg forever—the team listed every player whose name had appeared on their roster in a two-page spread of tiny newsprint. The total ran to *over 800 ballplayers,* and at that time *over 150 of them had played Major League Baseball* as well.

In such a rich talent pool there were bound to be standouts and memorable athletes. Among these were 30 players listed on veteran Manager Mel Roberts's "25th Anniversary Spartanburg Phillies Team." This team was as follows:

FIELD MANAGER	Bob Wellman (1966, 1971-72)	
INFIELD	Ron Allen, 1B (1966)	Greg Walker, 1B (1978)
	Denny Doyle, 2B (1966)	Juan Samuel, 2B (1981)
	Blas Santana, 3B (1971)	Keith Moreland, 3B
	Larry Bowa, SS (1966)	(1975)
		Ryne Sandberg, SS
		(1979)
OUTFIELD	Jerry Martin (1972)	Lonnie Smith (1974)
	Gilberto Torres (1966)	George Bell (1979)
	Barry Bonnell (1975)	
CATCHERS	Ozzie Virgil (1977)	Don McCormack
	Wilfredo Tejada (1983)	(1975)
DESIGNATED HITTER	Willie Darkis (1980-81)	
PITCHERS	John Penn (1966)	John T. Parker
	Tom Underwood (1973	(1966-67)
	Kevin Gross (1981	Willie Hernandez
	Mark Davis (1979)	(1974)
		Marty Bystrom (1977)
RELIEVERS	Pete Manos (1975)	Rocky Childress (1982)
	Ramon Carabello (1984)	Jerry Reed (1978)
GENERAL MANAGER	Pat Williams (1965-68)	

The Phillies were to play in Spartanburg another six years after Roberts compiled his All-Time list, so some of these names likely would be replaced during that time span. Most conspicuous would be the addition of **Scott Rolen** (1994) perhaps in place of Blas Santana (1971). Other players who might have been substituted for one of Roberts's listees include **Mickey Morandini** or **Andy Ashby** (1989), **Mike Lieberthal** (1991), and **Mike Grace** (1991-92, 1994).

Of all the Spartanburg Phillies who went on to The Show and had productive Major League careers, only two so far have been elected to the MLB Hall of Fame. **Ryne Sandberg** was elected to the Hall in 2005. Sandberg played short stop for the S-Phillies in 1979 as a 19-year-old, having played the previous year for the Helena, Montana, Phillies in the Pioneer League. He grew up in Spokane, Washington, and played there for North Central High School. A three-sport standout, Sandberg played quarterback on the football team and was named a *Parade* All-American. After being drafted in the 20th round of the 1978 MLB draft, he batted a noteworthy .311 in 56 Rookie League games at Spokane and then moved on to Spartanburg.

In the Hub City, Sandberg batted .247 in 138 games, with four home runs, 47 RBIs, and 64 bases on balls; he was also co-team leader in runs scored with 83. He had a fielding percentage of .945 and turned 80 double plays. Promoted to AA Reading in the Eastern League in 1980, Sandberg had a breakout year and was named a league All-Star. After a year in which he batted .293 and played both second base and short stop for the Oklahoma 89ers of the AAA American Association, as well as playing in six games for the Phillies, the 22-year-old was traded to the Chicago Cubs, with whom he played for 15 years and established himself as one of the sport's best players. His career stats include 10 All-Star games, one MVP title, nine Gold Gloves, seven Silver Sluggers, 1 year as Home Run Derby Winner at the All-Star Game, and seven years as the National League Assists Leader. In his SABR biography of Sandberg, Tim Herlich concluded with justification that he was "one of the greatest and most popular players in club history."

The other MLB Hall of Famer who played for the Spartanburg Phillies was **Scott Rolen**. Like his future batting coach and fellow Spartanburg Phillie Jerry Martin 20 years earlier, Rolen, a native of Jasper, Indiana, was a two-sport star in high school, being named Indiana's Mr. Baseball and winning state All-Star honors in basketball. Recruited by a number of universities to play basketball, he also was selected in the second round of the 1993 MLB draft by the Phillies and ultimately committed to the University of Georgia for basketball with an optimistic plan to play basketball in the winter and minor

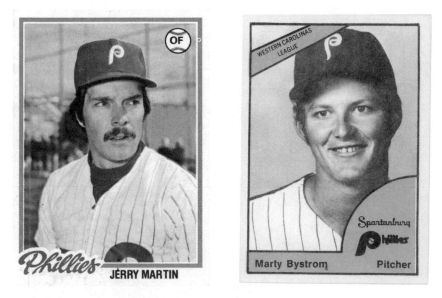

LEFT: *Columbia, South Carolina native Jerry Martin had his most productive baseball year in Spartanburg in 1972 and was MVP in the Southern Conference Basketball Tournament during his senior year at Furman.* RIGHT: *Marty Bystrom, one of Mel Roberts's All-Time pitchers, later pitched for Philadelphia and the New York Yankees.*

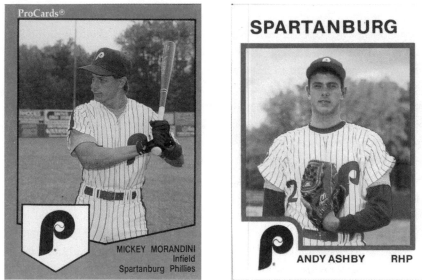

LEFT: *Mickey Morandini played more than a decade in MLB, mostly for Philadelphia.* RIGHT: *Andy Ashby played in two All-Star games in the Majors and three times placed in the top 10, in shutouts and in complete games.*

Ryne Sandberg, the first MLB Hall of Famer who was a Spartanburg Phillie.

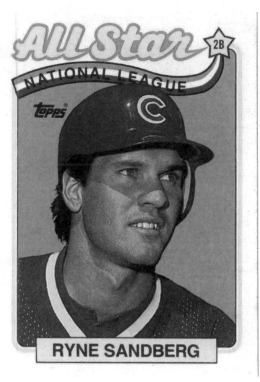

RYNE SANDBERG

league baseball in the summer. The Phillies had plans of their own, though, and talked him into devoting all of his time and energy to baseball. He then played rookie-league ball in Martinsville in the summer of 1993 before being sent to Class A Spartanburg for 1994. Rolen's first batting coach for the Phillies was Columbia, South Carolina, native Jerry Martin, who today fondly remembers the 18-year-old newcomer as "a nice kid" whom he still calls "Scotty."

Rolen had a good year in 1994. Having batted a respectable .313 in Martinsville the year before, he hit .294 in Spartanburg with a .462 slugging percentage, third highest on the team. He also had a .917 fielding percentage in 138 games at third base and was named team MVP. His next stops on the road to The Show were Class A-Advanced Clearwater, Class AA Reading, and AAA Scranton-Wilkes Barre. In spite of an injury to his glove hand in Clearwater, Rolen had recovered enough that by August of 1996 he was in Philly at the start of a 17-year career with the Phillies, the Cardinals, the Blue Jays, and the Reds. His career batting average in MLB was .281, with a .490 slugging percentage, 316 home runs, and a .968 fielding percentage. He was 1997 National League

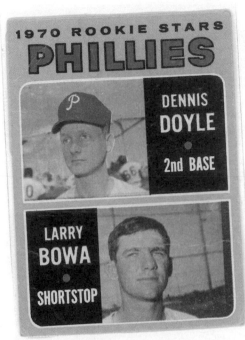

Denny Doyle and Larry Bowa, who were teammates in Spartanburg in 1966, were featured together as Topps "1970 Rookie Stars."

BELOW: *The 1994 Spartanburg Phillies, the last Phillies team that played in Duncan Park. Future MLB HOFer Scott Rolen is second from the right in row four.*

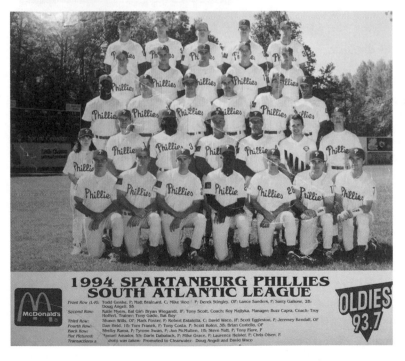

1973 Spartanburg Phillies

The 1973 Phillies, including Voice of the Phillies Warner Fusselle with his signature untamable hair; others included are GM Hub Blankenship, back row second from left, and coach Mel Roberts, third from right.

Rookie of the Year, was named to seven All-Star teams, and won eight Gold Gloves and a 2002 National League Silver Slugger. In January 2023 he was elected to the Major League Baseball Hall of Fame in his sixth year of eligibility. Rolen is also known for his charitable work, in Philadelphia for hospital visits to sick children and for other charities, including his family's Enis Furley Foundation.

Other standouts for the Phillies gained prominence off the field. John Gordon already has been mentioned as a longtime professional big leagues broadcaster, primarily for the Minnesota Twins; but there was also **Warner "The Fuse" Fusselle.** Fusselle began his broadcasting career after graduating from Wake Forest University and brief stints in the Army and a broadcasting school on the West Coast. After applying for more than 100 jobs, Fusselle was finally hired by a radio station in Salisbury, North Carolina, whence he came six months later to Spartanburg; here he worked for the Phillies and also broadcasted local high school and college games. One of the most engaging stories ever related by Fusselle is how he auditioned for the Phillies job in the 1970s by broadcasting a Spartanburg High School game into his portable tape recorder while lying recumbent on the hill behind center field as the Spartan High track team huddled around him to see what was going on. Fusselle worked hard in Spartanburg: Kenn Blankenship, whose father, Hub, was general manager of the Phillies, recalls the "huge notebook full of information on the players" that the broadcaster would pore over on bus trips between games.

The hard work paid off; from Spartanburg Fusselle was hired to broadcast the American Basketball Association Virginia Squires games and then moved on, eventually to a high profile job with *This Week in Baseball* (syndication, NBC, CBS, and ESPN) and play by play for the Brooklyn Cyclones.

Another Phillies broadcaster of note was **Ed Dickerson**, a local junior high school history teacher whose second job was in front of the microphone, not just for the Phillies at Duncan Park from 1967 to 1994 but also for Spartanburg High School and Spartanburg Christian Academy. When Dickerson was 5 years old in 1952, he won a Lone Ranger wristwatch for being the youngest fan at Duncan Park for a Peaches game, and he was hooked on baseball for the rest of his life. Although he left Spartanburg for a short period as a boy, he returned in 1963 and started going to Phillies games; he was alerted to the opening for a public address announcer at Duncan Park in 1967 by Joe Bowles, the announcer who was also dean of men at Spartanburg Junior College and who was leaving for a similar position at Brevard College. During the nearly 30 years that Dickerson sat at the microphone, he says he was there "when the stadium was filled to capacity and when it had only a few dozen fans," but that it was "enjoyable, exciting, entertaining no matter how many fans were there." The Phillies ownership clearly found his work enjoyable, exciting, entertaining, too.

Another indication of the Phillies' close connections to their Spartanburg community fan base was the hiring of Dickerson's predecessor at the old desktop microphone in the wooden "pressbox" perched above the roof of the grandstand. **Mack Amick** was a senior at Spartanburg High School in 1966, and although he was "not much of a baseball fan," he *was* "into the theater of it all" and had done on-air advertisements for WSPA radio's *Farmer Gray* show as well as some interviewing of outstanding Spartan High students for an interested public. Pat Williams had become aware of Amick and of the fact that the young man came to Phillies games, and the GM approached the student. "Mack, I know you can do this. I think you'd be perfect," he pitched. Young Amick found his future boss to be "very personable. Nicest guy in the world." He accepted the job offer and climbed the ladder up to the box on the roof during the spring of his senior year and the summer beyond until he traveled down to the University of South Carolina in Columbia as a freshman.

One other non-athlete who deserves to be mentioned in some detail for her

Local broadcasting legend Ed Dickerson in the Phillies press box.

place in Phillies—and Duncan Park's—history is **Rosie Putnam**. A native of Montana, Putnam first worked as the team's part-time receptionist but quickly impressed the team's owners, and "[e]ight months later, she was practically running the office operation and three years after that [in 1990] she was presented with the title of General Manager." She became office manager soon after being hired by minority owner Jeff Kurkis, who needed all the help that he could get when he himself had to step in as heneral manager upon the abrupt departure of his predecessor, Junior Ramsey. Putnam arrived for work early, was good at her job, and often assumed additional responsibilities, which even included painting stadium seats and office walls. Prior to being named GM, she became even more involved in the team by investing as a part-owner herself in 1988. The fit was a natural one for Putnam, who said, "This thing captured my heart so fully I don't know if I could walk away from it." When she was hired as the

Phillies GM, Putnam was one of only four women executives in Minor League Baseball. Field manager Mel Roberts depended heavily on her.

All good things come to an end, though, and from the time of their arrival in Spartanburg the Phillies faced challenges, especially monetary ones. Duncan Park stadium was already 37 years old when the Phillies began their tenure, and attentive readers will be aware that teams often abandoned ballparks in much less time; the Atlanta Braves, for example, departed from Turner Field only *20* years after it was opened for the 1996 Summer Olympics. It's one thing for a stadium to be a classic structure placed on the National Register of Historic Places. It's quite another for it to become an economic albatross around the neck of its owners and lessees. From the beginning, this tension was a very real aggravation between the City of Spartanburg, the Philadelphia Phillies, and the owners of their Spartanburg affiliate.

Even in 1963 income was uncertain, and finances were less than a guaranteed zero-sum prospect for the parties involved. Still, the city had committed its initial $20,000, guaranteed by Hughes and Littlejohn, and early on excitement over the new team helped to stimulate attendance, and then the success of General Manager Pat Williams—especially the relentless promotions that were a feature of his managerial practice—brought fans in in droves. By the beginning of 1967 nearly $50,000 had been spent to upgrade facilities at the ballpark, and the city planned additional repairs of $38,000. Spending on upgrades continued throughout Williams's time in Spartanburg. After Williams left, the team continued to do well for a while, winning Western Carolinas League Championships in 1972 and 1973, and the team's 1974 *Souvenir Program* boasted on its front cover of the stadium's "**NEW MULTI-VAPOR LIGHTS**," which it claimed were "**BRIGHT AS DAYTIME**." The new lights were part of a quid pro quo arrangement with the Philadelphia Phillies, who were not making money on their local affiliate and who demanded the new lights as a condition of remaining in the Piedmont. The City was to provide up to $20,000 for the new lights, to pay the electric bill, and to maintain the grass and grounds around the stadium; as the discussions continued, the city also agreed to provide police protection. The parties agreed to the terms, and the souvenir program optimistically proclaimed, "80 or More [wins, that is] in '74."

By 1978, a decade after Pat Williams's departure, the situation was not so rosy. In 1976 and 1977 the Phillies had told City Council that the grandstand needed a new roof likely to cost $40,000, and there was a need to demolish the right field bleachers. The Philadelphia parent club announced in February that it was interested in selling the team, and local powerhouse entertainers The

Marshall Tucker Band had even made an offer; Mayor Frank Allen and two others were also interested in acquiring the team. Howie Bedell, the assistant director of Minor League operations for the Phillies, would not negotiate a sale, though, until the issues surrounding renovations were resolved.

To complicate matters, only 22,000 fans attended games at Duncan Park in 1978, and 1979 attendance had been only 29,448. Owners Patty Cox and her partners from Oklahoma City, who had purchased the team from Leo Hughes and R.E. Littlejohn and had owned it for less than a year, wanted to sell. Cox, the owner of an advertising agency in Oklahoma City, previously had been the only woman GM in Minor League Baseball and had almost quadrupled attendance for the Oklahoma City 89ers, the Phillies' AAA affiliate in the Pacific Coast League. She and her two partners, Bing Hampton and Michael Carmack, had owned the 89ers and planned to buy the Phillies AA affiliate in Jacksonville, and had taken the helm in Spartanburg confident that they could turn around the team's dismal financial performance. Cox's daughter Blair had even been hired as the new Phillies business manager. Patty Cox's approach to baseball in Spartanburg notably echoed that of Williams in the 1960s: "We're promotion-minded. We don't believe in papering the town and giving our product away, but we do believe in making the ballpark a fun place to be."

The best laid plans of mice and men go oft astray, however, to paraphrase Scottish poet Robbie Burns, and the team continued to lose money. For one thing, attendance, although better than the year before, still fell short of the 35,000 fans the owners had estimated they needed. A major reason for this was probably the fact that the Phillies had not been issued a license to sell beer because the team had no local citizen among its ownership group. In addition, one of the primary financial backers of the team had died in a plane crash. The situation was dire, and the owners hustled to try to cut their losses. They had a number of options: to sell the team to the Phillies, to sell the team outright to a local ownership group, to sell some of the team to new partners, or to sell the team to the City of Spartanburg. The first and last alternatives were less than realistic since neither the big Phillies nor City Council wished to assume all of the risks of ownership alone.

The ownership issue was settled at last on Monday, November 5, 1979, when Dr. Frank A. Weir Jr. and attorney James Shaw, announced the purchase of the team, planning to implement a "fun for the family" atmosphere and to construct a new "clubhouse" containing a locker room, athletic treatment room, and manager's office, the cost of this facility to be borne by the city ($30,000) and the Weirs (the excess beyond $30,000). The Weirs also held a renaming contest, settling on "Traders" as the team's new nickname; implemented weekly bingo games; and pushed back the starting time of Wednesday night games to accommodate midweek churchgoers. In addition, they reapplied for a beer license that had been rejected the year before. The optimistic new owners hoped to replicate the success of Williams and to welcome 70,000 fans to the old grandstand during the coming season.

The Weir team were firmly grounded in the Spartanburg community, they loved baseball, and they worked hard to make their ownership a success. The legal corporation that owned the team included Weir, his wife, Janet, their children, and Shaw, who was both the general counsel and the doctor's son-in-law. Shaw related how the team management was indeed a family affair, regularly pitching in on game nights to keep the wheels turning. After securing their beer license, Shaw himself sold the beer at the stadium; Weir women cooked hot dogs, and the children worked at other stadium jobs. The family were full participants in team's business affairs as well, attending MLB winter meetings in Toronto and spring training in Clearwater, Florida, where a highlight for young Jim Shaw was getting to meet Phillies legend Pete Rose, still an active player.

The Weirs lasted three years, it turned out. After three more name changes—"Spinners" (ironically the former name of semipro teams in *Greenville*, South Carolina, a city with a history of considerably successful Minor League baseball), "Suns," and back to "Phillies"—and the start of a revolving carousel of team ownership groups, the handwriting was on the wall. In spite of the best efforts of local citizens hoping to save baseball and provide a long-term family-friendly environment for good, clean, traditional, community-based entertainment, the dice were rolling more and more often in favor of bottom line-focused city leaders concerned that public money not be spent on a facility increasingly unlikely to return a profit on investments. Nearly heroic exertions by Rosie Putnam and Mel Roberts and even the late-term creativity of almost non-stop promotions in the 1990s could not prevent the inevitable. Competition from Greenville (the AA Braves), Charlotte (the Knights), and Columbia (the Mets and Bombers) was fierce, and even Clemson University and the University of South Carolina had better stadiums with wider concourses, superior concessions, more exhibition space, and games and picnic areas for kids and their families; even the lights and public address systems were better than those at Duncan Park.

Facilities issues were obviously one of the factors in declining attendance. The clubhouse, dugouts, and storage areas were all subpar and already had been contentious points in negotiations between the city and the Phillies and between the city and the Oklahoma ownership group, and solutions remained elusive during the ownership of Weir. The increasing shabbiness and inadequacy of the ballpark was reflected in attendance, in fans' attitudes toward the stadium, and in the parent club's reluctance to shell out the progressively greater amounts needed to rectify the situation. In the glory days of Pat Williams, the Phillies always drew well more than 100,000 fans a season, from a low of 1,805 fans per game in 1968 to a high of 2,746 fans per game in 1966. By 1978, a critical year for the Phillies, attendance averaged just 382 fans per game, and by 1986 it was just 249 attendees per game. Also in 1986 the team suffered its most losses ever in a season—95—and only once thereafter did the S-Phils win more games than they lost. Clearly the combination of low attendance and mediocre performance both increased the inclination of owners to sell and drew the attention of prospective new owners looking for a cheap franchise they could relocate to a more attractive market elsewhere.

The financial bleeding was relentless. Spartan Sports Inc., the partnership formed by the Weir and Shaw families, delayed decisions on when to build a new clubhouse—the existing contract technically gave them until November 1981—as well as whether to apply for a beer license, and these delays had negative consequences. By early 1983 some of the wood in the grandstand was rotten, 33 lights on the field needed replacement, the concessions area had burned, and the city could not spare the labor and equipment necessary for it to shoulder some of the repair burden. What had at first seemed like a fun business opportunity had turned into little more than a troublesome tax shelter for the doctor. When the team was at last sold to a new non-local partnership—Dixie Professional Sports, owned by Robert Anderson, Clyde "Dixie" Wilmeth, and Dennis Bastien—in February 1983 and renamed the Spinners, the team was stretched so thin that the *Philadelphia* Phillies took the unusual step of providing allowances to the local Phillies for balls, bats, and new uniforms. Don Bramblett, a local electrical contractor, volunteered his time for electrical repairs, the Spartanburg Methodist College baseball team volunteered two days of labor on the playing field, and others volunteered as well. Neither Anderson, a New York attorney, nor Wilmeth, a textile executive from Philadelphia, had owned a team before, but Bastien, the third owner who became also the general manager, had worked for teams in both Macon and Gastonia. All three new owners were optimistic, and the city agreed to some limited assistance with repairs and maintenance; the partnership closed the deal with Weir for a purchase price of $63,000.

The 1983 season proved less profitable than all had hoped, however, and the Dixie Sports partnership in addition managed to alienate both American Legion Post 28, whose team also played at Duncan Park, and the city of Spartanburg by a curious event that occurred in mid-July. On the evening of Thursday, July 14, the Legion team arrived to prepare for their last game of the season against Mauldin, only to find that "[s]everal Spartanburg Spinners players' cars were parked in left field." The Legion team could not play, Spinners manager Bastien was out of town, and the Legion team had to forfeit its last game of the year. Post 28 coach Gene Campbell charged that the oversight—or prank or whatever it was—had been deliberate. Bastien countered that he had been out of town and had no prior knowledge of what had occurred. Spinners manager Rollie DeArmas admitted that his players sometimes did, in fact, park on the field but only when he had been told that the Legion team did *not* have a game and no one had told him about the Thursday night game. "They like us to park off the field," DeArmas said, "but sometimes we get lackadaisical and park them on the playing field." He went on, "I didn't figure there was a game because there wasn't anybody out there. It wasn't done on purpose, though. It was just a lack of communication." Spartanburg City Manager Bill Carstarphen added that the city was, "very disturbed with the way the Spinners representatives chose to handle the situation."

The car park in left field fiasco publicly soured the relationship between the city and the team's ownership and in addition highlighted earlier disagreements over the use of the field by the American Legion and whether and how much the Legion would have to pay for such use. Moreover the Dixie Sports partnership had not been as successful as early publicity had suggested it might be. Therefore by the end of 1983 the team was on the market again, and by Christmas the city was on the verge of approving a sale to new owner Lou Eliopulos. Eliopulos, another absentee owner headquartered in Jacksonville, Florida, had been "buying and selling teams for the past seven years." He owned two teams—in Jacksonville and in Elmira, New York—when he was negotiating the Spinners purchase, and recently had sold three others—in Florence, South Carolina; Hagerstown, Maryland; and Peoria, Illinois.

In retrospect, the spinning turnstile nature of Eliopulos's Minor League ownership history could and perhaps should have occasioned more careful examination, but City Council optimistically approved the sale, agreeing to rent the stadium to Eliopulos's Baseball Enterprises for $1 a year for five years, with the ownership agreeing to maintain the stadium. Eliopulos was also optimistic about the team's prospects. "I'll just say I'm very enthused about it," he gushed.

"All our people are sales oriented and our belief is if you work hard enough, see enough people and have enough sales, people will come see your product." Another promising sign was that the team's new general manager was to be Dan Overstreet, the 1981 Class A Baseball Executive of the Year—an accomplishment that must have reminded the Hub City establishment of Pat Williams's similar achievement a decade and a half before.

Two years later, although Eliopulos stated to the local paper that his team had been profitable, he found himself forced to sell it for reasons of personal health. He had had three strokes in four and a half years, the most recent in Spartanburg in October 1985, and now he was ready to "get out of baseball altogether." Offers were few and far between, though, in spite of the facts that "[i]t's been on the profitable side" and that preseason advertising for the coming season had been "very good." Absentee ownership had been a problem ever since the Weirs sold the team, however, and that had affected attendance. It was hard for local fans to care about a team owned by someone they did not know and run into at church or in the barbershop, a situation very different from the early days of the old Phillies, when they were owned by local businessmen R.E. Littlejohn and Leo Hughes.

With a valuation estimated by Eliopulos at between $200,000 and $300,000, the team finally found a new owner in Ellis "Woody" Erdman and his partners at Suns Sports Complex Inc. Once again, none of the principals in the partnership was local. Christina Wilhite, the new president of the club, did plan to move to Spartanburg, but Erdman was a Pennsylvanian (who also early on said that he would move to Spartanburg), board member David Lemon was a First Union Bank executive from Greensboro, and treasurer Ray Thompson was "also from out of town." Still, Erdman touted his team's commitment to the city, promised new uniforms and a new paint job for the grandstand, and practically guaranteed attendance better than 1985's 48,000 fans.

Flies settled onto the top of this ointment almost immediately. Ellis and Erdman failed to make the scheduled City Council meeting after the sale was announced to the media ("car trouble"); Erdman revealed that he did not know that Lou Eliopulos had agreed to pay for new lights for the stadium before he sold the team to Erdman's group and that Sun Sports was now similarly obligated; and it emerged that Eliopulos's Baseball Enterprises had incurred liens held by First Citizens Bank, Dr. Weir, and Jones Equipment Leasing Company Inc. Eliopulos had in fact generated considerable ill will in Spartanburg, one local hotel even encountering difficulty over payment for a visiting team's bill for their lodging during a series in the city.

Eliopulos's contract with Suns Sports Complex Inc., quickly became mired in a court battle by March 1986—the intended new owners sued for breach of contract and damages, and Eliopulos countered that he still owned the team since Erdman and his team had not paid the full purchase price of $200,000 or appeared at two scheduled court hearings—and by mid-April of that year the situation was so tenuous that the *Herald-Journal* headlined "Minor League Team Has Two Owners?" and a private citizen named Velma Wright actually came forward with the cash necessary to pay players' salaries herself, for one payday distributing 14 envelopes containing bundles of $20, $10, and $5 bills since neither ownership group would pay the salaries. By then also Phillies manager Rollie DeArmas had been locked out of the stadium, Weir had repossessed kitchen appliances and equipment that he said Eliopulos had never paid for under a seller financing agreement, and the Philadelphia Phillies' Vice President of Player Development and Scouting Jim Baumer had been quoted in the *Herald-Journal* as saying, "The Phillies and 25 players are left out in the cold and I don't give a damn what happens. I don't care if we have to work out the entire year in Clearwater..." rather than to continue to play in Spartanburg. To add insult to injury, Duncan Park stadium was broken into in May while the team was playing on the road in Asheville, and thieves stole "watches and jewelry valued at $5,514" and the contents of the players' wallets.

Eliopulos then won a court order by Judge Jonathan McKown restoring his ownership after the State Supreme Court had ruled temporarily in favor of the Erdman group, which had filed for bankruptcy protection. City Council was resigned that whoever ultimately was ruled the team owner could operate the team in Duncan Park, but the Philadelphia Major League team had had just about enough. In addition to issuing his four-letter-laced statement of frustration, Baumer was determined that if necessary, the Spartanburg players would just work out during the summer at the Phillies Florida Spring Training facility rather than play in Spartanburg as part of the South Atlantic League. The Sally League itself was seriously considering revoking Eliopulos's Baseball Enterprises club's membership in the league.

In the first week of June the Supreme Court's terse "petition denied" rejection of Suns Sports's motion to permanently decree their ownership of the team seemed to settle the matter, but the situation remained cloudy. Eliopulos apparently did owe creditors, and Suns Sports seemed both indecisive in proceeding and less than forthcoming in producing documents related to their bankruptcy and responses to Eliopulos. In addition, after the Supreme Court's decision rejecting Suns Sports, the Sally League had itself appointed a general manager to run the club until Eliopulos could find a new buyer and assumed the team's debts; the league also had ordered Eliopulos to pay the league $30,000 for the right to pursue a new owner.

For his part Eliopulos filed for a complete accounting of Suns Sports management of the Suns during the first half of 1986, and when Ellis Erdman and Kristina Wilhite failed to comply with the resulting court order, they were declared in contempt of court and sentenced to six months in the County Jail by Circuit Judge James B. Stephens. There the matter lay since neither of the Suns partners lived in South Carolina at the time and Jack Lawrence, their attorney, "does not know the whereabouts of either party." All Lawrence had as an address for his clients was a local post office box.

The Suns Sports debacle had the one positive effect of setting Eliopulos legally free to comply with the South Atlantic League's order to find a new owner, and he wasted little time. By mid-July he had found purchasers of the team in Bradford "Brad" Shover and Jeff Kurkis, two successful insurance salesmen from Harrisburg, Pennsylvania, who agreed to a purchase price of $200,000, of which $39,000 was to go to Weir as part of the price Eliopulos had agreed to pay the doctor when he purchased the team. The Harrisburg group paid Eliopulos a down payment of $10,00, with another $30,000 due in a matter of days and half the purchase price spread out over a five-year period. The Phillies were back in town, and the Harrisburg partnership would take over at the conclusion of the 1986 season.

It was the best of times and the worst of times for the team. Best was the fact that years of uncertainty and decline had finally come to an end. Worst was the dire condition of the franchise and its home field. At one point during the summer of 1986 the team drew only 10 fans to a game, and "crowds" of 50 were common. Promotions were virtually nonexistent that season as well. Starting from such a low base, however, improvement seemed practically inevitable, and the new guys forged ahead. For a while things seemed to be on the right trajectory: attendance was up 61 percent in 1987, and the team placed second in the league. The 1987 team had *seven* future Major Leaguers on it, too, the best known today being 14-year-MLB pitcher Andy Ashby.

There were indications, though, that all was not rosy. For one thing, although by May 3 the team already had drawn a third as many fans in 14 games as it had in all of 1986, average attendance was still only 439 fans per game. And while there were four other teams in the South Atlantic League with *worse* attendance—Sumter (428), Macon (351), Savannah (341), and Gastonia (186)—there were *seven* with *better* attendance, and two of those, including nearby rival Asheville, drew three times as many fans per game as Spartanburg. In addition, popular manager Mel Roberts, who had himself played shortstop for the 1966 Phillies, was on his way in June to Bend, Oregon, where he would become the manager of a rookie league team.

Roberts did return to manage the 1988 Spartanburg team, which won exactly as many games—69—as it lost and which featured Kim Batiste, who played four years at third base and short stop for Philadelphia, and for the second year Andy Ashby on the mound. In 1989 Roberts was back again to manage a team that went 62-79 and boasted as its second baseman Mickey Morandini, who would play 11 years in the Majors. The 1990 team had an almost identical 63-79 record, fifth in its division, but had only one future MLB position player, Tom Marsh, who played parts only of three seasons in Philadelphia, and three future Major League pitchers, only one of whom—Bob Wells—might be called effective.

By 1990 Brad Shover's Harrisburg Baseball Club Inc. partnership was able to extend its lease of Duncan Park stadium by a year after an initial term of three years. Shover had tried to sell the team to its general manager, Jim Pickles, but the directors of the South Atlantic League had refused to approve the sale. City Council had waived the Phillies stadium rent for 1988 and 1989, a sum of $16,250, in favor of payments on a debt for a new scoreboard that stood at almost $30,000 due to unpaid interest. The team had not contributed the full amount toward scoreboard debt for 1989, however, or any of the $15,000 stadium rent fee for 1990 by October of the year. As a result, the city had withheld some $7,700 due to the Phillies, mostly for utilities. Shover hung on, and the team posted records of 70-70 in 1991—when future MLB All-Star catcher Mike Lieberthal played in Spartanburg—and 70-68 in 1992.

Somehow Shover managed to survive and to mollify City Council until October 1992, when he was negotiating to sell the team to a Wilmington, North Carolina, group, which planned to either remain in Spartanburg if the city began needed improvements on the stadium or, failing that, move to Wilmington. The required "improvements" were substantial. According to a 1992 study commissioned by the National Association of Professional Baseball Leagues "to determine what improvements needed to be done to bring Duncan Park up to pro baseball's standards," the *minimum* requirements were:

- Widen the seats and space them farther apart [essentially replacing the seats].
- Improve home and visiting clubhouses.

- Enlarge dugouts.

- Improve media facilities.

- Improve administrative offices.

- Add storage to clubhouse area.

- Add enclosed hitting/pitching tunnels.

- Install dugout-to-bullpen telephones.

- Install dugout-to-press box telephones.

City Manager Wayne Bowers's response was unmistakable if oblique: "I don't think the attitude is that we'll build it and they'll come. We're not going to rebuild the stadium without a team." In other words, it looked like the Phillies would not stay without significant upgrades to the stadium, and the city was not about to spend the money required to make such upgrades without a firm commitment from the Phillies. Two additional factors argued against a solution to the standoff: the National Association of Professional Baseball Leagues would not consider *any* requests for expansion in the coming year, and Spartanburg's 32-mile proximity to Greenville argued against the construction of a new stadium or the in-migration of a new team since current regulations guaranteed "35-mile territorial rights to the area." Checkmate.

In the end Shover did not sell the team to the Wilmington group. Rather he signed a one-year lease with the city and almost in desperation put team president and minority owner Jim Pickles and General Manager Rosie Putnam to work to try to salvage the team. Pickles announced a ticket price rollback to just $1 per general admission ticket and $3 for a box seat, prices harkening back to those of the 1970s and possibly the cheapest in baseball, in an effort to draw at least a thousand fans per game. The City for its part agreed to work on field drainage, a backstop fence, repairs to the roof and improvements to the umpires' locker room and the lights on the field. In an eerily ominous and prescient admission, though, Pickles was also quoted as saying that even with their poor attendance and unprofitability the Phillies had been a "good investment, going from a value of $220,000 in 1988 to nearly $1.5 million" in 1992. He observed with alarming frankness, "I am not going to tell you that if the right offer came through the door we wouldn't entertain the thought of selling the franchise."

Pickles's comment about the partnership's willingness to sell the team under the right conditions might have reminded more attentive readers of the

Herald-Journal of his nearly vitriolic venting in an open letter in the newspaper the summer before. After reviewing the owners' and City government's valiant efforts to save the franchise, Pickles went on to attack Spartanburg's citizens:

> We have spent many thousands of dollars and incredible hours in this effort. The city has been nothing short of fantastic in their efforts, man hours and dollars spent. All this has been for naught. The people of this town just simply do not want a team, and with that attitude don't deserve one.

> The Phillies have spent an excess [*sic*] of $50,000 for promotions at the park, yet we have the second lowest attendance average in the league, barely 650 a game....

> We have concerts, but the people don't come. We have a circus, but the people don't come. The Chamber sells thousands of dollars in tickets but the people don't come.

> I am sure that General Manager Rosie Putnam would like to hear the reason why people don't come out just as much as I would.

Much to her credit, Putnam wrote no letter, and president Pickles's attempt to shame the fans into coming out and saving the team failed to have the desired effect. Sportswriter Jim Fair echoed the team's frustrations in his column: "Spartanburg baseball fans have spoken. Minor league baseball is not the thing to do and Duncan Park is not the place to be."

No longterm solution could be found, but both the team and the city of Spartanburg gritted their teeth and settled in for the 1993 season. Play opened on April 8, and a surprising crowd of 1,342 eager fans walked through the turnstiles, but two days later there were 80 percent fewer fans in attendance. By the end of June the Phillies were averaging 770 fans per game for the season, and that figure was the lowest in the league, a full 500 fans per game lower than the next-to-last team in Hagerstown. All but two teams in the 14-team league averaged at least twice as many fans as Spartanburg. "It's very disappointing," Putnam said, and Pickles agreed, saying, "I'm frustrated, and I have been for quite awhile [*sic*]." The existing frustrations only grew as the Philadelphia Phillies continued reluctant to spend significant additional funds on the stadium or to commit longterm to Spartanburg unless the city spent substantially more, and the city refused to step into the funding gap as long as the MLB team was unwilling to commit to stay longer than just a year. Without improvements to the stadium costing several hundreds of thousands of dollars, the outlook was bleak. As John Dietrich, general manager of the Phillies' Sally League rivals the Columbus, Georgia, Red Stixx, reported to the *Herald-Journal*, "that ballpark needs a lot of improvement. As charming as it is, it's not the kind of ballpark that will get you to the future."

Putnam continued to try. She met regularly with a group of local business leaders who constituted an advisory board that suggested ways to increase attendance. She also appealed to a local booster club, which in the past had helped young ballplayers find affordable housing and weather sudden personal financial emergencies; in its good years, though, this club had had close to 200 members, and here near the end it was lucky to be able to count 20. None of her efforts could overcome the many negatives: the condition of the stadium and the cost of upgrading it, the impasse between the city and the team over who would finance the necessary costs of improvement, the competition with nearby Greenville, the relative lack of local television coverage, and even the name the Spartanburg *Phillies:* locals had difficulty identifying with a team named for an MLB club that played *its* home games a thousand miles away.

Then, four days before Halloween 1993, there appeared in the *Herald-Journal* the unexpected headline "S-Phillies Changing Leadership." The news seemed both ironic and a little cruel. Deep in the quiet of a season known more for leaf changes, trick-or-treat, and the approach of the major holidays of Thanksgiving and Christmas, the Phillies had announced a real October surprise. Effective in five days Phillies President Jim Pickles and General Manager Rosie Putnam would "no longer run the team." Majority team owner Brad Shover "had no comment" and Putnam "could not be reached." Pickles would say only, "My feelings are there is nothing more I can do (in Spartanburg);" he would remain a stockholder and his decision to leave "had nothing to do with a real or fictitious sale"—it was only "a business decision."

In retrospect the announcement seems less surprising. Shover had let it be known for some time that he was open to selling the team if the price—typically now a million and a half dollars for a Minor League franchise—were right; after all he and his partners had paid only $200,000 when they had bought the team. Del Unser, the Philadelphia Phillies' director of player development, was quoted also as saying, "I don't think there is any evidence that the people [of Spartanburg] are willing to support minor league baseball, at least to the extent that it would make a club profitable." It had been rumored, too, that

Shover already had been talking with more than one group of potential new owners, the most likely being **NASCAR** owner Larry Hedrick, who seemed ready to move the team to Kannapolis, North Carolina, and was reportedly waiting upon local government backing for the construction of a spiffy, brand-new stadium in Kannapolis.

Before the end of November Larry Hedrick's business manager had confirmed that the sale to his boss was so nearly a done deal that Hedrick had hired a new general manager for the Phillies: Fred Palmerino, the assistant general manager of the Class **AA** El Paso Diablos in Texas. Putnam had "gone back to Montana," Ward announced. In addition, Hedrick had entertained or would entertain offers from four other cities to move the Phillies from Spartanburg. If Palmerino could make the team profitable where it was, Hedrick seemed open to keeping them in the Hub City. If that could not be done, he had no qualms about leaving. Palmerino, for his part, understood that returning the team to profitability where it was currently located was a condition of his hiring. The contingency did not seem too farfetched since Palmerino was leaving a job with "one of the most successful Minor League franchises in the country."

By early July Larry Hedrick had decided to move the team. Promotions like 22-ounce thermal coffee mugs and the presence of a **NASCAR** driver or car for each Monday home game—not to mention the *nine* recliners given away for Father's Day and the $3,000 diamond dug up from the infield dirt by a lucky mother for Mother's Day—were not resulting in the desired profitability, and the team was on its way to a losing season of 67 wins and 72 losses. The poor attendance and poor win-loss record belied a roster boasting a handful of future Major Leaguers, including notably future MLB Hall of Famer Scott Rolen, a fan favorite in Duncan Park stadium, and three other players who batted over .280 during the year. So although Larry Hedrick's business manager had said a year before that the Phillies still might play in Spartanburg after 1994, they did not. The new stadium in Kannapolis was too strong an incentive. The team left for the Tarheel State, playing as the Piedmont Phillies in 1995 and the Piedmont Boll Weevils after that until 2001, when they became the Intimidators after **NASCAR** legend Dale Earnhardt, the original "Intimidator," became a part owner. Today the team is known as the Cannon Ballers, they are a franchise of the Chicago White Sox, and they play in Atrium Health Ballpark, the *second* new stadium built for them since they departed Spartanburg.

In 1995, the first year after their move, the former Spartanburg Phillies record improved to 82-58, they were the second best team in the league, and pitcher Larry Wimberly had a 10-3 record and a 2.67 ERA. Their new ballpark,

Fieldcrest Cannon Stadium, held 4,700 fans, and there seem to have been no complaints about their profitability. From 1999-2000 the Boll Weevils' hitting coach was former Spartanburg Phillies player Jerry Martin.

The Phillies played their last game in Spartanburg on September 1, 1994. Spartanburg Mayor James Talley and former Mayor Bob Stoddard were there, as were former General Manager Pat Williams and Spartanburg American Legion Post 28 and Textile League legend Ty Wood. More than 1,500 fans attended the Phillies' swan song. It rained. The rain delay pushed the end of the game to after midnight. The Phillies won 6-3. The post-game fireworks violated a City ordinance prohibiting public fireworks displays after 10 p. m., so City Manager Wayne Bowers observed, "We might have to look at changing the ordinance…."

The American Legion Post 28 baseball team would continue to play at Duncan Park, as would local colleges, wooden bat league college teams, one short-lived (four games!) independent league team, and finally Spartanburg High School; but the days of official Minor League Baseball at Duncan Park were over. As Stewart Burgess, a fan sitting behind home plate, told *Herald-Journal* reporter Andy Friedlander, "There's plenty of blame to be spread around."

CHAPTER SIX

Love of Country AND Baseball: American Legion Post 28

AMERICAN LEGION POST 28 baseball was not the first team to play at Duncan Park stadium, but the team did begin play on West Park Drive just seven years after the stadium was built, in 1933. Legion ball nationally had begun in 1925 and from the outset became one of the most visible and most popular of all Legion programs. In Spartanburg, Post 28 is still an important presence. Chartered in 1921, the post is housed in an attractive granite structure built from stone quarried in nearby Pacolet, South Carolina. The building was designed by Lockwood, Greene & Company, which also had designed the landmark Montgomery Building in downtown Spartanburg. The cornerstone of Post 28's Colonial Revival style building was laid by South Carolina Governor Olin D. Johnston, on June 15, 1936. Construction by the Works Progress Administration was completed in 1937, and Post 28 held its first meeting in the structure on June 5, 1937.

There are two notable features of the Legion property on the small rise on West Park Drive that deserve mention in connection with baseball at Duncan Park. One is the huge baseball installed on a wheeled trailer that is rolled out to the Union Street entrance of Duncan Park before Legion home games. The giant ball was the original property of the Spartanburg Peaches and then passed to the Phillies; today it is lovingly curated by Post 28. In recent years it has been fully restored by Sherman Swofford of Skyvision Signs, its trailer built by Rick Conner and McElrath Trailers.

*Post 28 photo commemorating the centenary of American Legion Baseball.
Figures in the foreground include, L to R, Spartanburg City Councilman Jerome
Rice, Mayor Junie White, Post 28 longtime Athletic Director Jesse Campbell,
Post 28 Commander Carroll Owings, Post 28 Chaplain Ben Lineberry, Post 28
Assistant Commander and Athletic Director John J. Barron, and Post 28 Histo-
rian Ed Y. Hall. Teams are Inman Post 45 and Spartanburg Post 28.*

Another unavoidable structure at the Post 28 headquarters is the Confederate
War Monument, a statue of a Confederate soldier looking north erected atop
a large Corinthian column located in an open space outside the Legion hall.
Installed by the United Daughters of the Confederacy in 1910 on Kirby Hill
near the present location of the intersection of Henry and South Church streets,
the statue was relocated in the early 1960s at a time when sensitivities to me-
morials to the so-called "Lost Cause" were changing. In 1910 Confederate me-
morials had just been or were about to be raised throughout the South as part
of the reassertion of White dominance over Blacks in the former Confederacy
in the wake of the end of Reconstruction and the recapture of state legislatures
across the South by former Confederates and their sympathizers. In this context it should be remembered that Major Duncan, whose family donated the
land on which Duncan Park stadium now sits to the City of Spartanburg, had
been a senior Confederate officer and that a City ordinance forbade (White)
Spartanburg teams from competing in the park against teams with Black players. The irony is inescapable: the stone soldier, originally intended to memorialize White Southern soldiers and their society, was moved to a less publicly

American Legion Post 28 HQ, constructed in 1937. The 1910 Confederate soldier statue, relocated to Duncan Park in the 1960s, stands in the foreground.

viewable venue during the Civil Rights era that brought an end to Jim Crow segregation. Today it rises over a public park where white and Black citizens at first were not allowed to compete against each other and which was the home field of a team, the Spartanburg Peaches, whose owner threatened to shut down the team when it had to play against an integrated team in Tennessee because a City ordinance forbade such play—even though a popular completely Black team, the Sluggers, was playing in Duncan Park stadium against other Black teams, and many White fans came to see them play there. Today, of course, all teams that call Duncan Park their home—Post 28, Spartanburg High School, and the Spartanburgers (until the summer of 2022)—are fully integrated. Fans and the public, however, still can note the presence of a small, unmarked

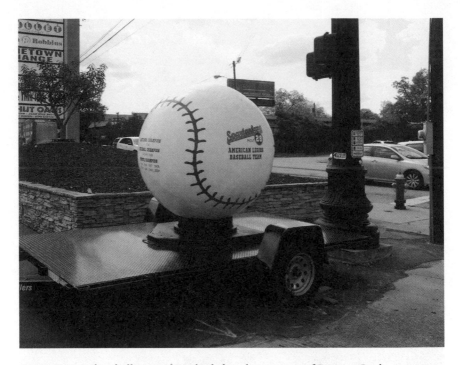

Iconic Post 28 baseball on trailer wheeled to the entrance of Duncan Park prior to home games

concrete block structure in place at the pull-off from West Park Drive above the stadium; this hut used to be the separate ticket box for Black spectators.

Today the American Legion is the organization that celebrates, commemorates, and promotes patriotism and service to country by *all* Americans, and it was largely Black soldiers' service during two World Wars that accelerated the integration of all aspects of American society when they returned home. In Spartanburg, Post 28 baseball is the legacy of many patriots, but the team's success and history are largely the ongoing legacy of two men who are remembered and celebrated today by the Post and by local residents as well: Sarge W. P. Hughes, the team's first coach; and Jesse E. "Gene" (or "Geno") Campbell—fondly remembered as "Mr. Baseball"—the Post's athletic director for 38 years.

Post 28 baseball began during the depths of the Great Depression, an optimistic move for a community which, in spite of its patriotism and love of country, was in dire economic straits. The other white team that played on the Duncan Park field, the Spartanburg Spartans, was having serious difficulties throughout the decade of the 1930s, finally departing for good in 1940;

their successors, the Spartanburg Peaches, would not take the field until 1946. Nevertheless, the Post 28 baseball team was launched on Friday, June 2, 1933, in a sloppy game against Pacolet that featured 11 errors and 27 men left on base. The crowd was small, so small that a fish fry scheduled for after the game had to be cancelled because only 37 tickets had been sold.

In spite of a less than stellar beginning, Post 28 baseball likely still benefited from its status as one of the few teams in town during the Depression. By 1939 the team had won five state championships, two regional and sectional titles, a *national championship* in 1936, and *national runner-up standing* in 1938. A large share of the credit for this success must be attributed to Athletic Director Mike Burgin, but even more was due to the hard work, energy, and love for both the game and his boys shown by Coach Sarge Hughes. A modest man, Hughes drove the team to away games in a hardy "woodie" station wagon well known to the team's families and their fans, and members of his team were themselves a familiar sight in the coach's downtown office after school. Back issues of Spartanburg newspapers, the archives of the Spartanburg County Public Libraries and the Spartanburg County Historical Association, and the family scrapbooks of many city residents are filled with photographs of the coach, the coach and his team, the coach and his station wagon, and his players' mementos. After their Little World Series triumph in 1936, Hughes even took the team to New York City to see the World Series between the New York Yankees and the New York Giants. To this day Spartanburg resident Susan Wood Pope, the daughter of 1936 bat boy and future Legion and Textile League stalwart Ty Wood, cherishes and preserves ticket stubs, programs, and team banners that Wood brought back from that MLB World Series. Pope also treasures her dad's red and gray Post 28 uniform, a garment remarkable not only for its fine condition 85 years after it was first worn but also for its heavy wool fabric, undoubtedly a burden during hot Upstate South Carolina summers.

The 1936 Little World Series, from which Spartanburg Post 28 emerged as National Champions, was a sporting event the likes of which had never been seen before in the Hub City and seldom has been seen since. Legion baseball had begun in 1926, when teams were fielded in 15 states. That year the American Legion World Series was held in Philadelphia. Post 321 from Yonkers, New York, defeated the team from Pocatello, Idaho, and was rewarded with a trip to the MLB World Series, a tradition that continues today. In 1927 cost overruns from the 1926 Series and the location of the American Legion convention in Paris, France, prevented a Legion World Series, but in 1928 Major League Baseball Commissioner Judge Kenesaw Mountain Landis—the same figure

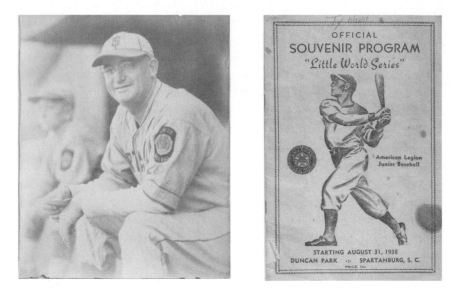

LEFT: *Coach Sarge Hughes, the father of Post 28 American Legion baseball*
RIGHT: *American Legion 1936 Little World Series program.*

MLB pennant from Post 28 Champions trip to the 1936 World Series

Ty Wood's American Legion uniform jersey

invited to Spartanburg for the banquet celebrating the opening of Duncan Park stadium in 1926—stepped up and pledged an annual $50,000 donation to the Legion, financial support that has continued, with exceptions during the Great Depression in 1933 and 1934, until the present day. Legion baseball today is one of the American Legion's most popular and influential programs, involving a total of more than 3,400 teams and 55,000 young players in the United States and Canada.

Attendance for the 1936 series in Spartanburg totaled more than 60,000 tickets sold, and for the series finale game five 20,000 diehards filled every seat in the grandstand and the bleachers, every available plot of standing room inside the stadium and beyond wherever there was a clear sight line to the diamond, and some of the branches in the trees past the outfield wall. Today there are still a few Spartan seniors who remember the thrills and excitement of that series and the joy of the championship.

The series *was* a big deal. Not only had Spartanburg won 15 games in a row, but the Los Angeles team that opposed them had a team batting average of .352, six members of the team batted over .400, and four of the West Coast pitchers were undefeated. Governor Olin D. Johnston threw out the first pitch, FDR's friend and future Secretary of State James F. Byrnes attended, and the crowd of more than 13,000 for the first game was up to that point the "largest ever assembled in Spartanburg for anything, according to press box estimates." The home team won the final game by a score of 8-1 in front of 7,000 *more* spectators than had watched game one, and total attendance at the five-game series exceeded three times that number. The official history of *The American Legion in South Carolina: The First Thirty Years* recorded that "All records for attendance at any baseball game in South Carolina fell…" when the 20,000 fans attended the final game. The paper reported that five members of the Post 28 team—Suvern Wright, Claude Thomas, Roy Prince, Pepper Martin, and Pete Fowler—were "ready to sign major league contracts as soon as the series is over." This mass signing did not, in fact, occur, but 1936 team bat boy Ty Wood did become a member of the Spartanburg Peaches, the Cleveland Indians Class A franchise, and for years was a standout in Textile League baseball, later becoming a founder of the annual Textile League Reunion games and an unofficial archivist of Textile League history. **Ray Linder** and **Furman Dobson** also played for the Peaches.

The Little World Series champions were amply rewarded for their achievement. They were given special American Legion jackets and dress suits from Belk's Department Store, then on Main Street in downtown Spartanburg. They also accompanied Hughes to New York City to attend the 1936 Major League Baseball World Series between the American League New York Yankees and National League New York Giants. Each player was given $2.00 per day spending money. The 1936 Little World Series trophy and vintage player uniforms are housed today on the landing of the staircase at Post 28 Headquarters at Duncan Park.

Two years after the Post 28 championship season, the team played again in the 1938 Little World Series. This time they fell short, losing to the team from San Diego, California, in three out of the four Championship contests. They rebounded in 1939, however, winning the American Legion Department of South Carolina state tournament for the fourth consecutive time. In 1940 Post 28 was supplanted as state champion by the team from Sumter, South Carolina, another perennial Legion power; among the players for Sumter that year was a young right fielder named Curtis Edens, the future father-in-law of the author of this history.

Ty Wood kept his World Series ticket stub from the Polo Grounds as a souvenir.

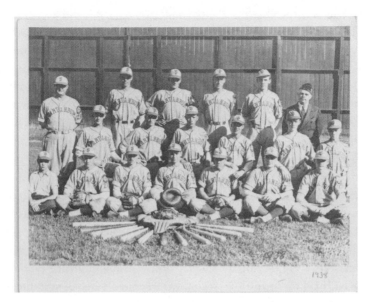

The 1938 Post 28 team that also made the Little World Series finals.

The war years were hard on Legion baseball. Not only were many potential players away on the battlefields of Europe, North Africa, Asia, and the South Pacific, but families and potential sponsors had less money and time to give, and the nation's attention was, of course, also focused elsewhere. Local Legionnaires continued to step up, however. Hughes coached through the first two war years, and others came forward as they could. At times Posts from smaller towns like Greenwood and Woodruff replaced teams from larger cities like Spartanburg as state champions. During World War II admission to a Legion game at Duncan Park was only 50 cents for the general public and a quarter for servicemen, many of whom were being trained not far from the ballpark at Camp Croft.

Several individuals have given extraordinary service to Post 28 baseball over the years. The dedication and love contributed by Hughes are legendary; current Athletic Director John Barron says that Hughes and former Athletic Director Mike Burgin "were responsible for the success of Legion baseball in Spartanburg" at the beginning. The depth of the community's regard for Hughes is reflected in the poem "Spartanburg's Champions," written by Harry

Russell Wilkins as "a souvenir" of the Little World Series and "Dedicated to Sergeant Hughes, the Coach." The poem celebrates the "wild acclaim" of the fans at "that great ball game" won by "a Legion team of high renown." Singled out for praise in the poem are virtually all citizens associated with the team: the players, the fans, Athletic Director Sam Bagwell, Post Commander Lentz, the Legionnaires, even the Legion Auxiliary and bat boy Ty Wood. Hughes's team had become heroes and the coach himself an icon. Today many public research collections contain black and white photos of the Sarge, and virtually every private citizen's collection of Little World Series memorabilia also contains photos and numerous newspaper clippings about the coach.

Another force behind the success of Post 28 baseball was local businessman and community leader R.E. Littlejohn. Littlejohn owned the Spartanburg Spartans and the Minor League Spartanburg Peaches and Spartanburg Phillies, and was an irresistible force dedicated to the improvement of life in Spartanburg. Longtime Post 28 Athletic Director Geno Campbell says that Littlejohn "was a big driving force here" and that his influence extended beyond the ballfield to the spiritual realm. He tolerated baseball at Duncan Park on Sundays but *only after church services concluded*, and during one Wednesday night playoff game he forced the suspension of the game when it became clear that it would last into the hours set aside locally for midweek church. Mr. R.E., as he was known to everyone in Spartanburg, was legendary for his kindness and quiet generosity, which were demonstrated in many anonymous donations to individuals and worthy causes in the city. When told about the universally unanimous testimony about Littlejohn's basic goodness and decency as a citizen, the businessman's son-in-law Bobby Pinson confirmed it: "I'm sure that everything you've heard about that is true."

By any measure the largest personal impact of anyone in Spartanburg on Post 28 baseball has been that of Geno Campbell, remembered by MLB veteran Wayne Tolleson—and many others—as "such a wonderful man." A native of Pacolet, whose history is tangled in the machinery of local textile mill culture and the white lines and red clay of mill village ballfields, Campbell connected with baseball early on. His granddaddy was a recruiter for the mill, and his "daddy played baseball with my mama's two brothers" and with **Ernie White**, who was born in Pacolet Mills in 1916 and played Textile League ball before moving on to a seven-year MLB career with the St. Louis Cardinals and the Boston Braves. Campbell himself played for the Pacolet Trojans before serving in the Navy during the Korean War but ironically only played one game at Duncan Park stadium, an All-Star game between County and City Textile League players.

*Jesse (Geno) Campbell,
Post 28's "Mr. Baseball"*

During his active duty Navy service as a master chief, Campbell played baseball for ship teams, and after he returned to Spartanburg he helped to organize the independent CO-OP Little League at Camp Croft and also assisted with Pony League teams. In the mid-1970s, a difficult time for Post 28, Campbell became involved with Legion baseball as well as with maintenance of the headquarters building, the management of the basement apartment which the Legion rented out, and ongoing efforts to provide a stable income and sound financial underpinning for Legion activities and programs. He also struggled to manage alcohol consumption at the two bars at Post headquarters, where "a bunch of World War II soldiers came to drink...although the Post was made up largely of reputable people."

In spite of the fact that Campbell worked hard at a series of demanding jobs after his active duty service in Korea and longterm service in the Naval Reserves—as a certified pipe welder at Kohler, an independent plumbing contractor, an engineer for Milliken and Company at Whitestone, and maintenance manager at BASF Chemical Corporation—he also devoted much time and effort to Post 28. "When I came in here," he reported, "they handed me the checkbook and they didn't have a penny." The situation was dire: "It was shambles. The windows and lights were busted out. The boiler was old. The kitchen roof was rotted and caved in. There were frozen pipes. I did all that on my own." Rental income from the family that "I kept …down there 15 years" helped, and other Post 28 members stepped up; conditions improved, and today the classic old granite building on West Park Drive proudly continues to serve veterans, their families, and the general public through meals, exhibitions, social gatherings, patriotic displays, and various civic and charitable activities.

During the hard times and the subsequent recovery of Post 28, the Legion continued to maintain a baseball team, a mission that Campbell saw as an almost religious duty. "Really I was not teachin' baseball," he said. "I was teachin' how to work together, how to respect one another, how to love one another. Plantin' a seed in little boys' heads that was planted in me." What was this seed? Its essence is expressed in the "Code of Sportsmanship" recited by Coach Campbell and both teams on the field before every Legion contest at Duncan Park:

> I will:
> Keep the rules.
> Keep faith with my teammates.
> Keep my temper.
> Keep myself fit.
> Keep a stout heart in defeat.
> Keep my pride under in victory.
> Keep a sound soul, a clean mind, and a healthy body.

How important was this code to Campbell? A story from the spring of 2010 is telling. During the third week of May that year Campbell had a health scare that sent him to the hospital for a week and forced him to miss the first Legion season opener in 37 years. This meant that he might also miss the recitation of the code for the first time in 37 years. Realizing the potential tragedy that was about to occur, Legion officials came up with a solution. A portable speaker was set up at home plate and connected to a cell phone. At the other end was Campbell on his cell phone at home, from which he led the recitation of the code as usual. "We were doing it for him," Post 28 coach Matthew West said. "I was told that when he found out that he could do that, his face lit up. I can only imagine how happy he was to find out he could be a part of it." Post 28 won the game, called early because of the mercy rule, by a score of 14-4.

Post 28 baseball has had a long and honorable history in the 90 years since it began. The agreement between the City of Spartanburg and Spartanburg

County School District Seven, which now guarantees the upkeep, maintenance, and improvement of Duncan Park stadium for the foreseeable future, will preserve Campbell's vision for many years to come. So will the leadership of current Legionnaires like Commander Carroll H. Owings, Athletic Director John J. Barron, and Coach Blake Burress. The table that appears as **Appendix V: Ninety Years of American Legion Baseball** lists, to the best of my ability to discover them, the names of the Post 28 Athletic Directors and the juniors and seniors coaches from 1933 through 2022. Many thanks to John Barron, athletic director of Post 28, for helping to uncover this history, some of which continues to be elusive and uncertain. Before 2013 there were not two divisions based on different age categories identified as "Seniors" and "Juniors." There was only one division for ages 13-19, and it was often designated as the "Juniors."

One more part of the American Legion Post 28 story deserves to be told here: the legacy of the Brian Peahuff Scholarship, awarded every year to the Legion's MVP. Brian Peahuff was a catcher for both Broome High School and Post 28, playing Legion Ball in 1990 and 1991. A month after the last game of 1991, Peahuff and a friend were driving to a job where they earned extra money for school when their car left Highway 29 and crashed into a tree near a shed owned by Pierce Motor Company, the city's Ford dealership, predecessor of Vic Bailey Ford. Both young men were hospitalized, and partial paralysis ended Peahuff's sports career and very nearly his life. Years of rehab followed, and by 1995 the determined ex-ballplayer was able to enroll in Spartanburg Technical College, from which he graduated with an associates degree, followed by a bachelor of arts in communications from the University of South Carolina Spartanburg in 2001. An 18-year career as a sports reporter for the *Spartanburg Herald-Journal* ensued, and today Peahuff works for GreerToday. com, writing about the disabled and their achievements. The journalist wrote a personal profile for the 2019 Post 28 baseball program in which he testified that "Spartanburg American Legion Post 28 played a huge role in this journey," particularly his years under the mentorship of Athletic Director Jesse Campbell, Head Coach John Daurity, and Assistant Coach Tim Wallace. In 1993 AD Campbell initiated the Brian Peahuff Scholarship; the year 2021 marked the 28th consecutive year the award had been presented to a Post 28 athlete, and Peahuff regularly gives motivational speeches to school and community groups. A complete listing of Brian Peahuff Scholarship award recipients is found in **Appendix VI.**

Although Spartanburg American Legion baseball has produced many

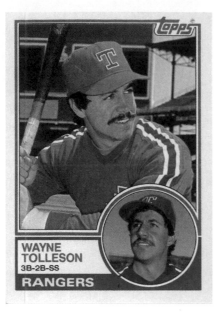

Post 28 and Spartanburg High School alum Wayne Tolleson, also an MLB veteran

talented players, a number of whom went on to extended careers in Textile League and Minor League Baseball, only three Post 28 players went on to play Major League Baseball in the first 90 years of its existence. The first of these was **Terry Hughes**, who played high school ball at Dorman High School on the west side of Spartanburg. Although Spartanburg Phillies General Manager Pat Williams, a Wake Forest University alumnus, aroused interest in Hughes from Wake baseball coach Jack McCloskey, the young player held out for a pro contract. Several MLB teams scouted Hughes, and although Bobby Richardson—himself a former Legion player in Sumter, South Carolina— urged his former Yankees team to draft the Hub City native, they passed, and Hughes was drafted by the Chicago Cubs, who then signed him with an attractive bonus offer. Hughes played Major League ball for three years but never became the star player many had foreseen him to be, the victim of injuries and interruptions caused by military service during the Vietnam War.

Two other Spartans went from Post 28 to the Majors: the father-son duo of **Wayne and Steven Tolleson**, the only MLB father-son team from South Carolina. Born in Spartanburg on November 22, 1955, Wayne Tolleson was the son of Jim Tolleson, who played seven years in Minor League Baseball, including for the Spartanburg Peaches, where he was a teammate of Rocky Colavito and witnessed the "strong throwing arm" that Colavito was known for. Wayne's brother **Mike** also played Post 28 Legion baseball and later played

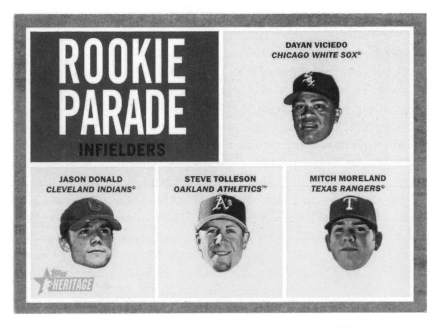

Young Steven Tolleson as a featured Topps rookie infielder

Minor League ball for the Spartanburg Peaches. Wayne Tolleson played foot-ball, basketball, *and* baseball for Spartanburg High School and frequently was mentioned in local press reports on all three sports. He played baseball for Post 28 in 1973 and 1974, playing short stop and occasionally pitching, also receiving notice for his powerful hitting; in 1974 he smacked multiple home-runs and triples.

Tolleson then attended Western Carolina University, where he was a two-sport standout and, in fact, led the nation in pass receptions in 1977. He was also the Southern Conference Baseball Player of the Year in 1978. On grad-uating, he realized that his body was better suited for the diamond than the gridiron, and after being drafted in the 8th round and playing for the Asheville Tourists, he was brought up to The Show in 1981 and had a 10-year MLB career with the Texas Rangers, the Chicago White Sox, and the New York Yankees. A dependable infielder, Tolleson had a career batting average of .241 and was a threat as a base runner: in 1983 he was eighth in the American League in sto-len bases (33), and the next year his stolen base percentage (84.62 percent) was second in the league.

Tolleson vividly remembers the first game he ever saw himself at Duncan Park. Already a staunch baseball fan, he was taken to an exhibition game between the St. Louis Cardinals and the Philadelphia Phillies. Eagerly anticipating the game between Major Leaguers he had only heard about before, young Tolleson became nervously sick to his stomach while sitting in the car waiting to enter the ballpark. He also remembers to this day how green the grass was and how crisp the field always looked. Later, when he became old enough to play on the nearby youth field beyond the right field fence as a member of the Optimists Little League team, he and his teammates were always taken to the Beacon restaurant for a hearty meal after every winning game.

Wayne's son, Steven Tolleson, played for Post 28 in the summer of 2000, going 7 for 12 in the first playoff round, including a two-run homer. The younger Tolleson played high school ball for his father's cross-town rival, Dorman High School, where he had a career batting average over .400. After high school, Steven attended the University of South Carolina and was drafted by the Minnesota Twins in 2005, playing in the Minors until 2010, when he was brought up to the Majors by the Oakland Athletics. An infielder like his dad, he played for parts of four seasons for the A's, the Baltimore Orioles, and the Toronto Blue Jays, compiling a .245 average in fewer than 200 games.

CHAPTER SEVEN

. . . .

Seventh Inning Stretch: Gotta Keep 'Em Coming

AS BASEBALL FANS KNOW, the success of *any* team depends on its ability to fill the stadium seats with the fannies of its players' families, their friends and followers, and local aficionados of the game. This fact is a truism at any time and anywhere, but it is especially true for teams playing in non-metropolitan venues in difficult economic times and in proximity to other teams competing for the fan dollar. In Spartanburg, South Carolina, trying times have included the 1930s (the Great Depression), the early 1940s (World War II), the 1980s and '90s (flight to the suburbs and the decline of downtown and the textile industry), and the recession of 2008 (municipal reluctance to spend scarce tax dollars on public facilities which do not draw the public). Complicating factors have been the increasing mobility of the population; the availability of baseball on home television, cable, and video streaming; and the proximity of other teams housed in sometimes superior facilities—the Knights in Charlotte, the Tourists in Asheville, the Drive and before them the Braves in Greenville, the Reds and the Bombers and the Fireflies in Columbia, and others.

Faced with these and other often daunting obstacles, resident teams—especially Minor League Baseball teams—and city fathers have at times proven to be extraordinarily hard-working and creative in their efforts to keep the turnstiles spinning. John Feinstein, one of our finest sportswriters and students of the game, puts it this way:

In every minor league ballpark, there is no such thing as nothing going on between innings. Fans expect entertainment that goes beyond hits, runs, and errors, and they get it.

There are all sorts of contests for fans to participate in, and there is always some kind of entertainment going on to distract those in the stands. To put it in perspective, one of the biggest disappointments of the 2012 season in Durham was when George Jetson Night was rained out.

Nobody in baseball understood the importance of ballpark promotions better than Pat Williams, the young marketing genius who managed the Spartanburg Phillies from 1965 to 1968. When he was hired to manage the Phillies, Williams was only 25 years old, and he was coming to Spartanburg to work for R.E. Littlejohn, whose own wife called him "Mister R. E." and "the greatest man in the world." Moreover, he was coming to work in a stadium that he recognized as "rundown, dirty, and unpainted." Williams was ambitious, though, and hard-working, and he almost immediately found Littlejohn to be an inspirational owner; he wanted to do well for his boss, so he buckled down and got to work. As he says, "I was going to sell baseball to that town and I was going to get the people to come out, see a great show, and have a good time." Almost 50 years after he was "thrown into the fire," Williams still remembered that "[o]ur mission was to get people into the ballpark," and he was eager to succeed. It worked: during his brief time in Spartanburg, Williams's team set attendance records, and he himself was named The Outstanding Class A Minor League Executive of 1967 by *The Sporting News.*

Although it has now been more than half a century since Williams left Spartanburg, his Duncan Park promotions are still fondly and famously remembered. One reason for this is undoubtedly the fact that another of the general manager's mentors was Bill Veeck, who at various times owned the Cleveland Indians, the St. Louis Browns, and the Chicago White Sox. Veeck was himself a legendary promoter who once threatened to create a Major League team composed only of Negro Leagues All-Stars and who also once inserted a player shorter than four feet tall into a game as a designated hitter because the opposing pitcher could not possibly stay within such a hitter's ridiculously small strike zone. Williams met Veeck on the recommendation of Bill Durney, the Phillies' farm team manager in Miami, for whom Williams had played during his two-year career as a Minor League player.

Williams often has told the story of the impact Veeck had upon him personally and professionally, most accessibly in his memoir *Ahead of the Game.*

The two met in the summer of 1962, not long after Veeck's own memoir, *Veeck as in Wreck,* was published. Over lunch beside the Chesapeake Bay, Williams listened to four critical pieces of advice from the older man, one of which was "Learn all you can about advertising and marketing." When he came to Spartanburg and assumed his duties as general manager of the Phillies, he applied this precept to his new job with a vengeance. Dan Smith, a native of Startex, South Carolina, and graduate of Wofford who became the Phillies official scorer in 1988 during his summer break from his junior high school math classroom, testifies to the effectiveness of Williams's efforts. "Every night there was some kind of promotion," he recalls, and as a result, "the place was packed every night." Morgan King, a retired educator who played second base for Wofford College at Duncan Park and later worked the hand-operated scoreboard during Phillies games, also recalled large crowds, especially for Stroller Nights and Christian Supply Nights. The Stroller was Seymour Rosenberg, author of a popular column of local news and opinion in the *Spartanburg Herald-Journal,* a feature later carried on by Lou Parris. Christian Supply was something like a local Bible superstore carrying, besides Bibles, other religious books, Sunday School supplies, coloring books and crafts for home use, as well as scriptural picture books, comics, paper dolls, chalk, easels, tempera paints, and pretty much everything else needed to help young Christians solidify their faith. The Stroller and Christian Supply might have been the only two Spartanburg institutions of the mid-1960s more popular than the Spartanburg Phillies, and Pat Williams was careful to take advantage of the popularity of both. If a fan brought a clipped image of The Stroller or an ad by Christian Supply to the stadium on their special nights, he or she was admitted free or at a reduced price—but, of course, concessions and the cost of a program were *not* discounted on these occasions.

Thirsty Thursdays were another popular promotion, especially with college kids who never had much money and while the legal age for drinking beer was still 18. These cheap beer nights were often a two-edged sword, though, likely to produce unforeseen consequences. King recalled one particularly entertaining evening when the Phillies hosted the Florence Blue Jays, whose third baseman Norm Tenuchi was ridden unmercifully by the fans all night long. Unable at last to just sit and take it any longer, Tenuchi turned to the fans and uttered a memorable "F*** you!" In reply, a drunken college kid displayed his agility by swiftly climbing the protective screen behind home plate, spread-eagling himself against the netting, and screaming back, "F*** ME, Norm! F*** ME!"

Ed Dickerson, the longtime public address announcer at Duncan Park, also remembers especially popular promotions. One was Max Patkin, the self-styled

"Clown Prince of Baseball," who performed for decades before both Minor and Major League audiences. Wearing a ball cap pulled askew across the side of his head and exhibiting a large catalog of goofy faces, the Clown Prince would pitch from second base, scuff the shoes of the sharpest-sighted umpire, make outrageous calls coaching third base, and wind up his arsenal of unbelievable pitches in motions never before seen on a mound. His baggy uniform trousers were a trademark, as was his love of America's pastime, and fans loved him as he did them. Dickerson said that the last time he saw Patkin, he had just stepped out of the locker room shower and was chatting with a couple of 19-year-old players about the finer points of the game.

Dickerson also recalled the meticulous preparation of the San Diego Chicken, a perfectionist who would always arrive early before a game because "he wanted to make sure his show was done right, his script was followed." The Chicken was very friendly, very personable, but "his livelihood depended on a good show" so everything had to work the way it was intended to.

Dickerson and King both mentioned Morganna, the "Kissing Bandit," aka "Morganna the Wild One," a nationally known "exotic dancer" who would dash madly onto a ballfield and enthusiastically smooch her unsuspecting victims, as a stellar attraction at Duncan Park stadium. Morganna was a mainstay in many Major and Minor League stadiums and other sports venues during a highly visible and profitable career in the 1970s and '80s. Her attendance at a game could easily double the usual gate, and she enjoyed herself as much as her fans did. Among others, George Brett, Nolan Ryan, Don Mattingly, Pete Rose, Kareem Abdul Jabbar, Bill Murray, and even Pat Sajak became her not so unwilling victims. Dickerson says that she was "one of the nicest ladies, very outgoing, very friendly." She was so nice, in fact, that she even brought a dog biscuit for Rookie, the Duncan Park mascot and after hours watchdog, when she appeared for the Phillies. King, who began to go bald almost as soon as he could throw a baseball, was particularly appreciative; the Bandit, who typically kissed her targets on one or both cheeks, planted a big smackeroo "right on top of my head."

Ed Dickerson, whose tenure at Duncan Park was the longest of any of my interviewees, had a genuine fondness for the group he called "some of the lesser professionals" among those hired to entertain the crowd between innings. One of these was Captain Dynamite, a character who actually would blow himself up out on the pitcher's mound. One night he positioned himself on the mound, began his countdown—"Ten-nine-eight…"—and then "Boom!" This time he had indeed hurt himself…by cutting his hand on a rock when he stumbled as he staggered off the mound. Later in the history of Duncan Park stadium after the Phillies had departed for Kannapolis, North Carolina, Dickerson was told another Captain Dynamite story by Billy Bird, the Louisville Redbirds mascot, who related how after one of his explosive performances a young fan came running up to the Bird yelling, "Mr. Bill! Mr. Bill! Mr. Dynamite's lying on the field and he's not moving!" The truth was that it was a hotter than normal evening, Captain Dynamite was tired, and he was resting peacefully asleep on the pavement in the parking lot.

Another slightly peculiar performer was Henri Lamothe, whose specialty was "diving" from a 30- to 40-foot tower into a small circular pool not unlike what most spectators at the game might have set up for their children in their own backyards. Walking out in a sequined jacket that he would don before his ascent, Lamothe climbed confidently aloft, turned around gracefully to face the crowd, and then bellyflopped magnificently into his pool. Dickerson reports that the "dive" was into a pool with telescoping poles, the whole act contained in a single car trunk.

Dickerson also recalls a game in which fireworks were set off *during*, not after, a game. The result was what anyone might have expected with a little forethought: the night was hot, the air heavy, and as a result of the ensuing atmospheric conditions smoke from the detonations hung trapped low in the air over right field. Fans' view of the right fielder was obliterated, and, of course, his view of home plate and any struck balls was totally obscured as well. The game had to be suspended until the smoke finally dissipated.

Joe Clarke, former principal at Spartanburg High School, which now plays all of its home games at Duncan Park, is a lifelong baseball fan who attended games at the old ballpark during 1966, the year when the Phillies set records and the legend of Pat Williams was born. In addition to outstanding players such as Denny Doyle and Larry Bowa, the other standout feature of the team that year for Clarke was its GM. "Pat Williams was a very energetic go-getter," he says, "trying to energize the Phillies base here." Williams's efforts even included bringing his well-known mentor Bill Veeck to Duncan Park twice for "Impress Bill Veeck" nights. On another occasion, in 1966, when the Phillies fielded a player named John Parker from North Carolina and another from Indiana named John Penn, Williams was inspired to schedule a "Parker Penn" night and secured a large supply of actual Parker pens as giveaways. Fate intervened, however: John Parker was called up to basic training the week before the scheduled Saturday night promotion, and John Penn's wife was in the later stages of her pregnancy; a rainstorm also popped up unexpectedly. The entire promotion had to be not only rescheduled but also reconceived into something a bit different. After consulting with Veeck, Williams decided to add a musical focus to the evening, which then became a performance tribute to the Ink Spots, for which the Parker pens were still an appropriate enough premium. As Williams said, "Bill was always there. He would put his twist on my ideas."

Williams's ideas began to pay dividends early in his days at Duncan Park, too. As he recalled, "We began to get some coverage. Not unlike Savannah, Georgia, in the two thousands—where the *nationally* beloved Savannah Bananas would sometimes field a player on stilts—Spartanburg became known as crazy, fun." Before his time was up, Williams had brought Bob Feller and Satchel Paige to Spartanburg, and there was an "A to Z Night," which featured Al **A**ber and George **Z**uverink, both former Spartanburg Peaches who went on to play Major League Baseball. William Eckert, the commissioner of Major League Baseball, came too, as did **NBA** star Oscar Robertson (the "Big O") and NFL players Johnny Unitas, Paul Hornung, and Bart Starr; Bobby Pinson, R.E. Littlejohn's son-in-law, played golf with Bart Starr on the weekend when he came to Duncan Park and was surprised when Starr actually recorded a six on the first hole. There were greased pig chases and other more usual Minor League Baseball attractions. By the time it was all over, people across the United States who had never before heard of Spartanburg, South Carolina, had not only heard of the city but also knew about the Spartanburg Phillies and their General Manager Pat Williams.

Even other players, managers, and executives admired what Williams was doing in the Upstate. Murray Cook, a former Minor League player, manager of the Pittsburgh Pirates affiliate in Gastonia, North Carolina, and MLB executive with the Yankees, the Montreal Expos, and the Cincinnati Reds, minces no words:

> Actually he was a real promoter. He was one of the few guys in that league that promoted baseball, that really had some promotional ideas. The rest of us pretty much were custodians.
>
> We all kind of looked at him like what is this guy really doing? You can't promote down at this level, but he did and he was successful doing it.

Other general managers—of the Phillies and of other teams who played at Duncan Park—also recruited performers and other kinds of promotions of course, even if they were not as good at it as Williams. One group that appeared several times was The King and His Court, a four-man independent touring fast pitch softball team composed of Eddie Feigner (the "King" and pitcher) plus his catcher, first baseman, and a shortstop (the "Court"), who would take on all nine-player teams who dared challenge them before a paying crowd. During a 40-plus-year tour from coast to coast, to the Middle East and the Caribbean and Australia and Hawaii and beyond, and over the airways with Steve Allen and Mike Douglas and Jerry Lewis, the King's quartet participated in more than 8,400 games, of which they won more than 7,300 and Feigner threw over 120,000 strikeouts, 7,003 of which he pitched blindfolded.

Gaylord Perry, the 300-game-winning, spitballing right-hander who is a member of the Baseball Hall of Fame at Cooperstown, New York, also appeared at Duncan Park more than once. After his playing career was over, Perry spent five years as the baseball coach at Limestone College just down the road from Spartanburg in Gaffney, South Carolina, and it was a short trek from there to the historic stadium. Another attraction for fans was the possibility of seeing unexpected celebrities at a game. Phil Niekro, the Atlanta Braves knuckleballing ace, came unannounced one night, and on another occasion fans shared the stadium with Julia Roberts and Kiefer Sutherland, an "item" at the time, when they were in town to film scenes from *Sleeping with the Enemy* at Converse College, now Converse University.

Some fans themselves were a draw to other fans: regulars at Duncan Park recognized the other regulars, looked forward to seeing them, and worried when they didn't appear in the grandstand. Among the most familiar of all the regulars was Libby Armstrong, whose family owned Armstrong Cleaners and who attended "just about every game" in her wheelchair, according to Morgan King. Armstrong was such a fan favorite herself that she had a reserved parking space beside the stadium, and she was such a devoted fan that she only missed three games from 1969 through 1991. The Phillies presented her a birthday cake on the field for her 19th birthday and celebrated the event regularly after that. When Hub Blankenship, the Phillies general manager in the early 1970s, organized a trip for Spartanburg fans to Veterans Stadium in Philadelphia, Armstrong was there.

Chip Rivers, one of four teachers at McCracken Junior High School who worked at Duncan Park during the summers in the 1980s and '90s, remembered that during this time there was a core group of 20 or so regulars who could be counted on to be at every game. "These people just never left the stadium," Rivers said. One of them, "Reverend," who worked for the railroad, would always bring Rivers, who stood taking tickets at the turnstile, fresh vegetables. Another, a part-Cherokee native American named Marge Scales, would come in a Cherokee headdress.

Another fan regular in his attendance was "this one guy who sat up there in coveralls [who] used to get on *every*body," according to former Phillie Jerry Martin from Columbia. Bob Wellman, the Phillies Manager, whom Martin remembered as "a big ol' guy," as payback for the fan's habitual verbal abuse of players and coaches during games, "found out where he was workin' as a brickmason. So Wellman on an off-day went over there and got him a lounge chair, and sat out there where the guy was workin' and gave it to *him* for a while."

Some fans of Minor League Baseball have become the subjects of Hollywood movies. One in particular was the legendary, if fictional, Annie Savoy (Susan Sarandon), whose affections were solicited by both Crash Davis (Kevin Costner) and Nuke LaLoosh (Tim Robbins) in the 1988 film *Bull Durham,* parts of which were filmed at the Asheville Tourists' McCormick Field just an hour up I-26 from Spartanburg. Annie has had her counterparts in the Hub City over the years, although none were likely as cerebral as Annie herself in the movie. One in particular in the 1990s liked young professional ballplayers a lot and would often go home with different players at the conclusions of different games. Other fans noticed, and some began to play the game of watching to guess who the young woman would leave with on a given night. Sometimes young women hoping for a date would enlist the aid of team employees, even recruiting the bat boys for help. When he was the Phillies bat boy, Jimmy Tobias often carried notes from players to female fans in the stadium, hoping to score a post-game date via pencil and paper.

Serendipity also paid other kinds of dividends for fans. Eula Williams, a retired English teacher in Spartanburg School District Seven, had two sons who "have good memories of going to games there with their dad and also playing in little league games." She related one special night game:

> One night my son, Truett, sat and talked to a guy during his brother's game but he didn't know who he was. The next night he was at a game and Bob Feller was introduced, and my son said, "Hey, I sat with him at the game last night," which was a big deal for him.

Williams also remembered birthday parties celebrated at the ballpark.

The Phillies office staff were also attractions in themselves. Already mentioned have been general managers Pat Williams and Rosie Putnam, and early on Pat Williams's mentor "Mr. R. E." Littlejohn was well known and widely respected for his prior ownership of the Spartanburg Peaches and his petroleum carrier business, which had begun with a single truck driven by Littlejohn himself and made him millions during his lifetime. Another group of favorites was the crew of teachers from McCracken Junior High School who for years worked at the ballpark during the summer. Morgan King, Dan Smith, and Chip Rivers were all popular teachers, and many of their students and their students' families were on the lookout for their faculty members in the grandstand—or above it in the sweltering wooden broadcast booth or hunched down changing the score on the hand-operated scoreboard above the fence—during ballgames. Smith, who was the official scorer at Duncan Park for a decade, often claimed that since he and his colleagues were all teachers, the Phillies had "the most grammatically correct scoreboard in baseball."

Another member of the McCracken faculty who was highly visible at the ballpark was Jean Lomax, waitress to the box seats, who could bound across and over the stadium seats and hustle back and forth from the concessions stand with the agility of a deer. Lomax also could juggle bags of popcorn and peanuts and Cracker Jacks with ease and balance hot dogs and fries in one tight fist against deftly hoisted plastic cups of draft beer in the other. Lomax was a sight to behold, and I for one never saw her spill a customer's beer.

Perhaps unsurprisingly, some of the best years for promotions were during hard times when the business of baseball was not going well at Duncan Park, and management had to exert itself with greater imagination and effort to bring fans through the turnstile. In 1988, for example, the Phillies were coming off a year when their record had been 67 wins and 74 losses, and attendance, although more than twice what it had been in 1986, was only 36,286 or a paltry 518 fans per home game. Owner Brad Shover, General Manager Jeff Kurkis, and Director of Marketing Dan Kable tried their best to right the ship, planning no fewer than 61 home games with pre-announced featured promotions. These included Thirsty Thursdays each week sponsored by Union Street favorite Clancy's Bar and Grill, five Westgate Mall Nights, three *Herald-Journal* Youth Baseball Clinics, three Stroller Nights, two Christian Supply Nights, a jalapeño pepper contest, a cow milking contest, giveaways sponsored by Betras Plastics and Bi-Lo/Eagle Snacks and Moo Bars, and the Phillies themselves (an S-Phils alumni baseball card night on July 15 and a big Fan Appreciation Night on August 23). One night in May the price of admission was a can of Campbell's Soup for the Food Bank, and on April 19 all Little Leaguers were admitted free. On July 2 there was a doubleheader with a game played by American Legion Post 28. There was a fundraiser on June 5 for the American Red Cross and another for the United Way on August 9. Miss Spartanburg came on May 15, as did Gaylord Perry on June 28; there was a fireworks display on July 1 and an exhibition softball game between the "Arch Rivals" and the "Men of Steele" on June 29. The main sports promotions were the Phillie Phanatic on April 18, the Famous Chicken on July 24, the University of Miami Maniac on August 12, and, of course, Carolina-Clemson Night on August 6. There was even an appearance on May 14 by a group called the Hollywood Starlets, whose photograph shows two dozen attractive young women in shorts, sneakers, and V-neck shirts; the girls don't look especially athletic and they're not carrying bats or balls or gloves, but they all look happy and pleased with themselves, and they must have been a hit at Duncan Park. It is hard to draw any cause-effect connections here, but *some*thing worked for the 1988 Phillies: they won three more games than they had in 1987, and attendance at the ballpark was up by more than 350 fans per game.

Five years later the Phillies faced a similar situation in the penultimate year of their tenure in Spartanburg. Attendance *had* recovered some in 1988, and in 1989 it was actually about two and a half times what it had been in 1987, but in 1992 it stood back at a little more than 750 fans per game, and there was a Wilmington, North Carolina, group that wanted to purchase the team and move it to the Tarheel State. Team President Jim Pickles, General Manager Rosie Putnam, and first-year Corporate Promotions Director Chuck Allsbrook regrouped and planned a razzle-dazzle schedule of promotions for 1993. Many of the 1988 sponsors were still on board: Betras Plastics, Christian Supply, and The Stroller provided free entry or giveaways; city merchants gave away Phillies caps, free beach towels, free baseballs, free bats, free game tickets, an expensive set of golf clubs, even furniture worth $1,000 and $2,000. Spartanburg County public school students and A-students were admitted to games free, there was an auction of autographed MLB equipment and memorabilia to benefit a scholarship fund, and the Phillies gave away sets of team baseball cards twice. The Phillies Phanatic was back on April 16, and Billy Bird from the Louisville Redbirds appeared on May 5. Max Patkin returned on July 15, and on June 17 a pinnacle of sorts was reached when Morganna, "The Kissing Bandit," was scheduled.

Attendance did increase in 1993, by about 6,000, and it went up by another, 5,000 or so in 1994. It was too little, too late however. The city would not commit the funds necessary to fully rehabilitate the stadium, the S-Phils could not afford improvements on their own, the Philadelphia Phillies were looking around elsewhere, and Minor League Baseball would not entertain an invitation to another team so close to Greenville. In the end, owner Larry Hedrick accepted the offer to relocate the team to Kannapolis, North Carolina, and in 1995 the renamed *Piedmont* Phillies played there in a spanking new stadium, which ironically was itself replaced 25 years later by state-of-the-art Atrium

Health Ballpark. Today official Minor League Baseball is alive and very well in Kannapolis, but it will not return to Duncan Park. Spartanburg recently announced a new team for a new downtown stadium.

A final sadness, recounted by former Spartanburg Mayor Bob Stoddard, involved a promotion of another kind. One of the most popular fan promotions anywhere has always been the chance to see celebrities at the ballpark, and local citizens could see several on opening day for the Phillies. Stoddard, who had been instrumental in bringing the Phillies to Spartanburg in 1965, was invited back to Duncan Park stadium to throw out the first pitch for the final Phillies game on September 1, 1994, as were former general manager Pat Williams and then-current Mayor James Talley, the city's first Black Mayor. In recalling the Phillies' 31 years in his city, Stoddard recalled for the *Herald Journal* the first time he pitched for a Phillies game:

> "I was pitching, Greenville Mayor David Traxler was catching, [Senator] Strom Thurmond was batting and Ms. South Carolina Nancy Moore was umpiring," Stoddard said. "I threw three pitches that Strom Thurmond fouled off, and Miss Moore (later Thurmond's wife) called him out."

Many Spartanburg citizens still remember that opening day in the spring of 1965. Of the celebrities on the field that day, Talley is the only one still with us; even for him, though, there will be no more Phillies games.

CHAPTER EIGHT

. . . .

Later Innings: Newcomers and a Revolving Carousel of Players

WHEN THE SPARTANBURG PHILLIES left town after the 1994 season, it was not the end of baseball in the city. The post-Phillies history of Duncan Park stadium, although it now stretches beyond the quarter-century mark, is both less familiar and less illustrious than that of the teams that played here before 1994. It is a little easier to follow, too, but it is pretty apparent that market forces and community support still drove and continue to drive fan attendance and, to a lesser degree, team success on the field.

There have been eight resident adult teams at Duncan Park since 1994. Their tenures at Duncan Park are briefly summarized in **Appendix VII.** More of their stories are included in the following:

USC SPARTANBURG RIFLES. As a regional campus in the University of South Carolina system, the University of South Carolina Spartanburg opened in 1967 as a two-year institution that would replace the nursing school previously operated by Spartanburg General Hospital. Expanded to a four-year university in 1975, the size of its student body and budgetary constraints caused it to proceed slowly and cautiously in offering competitive athletic programs. In 2004 the university opened its current Harley Baseball Park, at the time a state-of-the-art collegiate ballpark, named after longtime college benefactor and member of the Spartanburg County Higher Education Commission **Cleveland S. Harley.** Prior to the opening of Harley Park, the Rifles played at Rifle Field, located where The Magnolia and Palmetto dorms are currently on the University of South Carolina Upstate campus, and after that at Duncan Park.

The USC Spartanburg residency at Duncan Park stadium was not an auspicious one by any means. During the years 1995-2003 the Rifles compiled a dismal 146 wins-307 losses record overall and could do no better than 49-195 in the Peach Belt Conference. The team's best year during this time was 2003, when it posted a record of 28-26, the only time during the nine years that wins exceeded losses, and even that year the team won only half as many games (nine) as it lost (18) in its conference. **Bubba Dorman** coached the team from 1995 through 1997, and **Matt Fincher** was at the helm from 1998 through 2003. After the Rifles returned to the Upstate campus in 2004, their team and mascot became known as the Spartans.

SPARTANBURG ALLEY CATS. Even more dismal than the record of the USC Spartanburg team was that of the Spartanburg Alley Cats, a nearly apocryphal team that belonged to the equally ephemeral Atlantic Coast League in 1995. A brave attempt to preserve a more or less official professional team presence at Duncan Park after the departure of the Phillies, the Alley Cats were formed as one of only four teams in the new league; the others were the Gaston King Couriers, the Florence Flame, and the Greenwood Grizzlies. The entire league played a total of only 32 games, a season of only 15 or 17 games, depending on the longevity of the teams. The Alley Cats compiled a record of 7-8 under manager **Buzz Capra**, who had pitched for the New York Mets and the Atlanta Braves in the early 1970s and who also had served as pitching coach for the Spartanburg Phillies. The 14 players on the team compiled a .237 batting average; 10 players pitched, with only one winning as many as two games. None of the players ever played in MLB. Never on a very firm financial footing, the league utterly collapsed and disappeared after 1995.

WOFFORD TERRIERS. Like the University of South Carolina Spartanburg prior to the construction of Harley Baseball Park, Wofford College played at Duncan Park from 1996 through 2003 before the construction of Russell C. King Field on the Wofford campus. Previous to playing at Duncan Park, the Terriers played on Law Field, located where the new Russell C. King stadium was constructed.

The Terriers' years at Duncan Park stadium were not their best seven-year stretch in the team's history. In fact, the *2021 Wofford Baseball Media Guide* lists the following *negative* records established during these years: fourth most hits allowed (623 in 2003), third most runs allowed (482, also in 2003), fifth most earned runs allowed (403 in 2003), first in most walks allowed (313 in

2000), first *and* second *and* third in wild pitches (102 in 2000, 80 in 1995, and 75 in 1999), and first in errors (115 in 2000). To give the team its due, however, it must also be noted that at Duncan Park in 2002 the team produced its sixth highest total of walks received, in 1999 its fifth highest ever total of sacrifice flies, its second *and* third highest totals of assists (631 in 2000 and 626 in 2002), and its highest number of double plays ever (64 in 2000). Moreover, in 2001 the team set single-game records for doubles (seven, a feat achieved against four different teams in different years), sacrifice flies (four, against Davidson), and assists (24, against Georgia Southern).

The overall record of the Wofford Terriers while Duncan Park was their home field was 119 wins versus 276 losses. In 1997 the college joined the Southern Conference, and their record within the conference from 1998 through 2003 was 54-112. The baseball coaches at Wofford during the Duncan Park era were **Mark Line** (1995), **Ernie May** (1996-1999), and **Steve Traylor** (2000-2003). Two Wofford players were drafted by MLB teams during this period: **Anthony Salley** by the Toronto Blue Jays in the 24th round in 1997 and **Kevin Blocker** by the Colorado Rockies in the 25th round in 2000; neither player advanced to the Major Leagues.

SPARTANBURG CRICKETS. The Crickets were members of the Southern Collegiate Baseball League, an independent summer wooden bat league composed of teams from North Carolina and South Carolina, Georgia, and Tennessee, from 2001-2005. There was also a Spartanburg SCBL team in 2010, but that team (the Blue Eagles) played at Russell C. King Field at Wofford. The 2001 Crickets played in a 7-team league at Duncan Park, featuring players from two- and four-year colleges, most located in South Carolina. Coached by **Mike Noble**, the team finished tied for first place in a season marked by disappointing attendance and publicity. As columnist Lou Parris noted, "words of disappointment at the lack of community support for the first-year team were being spoken like a broken record." Even owner Steve Cunningham was open in expressing his frustration: "We need some support from the public....We're not asking people to lie down in traffic and give up their lives. We just need some help paying the bills." These words from a successful businessman who owned Veteran's Lanes and the Hillcrest Sports Club and who was also president of the Spartanburg Touchdown Club are revealing.

Still, the Crickets returned in 2002, in an eight-team league, with an apparently expanded corps of local business supporters; Coach Mike Noble was back, along with players from USC Aiken, USC Columbia, USC Spartanburg, USC Union, Coastal Carolina, Wofford, Furman, and smaller area schools.

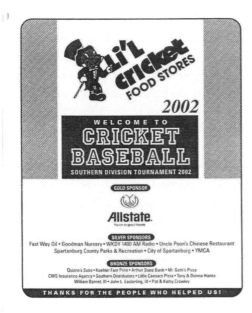

The Spartanburg Crickets benefited from their connection to local convenience store chain Li'l Cricket.

The Crickets hosted the SCBL tournament in 2002 and placed 10 players on the South Division All Stars Roster. By 2004 the Crickets were looking for creative ways to draw fans to the stadium, prominent among which was "Cricket's Baseball Bingo," featuring prizes such as a free lunch at Uncle Poon's, wraps at Sandella's on Main, a $50 savings bond from Arthur State Bank, free oil changes from Fastway Oil Change, and gift certificates from Fatz Cafe and Your Dollar Store With More. The team finished with a 27-23 record in the SCBL.

The Crickets continued to be optimistic as the 2005 season approached. The team had seven returnees from 2004, and Cunningham expressed hope that the fact that all of his players reported early to the team's first practice augured well for 2005: "That's the first time in five years that everybody has been early. I couldn't believe it," he reported. Cunningham's son, Mike, the new coach, agreed: "We have guys from all levels of college and they can leg it." By 2006, though, the magic was gone from Duncan Park, and needed repairs at the structure accelerated the team's departure to USC Upstate that summer. After the unexpected death of owner Steve Cunningham in October 2007, the

Cunningham sons sold the team to RBI Sports, which relocated it again to Wofford College as the Blue Eagles.

SPARTANBURG STINGERS. The Spartanburg Stingers, who played at Duncan Park from 2003 through 2006, belonged to the Coastal Plain League, another summer collegiate wooden bat league with members spread from Virginia to South Carolina. The original general manager of the team was **Lenny Mathis**, one of the founders of The Friends of Duncan Park and associate athletic director for marketing at Wofford College; **Brandon McKillop**, the Wofford baseball coach, was the Stingers first manager. Among the Stingers players were two local favorites: **Steven Tolleson**, who played for the University of South Carolina and then graduated to professional baseball—and whose father Wayne had played for the New York Yankees and other MLB teams—and **Hank Parks**, who in addition to also playing for USC had played American Legion baseball in Spartanburg and was an All-Region star for Spartanburg Methodist College. Other Stingers played for Clemson, Virginia, Vanderbilt, Coastal Carolina, University of North Carolina Asheville, The Citadel, and smaller regional schools.

The Stingers tried hard to draw fans into Duncan Park stadium. Among the attractions were "Daycare Day at Duncan Park," when daycares and summer camps could bring their charges to the stadium for an unusual summer noontime game, a hot dog, chips, and a soda for the bargain price of $5 per person. Another deal was "Spartanburg's BEST Birthday Party," for which 10 kids and two chaperoning adults could enjoy a game, a free Stingers pennant, reserved seating, a free pass to Hollywild Animal Park, and a visit by Dinger the Stinger—and the birthday child also would receive a signed baseball and PA announcement—all for $99.

The team also tried hard to help out the players, who, like all summer college league players, played for nothing since NCAA rules at the time forbade payments to student-athletes. In addition to free housing with local families, the team also solicited part-time jobs for team members "in offices, retail stores, or recreational facilities (like golf courses)" and other experiences for players having "targeted interests pertaining to their majors."

During their four years at Duncan Park, the Stingers enjoyed modest success on the diamond. In 2003 the team won 19 and lost 26 under coach McKillop, but they did have a winning 12-8 record in their division. In 2004 the record was 17-29 with coach **Kevin Flanagan;** in 2005, 31-23 under **Garrett Brown**— they made the tournament this year but were defeated—and in 2006, 21-29 under **Matt Hayes.** In 2006 the writing was on the wall though: the City of Spartanburg would not undertake needed repairs, and the Stingers could not

The Spartanburg Stingers official "Souvenir Score-card" featured a photo of Duncan Park stadium.

afford to make them on their own; estimates of what might be needed ranged up to $3,000,000. In 2007 the Stingers played at Wofford.

TURNING POINTS. It looked indeed like the game might be over for "Beautiful Duncan Park Stadium" in 2006. The stadium was ancient—it had been just a little short of 40 years old in 1963, the *first* year the Phillies played in the stadium, after all—and maintenance and repair had always been contentious issues: who would pay the costs, on what basis would the interested parties share the costs, what priority would be put on prevention versus repair and replacement, and to what extent could the public be expected and/or persuaded to buy into the costs? In the years that official Minor League Baseball teams played at Duncan Park—1938-1940, 1946-1955, and 1963-1994—there was an additional consideration: what were the minimum conditions acceptable to professional baseball before the responsible governing bodies would require the removal of the team?

As early as 1966, when Pat Williams in his second year with the Phillies was trying to persuade the city to fund upgrades in anticipation of moving up from

Stingers "merch" included baseballs with the official team mascot and refrigerator magnets.

A to AA classification, the team was asking for $35,000 for new lighting and another $50,000 for wiring; the city did *not* apply for a AA franchise. In 1970 the city learned that its population had actually *declined* by 816 individuals (1.6 percent) in the previous decade, while Spartanburg *County* had *increased* its population by 12,915 during the same period. The population trends and implications for tax revenues were not encouraging. In 1976 Phillies General Manager Billy Williams told the city that the ballpark needed a $25,000 new roof, an unfulfilled request that he repeated in 1977. Williams reported that although the Phillies were "happy here," 15 years after first hosting the team in Spartanburg the stadium was "just not the bright, homey spot it used to be." Howie Bedell, the assistant farm director of the Philadelphia Phillies, told the city that the big Phillies were "not interested in making money" but that their losses had been "sizable" during their seven-year term of ownership. As a result, he said, it was time to "find out if Spartanburg wants to support baseball." Wrangling, bargaining, and jockeying for position continued off and on among the city, the Philadelphia ownership, and subsequent local owners for most of the rest of the Phillies' time at Duncan Park. A late 1980s attendance resurgence was not to endure, and as the 1990s progressed, ownership became more and more restive, hearing the siren call of better facilities across the state line, and City Council was unable to rise sufficiently to the challenge; neither did the Phillies have sufficiently deep pockets. So the marriage between the City of Spartanburg and the Spartanburg Phillies, originally a match seemingly made in heaven that blossomed into a productive and profitable partnership and then a marriage of convenience only and finally a loveless arrangement that endured out of little more than inertia, came to a cheerless end.

STOP-GAPS AND A LONG DECLINE. After the Phillies departed Spartanburg in 1994, the future of baseball in the historic stadium and the long-term stability of the structure itself seemed dim indeed. American Legion Post 28 still played its home games at Duncan Park, bur the Legion itself had never been able to contribute much, if anything, to stadium upgrades or improvements. The city's agreement with Post 28 stipulated that the municipal budget would contribute to maintenance of the stadium and field but that Post 28 would bear the cost of baseball operations for the team, i. e., uniforms, balls and other equipment, travel, etc. Costs incurred for ticketing, concessions, stadium cleanup, programs, etc. would be covered by donations from players' parents, legionnaires, the Legion Auxiliary, and the general public. In fact, too, although the city was to provide for facilities maintenance, such provision was often minimal at best, and during his long association with Post 28 Baseball, former Athletic Director Geno Campbell himself often took care of plumbing repairs and replacements, painting, and occasional electrical repairs. It takes a village to run an American Legion baseball team, but in Spartanburg it has often been a small village.

From 1995 until 2008, to be sure, some other teams did play baseball at Duncan Park stadium. The University of South Carolina Rifles played there from 1995 through 2003, and the Wofford College Terriers were tenants from 1996 through 2003, for example, but institutional teams at heart want to host competition on their own campuses; scheduling can also be difficult when there are *two* teams that call a stadium home, and during these years Legion team preseason practice and competing city recreational programs were often at odds with the colleges. In the end neither Wofford nor USC Spartanburg would be willing or able to spend big money on the physical plant, and both teams ultimately moved into brand-new facilities on their own properties.

The independent Atlantic Coast League Spartanburg Alley Cats played at Duncan Park in 1995, too, but only briefly. The team and its league were underfunded from the get-go and did not even complete their planned inaugural season. The wooden bat collegiate league Spartanburg Crickets (Southern Collegiate Baseball League) and Spartanburg Stingers (Coastal Plain League) played a few years at Duncan Park, but their contracts with the city stipulated "seat tax" payments of only $2,500 plus a token per game fee of $65 for utility costs, also $4,000 "annual rent" in 2003. This income to the city, balanced against necessary expenditures over the years, could never produce sufficient funds for the kinds of substantial outlays that might save the stadium for future generations.

WHAT NEXT? The consequences of inattention to needed maintenance and repairs became plainly apparent as early as May 1995, when one wall of the stadium literally came tumbling down. Under pressure from an exterior mound of dirt that apparently had been building for years, a 50-foot section of the 16-foot-high concrete right field wall spontaneously gave way and fell inward. Because the wall had been built at a time when steel rod reinforcement was not required by building codes, the unreinforced concrete could not withstand the outside pressure. Luckily no one was injured in the collapse, but the event signaled what might happen in the future.

In the absence of a MiLB tenant, the city was becoming increasingly concerned about the costs of operating Duncan Park stadium. In October of 1996 Mayor James Talley asked Assistant City Manager Evelyn Tice to report "on the financial status of Duncan Park stadium." Tice reported that the stadium had been busy: from February through mid-October of 1996 95 events or dates had been scheduled at the stadium with a total attendance of around 10,000. These events included Wofford and USC Spartanburg baseball, company picnics, family reunions, fundraisers for local nonprofits, etc. Revenue generated by these events amounted to only $11,832, however, although operating costs were more than four times that amount at $48,269. Other information supplied to council was inconsistent: expenditures were "comparable to Minor League Baseball expenditures," revenues were down only $5,000, and only minor capital improvements—for the continually deteriorating outfield wall and grandstand seating—were needed; but "it had been a challenge to keep the stadium available for community use," a task achieved only by "shifting some staff responsibilities."

Two years later the situation was more dire, and the city was trying to decide the "fate" of the stadium. At this point it was costing the city $150,000 a year to maintain the stadium and grounds, but use of the facilities was generating only $30,000 in rentals. An 11-member committee of "private citizens and city officials" had been studying the problem for six weeks and was due to report to the city in two more months. An outlay of $300,000 was needed for repairs and to "spruce up the stadium," but factors that argued against committing more money to stadium projects included the **MLB** territorial boundary agreement with the Greenville Braves, the $6 million to $8 million cost of constructing a new modern facility, and the anticipated departures of Wofford and **USC**

Spartanburg because of new home stadiums on their campuses. Other options were being discussed actively. One, the stadium's potential conversion to some kind of music venue, had been discarded because of the amphitheater at the new downtown Barnet Park. City Manager Roy Lane told council that "[t]here are still a number of options we're looking at," but he also admitted publicly that "[t]earing down the stadium" was one of them. The situation had become so worrisome that a poignant personal appearance was made at this meeting by Ty Wood and Ray Linder from the 1936 American Legion team that played before more than 20,000 fans in the championship Little World Series game at Duncan Park. Both men made heartfelt appeals for the preservation of the stadium.

As the 21st century neared, then, the problems faced by those who wished to preserve the classic old wooden grandstand stadium at Duncan Park were well nigh insurmountable. In addition to issues extending backward to the later period of the Spartanburg Phillies tenure and later developments described in "Stop-gaps and a long decline," other concerns arrived with the new millennium. Although the years spent in Duncan Park by the Spartanburg Stingers and the Spartanburg Crickets saw an infusion of new cash, it was not a major infusion, and both teams had departed by the end of the summer of 2006 in any event. Post 28 remained, but the American Legion was not obligated to contribute to maintenance, repairs, or new construction at the ballpark in any substantial way. And although there was occasional discussion of Spartanburg County School District Seven relocating to Duncan Park as its home stadium rather than improving facilities at Spartanburg High School on its Fernwood campus on the East Side of town (there was not really room to do this on Sydnor Road, and Lawsons Fork Creek was a formidable barrier to expansion in another direction), nothing much ever came of a serious plan for this.

By the fall of 2002, although the Crickets had been in Spartanburg for two years already and the Stingers were to begin their first season the next summer, attorney Michael Duncan—grandson of the Major Duncan—whose family had donated the property on which the park and stadium are located to the city was writing to Steve Cunningham, the owner of the Crickets, that "My grandfather's gift has been sorely neglected by the city." Duncan and Cunningham had talked about the stadium before, and Duncan was writing to say that he was "very concerned about the deteriorating condition not only of the ballpark, but of the American Legion Home which is also located on Duncan Park (City) property." Duncan agreed with "your assessment that the walls need to be repaired and the facilities improved" and hoped that since there recently had been major improvements made to Cleveland Park on the Asheville Highway, "perhaps the city can turn and focus its attention on another 'hidden jewel' inside the city limits." In order to bolster his case, Duncan wrote that he was forwarding copies of his letter to Mayor William Barnet III, and City Councilman Bob Allen.

CHAPTER NINE

. . . .

The Sun Rises on a Whole New Ballgame

MICHAEL DUNCAN'S VISION FOR the stadium that he saw as part of his family's legacy to the city of Spartanburg and its citizens was to come closer to being realized beginning in 2008. This outcome, the impact of which continues as these words are being written, was the result of the hard work of two organizations and several determined individuals. The organizations were the Friends of Duncan Park and Spartanburg County School District Seven. The individuals were Dr. Thomas White, former superintendent and later assistant superintendent for planning of School District Seven; Myles Wilson, former athletic director of Spartanburg High School and director of athletic facilities for School District Seven; Lenny Mathis, founder of the Friends; Terry Haselden, local attorney who spent hours on the telephone and at his computer keyboard campaigning on behalf of the Friends and Duncan Park stadium; Donnie Love, principal of MacMillan Pazdan Smith, and of course many others.

THE FRIENDS OF DUNCAN PARK. By the fall of 2005, with the departure of the Spartanburg Crickets leaving the Spartanburg Stingers and American Legion Post 28 as the only teams committed to Duncan Park stadium, and the City of Spartanburg's intentions regarding the ballpark's future uncertain at best, a group of local citizens spearheaded by Mathis stepped up to the plate on behalf of the historic facility. An honors graduate of the University of South Carolina, Mathis had become associate athletic director for marketing at Wofford College in 2003 and in the same year had also become public relations coordinator for the Carolina Miracle League. He was active in Spartanburg Young Professionals and the Arts X Society of the Chapman Cultural Center. His professional and civic duties connected him with local media; and he had firsthand experience with Minor League Baseball, having served as director of ticket operations of the Savannah Sand Gnats in 2001-2002, and with independent college league baseball, having been the general manager of the Spartanburg Stingers Baseball Club in 2003. As the potential abandonment of Duncan Park stadium became a more and more likely eventuality and as awareness of this possibility gradually spread into public consciousness, Mathis "sent an email to a couple dozen friends in May 2005 and it originally was the Spartanburg Baseball Historical Society (or something like that); quickly it turned into the Friends of Duncan Park." Mathis became the natural choice as head honcho and spokesperson for the group.

Mathis had many allies in his efforts to save Duncan Park stadium, some more active and publicly visible than others. Early on, in September 2005, the Friends email header included around three dozen names; by the middle of the next summer, July 2006, it had expanded to more than 120 names. Not all of these were official "Friends;" many of them were, however. Among those who aided Mathis in significant ways were the following:

- Local attorney Terry Haselden, whose son, David, was to become a first-rate pitcher for Clemson University and then went on to play Minor League ball for the Chicago White Sox.

- Don Camby, vice president of the Friends of Duncan Park, a former assistant principal at Broome High School and historian of Textile Leagues baseball and other fast-disappearing aspects of historic Spartanburg, who remembered Rocky Colavito playing in 1952 in a Spartanburg Peaches game his grandfather took him to.

- Cindy Carter, treasurer of the Friends of Duncan Park.

- Susan Wood Pope, whose father, Ty Wood, was bat boy for the 1936 Post 28 American Legion Little World Series Champions and played for the 1938 Post 28 team that also contended for the Little World Series Championship, as well as for the 1952 Spartanburg Peaches and local Textile League teams.

- Luther Norman, local Black businessman, Director of the Youth Sports Bureau, and son-in-law of "Little" Newt Whitmire, owner of the Spartanburg Sluggers.

- Jeff Kurkis, former general manager of the Spartanburg Phillies during a difficult time for the Minor League franchise.

- Journalists like WSPA-TV's Russ Bradley and the *Herald-Journal's* Gary Henderson.

- Professors at Wofford and USC Upstate, first and foremost probably Tommy Ordoyne of the math department at USC Upstate.

- High school coaches and teachers.

- Local baseball historians who wished to preserve the stadium's connections to the old Sally and Western Carolina Leagues, to the Peaches and Phillies, and to the Black semipro Spartanburg Sluggers.

- Adults who had themselves played at Duncan Park in their youth and whose sons currently played there.

- Architect Donnie Love, historic preservation specialist at McMillan Pazdan Smith, who prepared the application for the stadium's recognition on the National Register of Historic Places.

- Local citizens with a love of the old ballpark.

- Residents of the Duncan Park neighborhood who viewed the continuation of an active baseball presence as a condition necessary to the stability, safety, and vitality of their surroundings

The Friends' campaign to save Duncan Park proceeded slowly but in its way relentlessly. On September 8, 2005, Mathis announced an open town hall-style meeting scheduled for later in the month, a meeting whose time had come after a series of newspaper articles and Friends meetings during the previous several months. Friends membership had doubled, and there was already substantial behind-the-scenes discussion of potential uses of the stadium that might stave off the wrecking ball. The message received significant response, but the meeting had to be rescheduled to accommodate potential attendees who could not come at the scheduled lunch hour time. In the end around 15 of the 55 official Friends attended the September 24 meeting at the ballpark. Mathis opened the meeting with the observation that the city had no clear idea or "vision about what they want to do here." Whatever the plan became, though, the minimum amount needed to bring the stadium up to playable conditions in the short term was $500,000 to $800,000. Among the ideas discussed as potential ways to utilize the stadium were the following:

*Local historical archi-
tecture specialist and
principal at McMillan
Pazdan Smith Donnie
Love prepared the appli-
cation for recognition of
Duncan Park stadium on
the National Register of
Historic Places.*

- A late February college baseball tournament.
- A March JV and Varsity high school baseball tournament sponsored by the Spartanburg High School teams.
- Games featuring the popular Spartanburg Methodist College baseball program.
- A junior college Carolinas/Virginia Athletic Conference Regional Playoffs tournament.
- Field conditioning in May.
- Summertime play by Post 28, the Stingers, and the Crickets.
- September Little League football and/or Little League soccer.
- A Gospel Fest.
- A community flea market in October in the parking lot, with the concourse as a backup in case of spillover or bad weather.
- Reunion games featuring former Phillies or Legion players.

There was even discussion of a possible "Hispanic" soccer league playing at the ballpark—migrant laborer and immigrant teams had been playing at the Highway 295 field for a while, and there was no seating there or concessions— and a reminder that from time to time it had been suggested that Spartanburg

High School might play at Duncan Park. Someone recalled that the high school would prefer to play on its own campus although there was not really space available there. The most discouraging comment during the meeting was the observation that it looked like the Friends or others had about 18 months to come up with a plan or plans to save the stadium.

By the next May not much had been accomplished. The city had not responded to requests to publicize the results of a "structural study on the ballpark," the outfield grass had been cut but only recently for the first time that spring, nothing had been done about the outfield wall, and planking along the concourse to the men's restroom had not been replaced. Before the end of the month, though, some progress had been made: a 20-foot section of the outfield cinder-block wall had been replaced by a wooden wall, repairs had been made to the concourse flooring and to the wall on both sides of the concourse, the field had been improved, exit signs and lights had been added to both ends of the grandstand, and both Post 28 and the Stingers were prepared to begin their seasons.

The next month saw Edition 4 of the Friends Newsletter in near-panic mode. The City "do not plan to operate the park next year—basically locking it up, but not razing it. Yet." Friends members were calling city officials in Greensboro, Chattanooga, Birmingham, Evansville (Indiana), and Wilson (North Carolina)—in all of which cities there were old ballparks or fan bases with demographics and/or histories similar to those in Spartanburg—for ideas that might lead to a longterm solution for Duncan Park. It was, the newsletter announced, "do or die time for South Carolina's oldest ballpark," and as many Friends as possible needed to rally and bombard the city with phone calls and letters urging support for the old stadium. A meeting would be held on June 25, 2006, to form committees and to develop a specific action plan.

In fact, a meeting was held at 6 p.m. on June 28, 2006, prior to the Spartanburg Stingers game, admission to which was free for attendees to the Friends meeting. The most critical need was how to raise the $1.1 million essential to Phase 1 of the $4.7 million total identified in the recent engineering analysis of the stadium. The Friends issued a summary of the meeting's outcomes on July 1. Not only had about 80 individuals attended the meeting, but 20 new names had been added to the email list as well. There was now an official slate of officers: President—Lenny Mathis; Vice President—Don Camby; Treasurer—Cindy Carter; Secretary—Leann Dixon; and an advisory committee consisting of Russ Bradley, Jeff Kurkis, Scott Bryant, Luther Norman, Travis Woods (media), and Jim Harbison. Dixon had updated the www.saveduncanpark.org website, the organization was transitioning to a new email platform (info@saveduncanpark.org) for space reasons, the *Herald-Journal* was soliciting photographs for a feature story to be run later in the week, and the Friends were planning to attend a number of upcoming Stingers and Post 28 games as a way of maintaining a visible presence of interest in the stadium. Mathis was also meeting with the Spartanburg County Foundation in order to establish a 501 (c) (3) account that could hold funds earmarked for stadium preservation, such as the $30,000 grant secured by Senator Glenn Reese.

Progress was being made. An email of July 6 encouraged Friends members to write to City Manager Mark Scott on behalf of the stadium, to attend the city council meeting coming up on July 10 in support of an appeal to Council, and to attend the Stingers game on July 8, at which the Stingers would be wearing Phillies practice jerseys and the Friends would be selling Friends of Duncan Park tee shirts. At the Stingers game the Friends sold all 108 "Save Duncan Park" shirts it had printed, and there was a strong show of support for the stadium at the council meeting. The city would not cave, of course, and it still planned to lock the stadium gates at the conclusion of the 2006 season, but, significantly, it announced that it *had* found *some* money that could be spent on Duncan Park. The funds in question were some $200,000 in hospitality tax income that had been allocated for the stadium but remained unspent because "we felt, over the last few years, that spending it on stopgap measures would be akin to throwing it away." The money in question would not be enough to make all of the repairs and maintenance that were required to make the stadium whole, but the city now regarded it as a seed money match for private fundraising efforts that might make enough of a difference to turn the situation around.

On the same day that Lane Filler's article appeared in the newspaper, the Friends email account reported that Mathis and Bradley had met in Birmingham with David Brewer, executive director of the Friends of Rickwood, which had saved and revitalized historic Rickwood Field, the oldest stadium in the country (1910), former home to both the Birmingham Barons and the Birmingham Black Barons of the Negro Leagues. Mathis and Bradley had also met with current Birmingham Barons general manager Jonathan Nelson, and when they returned to Spartanburg they were genuinely encouraged. "The Friends of Duncan Park," they said, "will continue its efforts in the local Spartanburg community as well as work with the City of Spartanburg in a public-private partnership."

The local press was unconvinced. In August in a piece titled "Too Little, Too Late?" *Herald-Journal* staff writer Robert Dalton contrasted Buncombe County, North Carolina's *salvation* of its Minor League team with

Spartanburg's *failure* to keep the Phillies in the 1990s. Dalton's article actually said little about Duncan Park beyond a few paragraphs near the end, but it concluded that Asheville's success was due to its forward-looking attitude, whereas Spartanburg was always looking to its past. In the same issue of the newspaper, Filler emphasized another problem in an analysis of the successful construction of the Chapman Cultural Center compared to the failures of a proposed NASCAR museum, the choice of Spartanburg as the site of a South Carolina Sports Hall of Fame, and the renovation of Duncan Park stadium. After discussing the generosity of the city's philanthropic community in financing the Chapman Center, Filler went on to quote businessman Jimmy Gibbs on Duncan Park: "...Spartanburg needs to be progressive in putting things up that will put money in people's pockets or help make their lives better. There are a lot of poor people here, a lot of needs, and only so much money. I just can't see the ballpark as a priority."

The final chapter was yet to be written though. Four days after the two stories appeared, the Friends of Duncan Park announced that Jaycees Charities Inc. had agreed to permit the Friends to operate within their 501 (c) (3) corporation umbrella as a registered nonprofit. The Friends newsletter quoted Mathis as saying, "We are grateful for the support of the Jaycees for allowing us to work with them in this manner. It helps us have one more piece of the puzzle in place as we look toward kicking off this fundraising effort." Thus matters stood.

SPARTANBURG COUNTY SCHOOL DISTRICT SEVEN. Matters still stood thus less than a year later when suddenly, out of the unsuspecting blue, the *Herald-Journal* made the surprising announcement that "District 7 Might Revive Duncan Park stadium." According to reporters Lynne Shackleford and Ashlei Stevens, all but one member of the District Seven Board of Trustees had met with City Manager Mark Scott to discuss "a deal that could include renovating Duncan Park stadium." Scott, moreover, had been supportive: "I'm excited about it, and I think it's a real possibility now that the district would be able to use the field and put it back on our radar. We'll both be winners if we can make it happen." Neither the city nor District Seven announced any details regarding the discussions, what decisions regarding repairs and maintenance might be made, or who might pay how much to restore the stadium to playing condition and remove the padlock on the gates. Mathis had not been notified of the meeting between the city and the district, and two parents of ballplayers at the high school, Terry Haselden and Kit Jennings, spoke out in favor of maintaining some kind of baseball presence at the high school campus as well. Still, support for a stadium partnership between the city and the District seemed pretty solid according to the paper.

It was solid largely because it had been carefully prepared for. In an interview in 2017 Myles Wilson and Dr. Thomas White confirmed that they had worked for some time to lay the groundwork for the agreement with the city. For one thing, White said, the district was "always looking at facilities;" and he and Terry Gilmer, the district's director of maintenance and operations, visited with principals around twice a year to determine their maintenance needs. They in turn passed their assessments along to Assistant Superintendent for Business Affairs Glenn Stiegman, who relayed them to the superintendent and the board. District officials began leaning toward Duncan Park as their preferred home for baseball for several reasons. The main one was that the District needed room for games and/or practice fields for two football teams and four soccer teams *in addition to room for JV and varsity baseball,* and the existing Hillbrook campus simply could not provide such space. Another impetus for moving to Duncan Park was that it was the right time: Stiegman was nearing retirement, and helping to stabilize district facilities at Duncan Park would be "a good step to go out on."

"If you didn't plant a seed, it wouldn't grow," said Wilson, and it was time to plant the seed.

The devil is always in the details, of course, and apparently this was the case in the deliberations between the city and District Seven. The city had called a halt to any actions regarding demolition of the ballpark for the time being, but immediate implementation of any measures to upgrade the facility were not in the works. There was an expectation that the Friends would continue their efforts to raise money for the stadium, and everyone involved knew that any improvements made would be expensive. Preliminary steps were being taken though: the Friends had commissioned a study of proposed changes from McMillan Pazdan Smith & Partners, state Senator Glenn Reese and Representative Doug Smith had secured grants from state government, and the Greenville Drive had even sponsored a "Spartanburg Night" at West End Field with proceeds from the auction of replica Spartanburg Peaches uniforms going to the Friends stadium revitalization fund.

One thing was clear: Spartanburg District Seven was committed to the process. Although deliberations were mostly conducted in private and behind closed doors, the prime movers in this process were Superintendent Dr. Thomas White and Director of Athletic Facilities Myles Wilson. White had served the district since the 1980s, worked in other Upstate districts, was an

Spartanburg County School District Seven's Myles Wilson inspects stadium details during restoration. Former Athletic Director Wilson, who was taken early by the COVID virus, loved Duncan Park stadium.

experienced project planner and manager, and had valuable additional experience negotiating the often politically fraught landscape of policies impacting a variety of communities. Wilson had been athletic director at Spartanburg High School, had knowledge of wide-ranging athletic projects statewide as a leader in South Carolina athletic administrators' organizations, and—most importantly—loved Duncan Park stadium. Wilson was also good at seeing projects through from beginning to end and was a consummate people person: when he succumbed to COVID during the early stages of the pandemic in Spartanburg, he was beloved in the District Seven community.

Other leaders in District Seven also supported the District's strengthening attachment to the stadium. Dr. Russell Booker, soon to become Superintendent himself, had a strong commitment to diversity and to serving all constituent communities within the District and had a clear vision of the value of Duncan Park stadium to the center city neighborhoods around it and to the possibility of increasing Black student participation in District Seven baseball since Spartanburg High School had a student body composed of 70+ percent majorities of both minority and economically disadvantaged students. Principal Jeff Stevens at Spartanburg High School, a graduate of the school and himself a baseball player, having attended Western Carolina University on a baseball scholarship, understood the historical significance of Duncan Park stadium. Stevens would also follow Booker as district superintendent so there would be a sustained continuity of commitment to whatever the district would agree to.

On the city side of the stadium negotiations there was no publicly committed advocate pledging significant ongoing funding to save the stadium. Lenny Mathis recalled, "I honestly can't remember an advocate. From the city [sic]." Mathis did emphasize, though, that Mayor Bill Barnet, although skeptical about the Friends chances for success, was respectful as he listened to the Friends plans and proposals. Another member of City Council suspected that Mathis, former general manager of the Stingers, might be interested in the ballpark for the Stingers' sake rather than for its own value to the community. There were also persistent rumors that "someone" had plans to build a new stadium on the vacant property behind the site of the Marriott Hotel downtown on Church Street, a hope that might clearly have influenced some members of City Council's thinking on the issue.

In any event, even in the absence of a groundswell of support from city leaders District Seven officials persisted and seem to have pressed their position. The result was that on Monday, May 12, 2008, City Council approved an agreement with Spartanburg County School District Seven for shared respon- · sibility for the Duncan Park stadium. The agreement specified that the city and District Seven would each commit $750,000 out of a projected total renovation cost of $3 million or more, additional expenses to be paid from "fundraising." The district already had spent almost a quarter of a million dollars on demolishing the old concrete outfield wall, constructing a new wooden wall, and readying the field for play in the summer of 2008. Moving forward, the city would maintain the stadium, fields, and trails at the park; District Seven would maintain portable toilets and bleachers. The partners would share utility costs. There were no stated arrangements regarding the grandstand.

The 2007 agreement between the city and District Seven was formalized in a memorandum of understanding between the two parties dated January 7, 2013. This document stipulated that District Seven would have first priority of use of the stadium except during Post 28's American Legion season in the summer; that the school district also would be entitled to non-exclusive rights to the softball fields and nature trails at the Park; that the city would maintain the stadium and softball fields to the district's "reasonable satisfaction" as well as the outfield wall and nature trails; that the district would supply and maintain

Structural safety issues such as roof strut supports and the integrity of other stadium ironwork were addressed by District Seven.

portable toilets and temporary bleachers; that the city and district would jointly share "the pro rata expenses for utilities, lighting and water;" and that the district would provide liability insurance for park facilities. The memorandum also specified that "THE CURRENT GRAND STAND AREA WITHIN THE STADIUM IS EXCLUDED FROM USE UNTIL SUCH TIME AN AGREEMENT IS REACHED WITH THE CITY CODE ENFORCEMENT OFFICIALS THAT SUCH AREA MAY BE USED [sic]."

As time passed and the district's use of the stadium and other facilities became more regularized, responsibilities also evolved. Today—the original memorandum of understanding is still in effect as of fall 2021 without alteration in its terms—the city maintains the fields within and beyond the stadium, and the district maintains the stadium itself, utilizing its capital budget for repairs and to maintain the character of the stadium and its safety for both students and district personnel and the general public. By February 2019 the district had spent more than a million and a half dollars on renovations called for by virtually every team that had occupied Duncan Park stadium since the departure of the Phillies in 1994. These included new locker rooms, showers, restrooms, and storage space for both baseball and girls softball, also new dugouts with restrooms on both sides of home plate. Many of the vintage wooden seats from Shibe Park in Philadelphia have been restored and reinstalled as well, and the grandstand is becoming structurally secure. Most recently, drainage and sewerage issues were addressed in 2019—as Thomas White observed, "Once you start peeling back the layers here you find other structural kinds of issues that turns [sic] into another project."

More work still needs to be done. The grandstand roof and concourse need additional attention, and there is no available acceptable concession area under the roof. The "press box" is subpar, and although there are new signage and banners, the "office" area just inside the gate has an ad hoc feel to it. There is also the need for upgrades in case of a need for sudden emergency exiting, and handicapped access is not what it ought to be. These needs have to be addressed in order for spectator capacity to increase from the current 500 to 600 fans per game to the 2,500 or more that the new tenants, The Spartanburgers, would like to see. The arrival of The Spartanburgers, a wooden bat collegiate league member of the Coastal Plain League, in summer 2021 already had resulted in some improvements: increased attention to field preparation, closer regard for and recognition of the historic features of the stadium and its former tenants, better restrooms and bleachers, fencing along the first base "bullpen" area, and craft beers at the beverage station. Luther Norman's Youth Sports Bureau was also coordinating with students and teachers at Mary H. Wright Elementary School and Carver Middle School on plans for a large historical mural for the exterior wall alongside Duncan Park Drive.

THE SPARTANBURGERS. The return of summer wooden bat league baseball with The Spartanburgers, welcomed enthusiastically by local fans, promised increased long-term funding for the stadium and the potential for the implementation of new programs, the construction of new facilities and rehabilitation of older ones, and greater giveback to Spartanburg communities. Media attention—both print and digital, local and regional—was encouraging. For years, too, there had been discussion among local historians, city officials, and organizations such as the Spartanburg County Historical Association of the possibilities for an historical display area or even a museum of some sort to celebrate the long history of Duncan Park stadium and the teams that have played there. There was some room for such a space already along the old concourse at the top of the grandstand, and there was a rich history of semipro and Negro Leagues Baseball, a nearly 90-year presence of American Legion baseball, the tenures of two official Minor League Baseball teams, and almost forgotten connections with the former Black downtown business community that were all under-commemorated and memorialized.

The Spartanburgers ownership was not local. They hailed from the Northeast, the Mid-Atlantic, and the Midwest, but they were consummate sports professionals. Individually or corporately, they had owned, currently owned, or had helped develop a variety of Minor League Baseball, independent league baseball, collegiate summer league baseball, professional and junior hockey league, **NBADL** basketball, and arena football teams across the country. They also provided marketing analysis, facilities management and renovation, and other services to teams in many different leagues. They appeared to have the know-how to succeed at Duncan Park, and their top priority plans included increasing stadium capacity, initially reported at 850 fans for summer 2021, to 1,700 and more. Since the stadium was designed with a capacity of 2,500, there was potential for more growth in the future. Facilitating these plans were near-term renovations in safety and fan amenities, and team management were committed to engaging fans in a family-friendly way designed to make the ballpark a destination of choice.

The Spartanburgers inaugural season, planned for 2020, was derailed by the **COVID** pandemic, and 2021 attendance was smaller than desired. The team's record was only 12 wins against 31 losses, a success rate of only 23.5 percent. Still, hundreds of fans attended most games, and team owners seemed committed to working hard to promote a larger attendance. The outlook, while not guaranteed, was encouraging. The addition of the Spartanburgers to the mix in any case promised to strengthen the commitment of the City of Spartanburg and Spartanburg County School District Seven. As Lenny Mathis observed, "The park is in good hands now and I know people have it's [sic] best interest at heart. Thankfully too much has been invested in it now to see it wither away and the Spartanburgers relative success this year only helps that cause."

CODA. Subsequent to the completion of the finished manuscript of this volume in summer 2022, things changed again for Duncan Park stadium and its long-suffering supporters. After the disappointing 2021 season, the Spartanburgers decided to regroup. To begin with, the decision was to take a year's hiatus while the city worked in summer 2022 on its part of further restoring and renovating the grandstand in order to draw more fans in years to come. There was also consideration by some members of the partnership of forming a new ownership group to take over the team, and this proposal got so far as to actively consider turning management over to an individual who had been successful in creating one of the most exciting wooden bat league teams in the country. When this idea was floated with the Coastal Plains League itself, however, the league apparently refused to accept the terms of the deal, took over ownership of the franchise as a league property, and announced that it would sit out the 2022 season while the city worked on the stadium. There were no additional public announcements of anyone's plans regarding the Spartanburgers, including either the team's continued existence or its tenure in Spartanburg.

As of the end of May 2023 rumors had continued to surface for two years of the impending proposed construction of a new stadium downtown in the recently designated "Grain District" on currently vacant property behind the AC Marriott Hotel. Suddenly, on Tuesday, May 23, GoUpstate.com, the on-line presence of the *Spartanburg Herald-Journal* announced that the Kinston, North Carolina, Down East Wood Ducks, a Low A Minor League affiliate of the Texas Rangers, would be relocating from their 75-year-old home stadium of Grainger Field to a new 3,500-seat stadium in the long-rumored downtown site. The stadium would be owned by the city and developed by Spartanburg's The Johnson Group, an experienced and highly successful presence in commercial property development in a large number of national locations. In addition, other sites adjacent to the stadium would see extensive construction of additional recreational, residential, and commercial office properties, the whole representing what County Councilman David Britt was reported to have called "the biggest development project to happen to Spartanburg since BMW's 1992 announcement that its North American manufacturing plant would be built in Spartanburg County."

The total project announced on May 23 had been in the works for many months on the QT and represented a sophisticated collaboration among many entities. In addition to the Wood Ducks and the City of Spartanburg, partners included The Johnson Group, county and state government, One Spartanburg Inc. (the local chamber of commerce), and Diamond Baseball Holdings, the Major League Baseball partner which was formed in 2021 and initially managed nine Minor League affiliates of MLB teams, including four belonging to the Atlanta Braves. The Wood Ducks, likely to be renamed, will be members of the Carolina League, an organization that includes the nearby Columbia Fireflies, Charleston River Dogs, and Myrtle Beach Pelicans, all of whose relative proximity to Spartanburg should generate some lively rivalries.

The remaining question for readers of this volume, of course, is what next for Duncan Park stadium? Just a week after the stadium announcement, Spartanburg Deputy City Manager Mitch Kennedy hosted a meeting at City

Hall that convened a number of individuals with longstanding interests and commitments to the old ballpark. These included Dr. Thomas White, special consultant to and former superintendent of Spartanburg County School District Seven; David Theiss, the trails coordinator of PAL Spartanburg; John Barron, athletic director of Spartanburg American Legion Post 28; Brad Steinecke, assistant director of local history at Spartanburg County Libraries; Todd Stephens, County Librarian; Luther Norman, director of the Youth Sports Bureau; Kim Moultrie, parks and recreation director of the City of Spartanburg; Bill Cummings, a director of the Harry Dallara Foundation; and your author. In an open and frank discussion both the city and School District Seven expressed their long-term commitments to the stadium. Without a new resident team, however, the district stressed that its efforts to upgrade the stadium's grandstand integrity, restrooms, and emergency egress would have to take a back seat to other district priorities; progress would be less immediate and take longer to accomplish. The city recommitted to its ongoing maintenance procedures and to support for the Dallara Foundation's renovation of the park's youth ballfields and other park initiatives, but it also stressed that its attention would be significantly diverted to the new comprehensive downtown development. Neither the school district nor the city saw the anticipated return of wooden bat league baseball—that is, a team like the 2021 Spartanburgers—to be realistic given that such a team would compete directly with Minor League Baseball for attendance, concessions, merchandise, and promotions.

The upshot seems to be that Duncan Park stadium is safe for now, but its future is less optimistic than it would have seemed just a couple of weeks ago. Plans and actual designs for the new stadium and surrounding areas are still in the early stages, however, and the soonest the new facility could open would be the summer of 2025. In the meantime the PAL organization is convening a new Friends of Duncan Park committee to facilitate planning for the larger park property and surrounding neighborhoods. It looks like something will be done to renovate and memorialize the old Black ticket office at the upper entrance to the stadium and renovation and improvement of the youth fields seem assured. Stay tuned, baseball fans!

APPENDIX I

· ·

Spartanburg Sluggers Games, 1911-1961

The following chart documents 364 games played or at least scheduled by the Spartanburg Sluggers from 1911 (15 years before the construction of Duncan Park stadium) through 1961, the last date on which I have been able to document a game by a team named the "Spartanburg Sluggers." Games listed were documented in at least one printed source, but whether listed games without scores actually occurred in all cases is problematic, as are such data for most Black independent/semipro/exhibition teams during this era due to their irregular coverage in what were mostly White-owned media.

"BDP"=Beautiful Duncan Park stadium; "A'ville"=Asheville, NC; "G'ville"=Greenville, SC. "P" in the "Comments" column designates the name of the pitcher in the game; other positions are noted with similar abbreviations. A series of three question marks (???) indicates information missing in the original source. Three question marks in the "Outcome" column indicates that a source recorded that a game would be played on this date but that no subsequent source carries a final score; this could mean that the game was not covered by a documented source, usually a newspaper, OR that the game might have been canceled because of weather OR that one team did not show up and the game was not played. The actual reason is unknown.

DATE	WHERE PLAYED	OPPONENT	OUTCOME	COMMENTS (quoted, para-phrased, or summarized from newspaper accounts)
8/19/1911	Sptbg Fairgrounds	"Railroad Bill's team" from Columbia	???	Part of "negroes' Emancipation day celebration;" $50 purse for the winning team
4/14/1913	League Park, Greenville	"the Greenville Baseball team"	???	Large number of White fans expected; "an exceptionally good game is more than likely to be seen this afternoon."
4/21/1913	League Park, Greenville	Greenville Stars	???	"special reservations for White people"

5/7/1916	Oates Park, Asheville; Oates Park was founded by Black Asheville entrepreneur Edward W. Pearson Sr.	Young Men's Institute (Y. M. I.) Thorns; the YMI was founded for Black con- struction workers at the Biltmore Estate and funded by George Vanderbilt in 1892.	L: 1-12; L: 5-6	DOUBLEHEADER; "large crowd of White people expected;" Sluggers will bring "one of the best allotments of ball players seen here in the colored teams for many a day." Greenville pitcher Chatman pitched ALL 18 INNINGS, striking out 12 in the first game and nine in the second. Spartanburg pitcher "No Hit" Hamilton lost first game.
7/4/1917	Oates Park, Asheville	Y.M.I. Thorns	???	"the stellar attraction of the day for the colored people"
7/12/1917	Oates Park, Asheville	Y.M.I. Thorns	L: 1-5	
8/13/1917	Riverside Park, Greenville	Greenville Stars	???	"The Greenville Stars have played a number of games this season."
9/3/1917	Oates Park, Asheville	Y.M.I. All Stars	???	large crowd expected
6/11/1918	Wearn Field, Charlotte	Charlotte Red Sox	L: 2-3	Sluggers battery: Phifer and Rogers
7/4/1918	Wearn Field, Charlotte	Charlotte Red Sox	???	
7/24/1918	Oates Park, Asheville	Y. M. I.	???	
7/25/1918	Oates Park, Asheville	Y. M. I.	???	
8/4/1919	Wearn Field, Charlotte	Charlotte Red Sox	???	Charlotte's "champion colored baseball aggregation"
8/14/1919	Oates Park, Asheville	Asheville Giants	???	third game in a four-game series; both teams havewon several games since their last contest.
8/15/1919	Oates Park, Asheville	Asheville Giants	L; 2-6 L: 0-7	Double-header; was the first game the rained out game from the day before? Third and fourth games in the series?

6/21/1920	Poe Mill Park	Greenville Stars	???	Reference to the Stars' not losing "since the Blue Ridge League was formed;" "consideable rivalry" between the teams
7/21/1920	Oates Park, Asheville	Asheville Royal Giants	???	
7/30/1920	Unknown	Atlanta Deppins	W: 14-6	
7/31/1920	Unknown	Atlanta Deppins	???	"Seats again will be reserved for white people, who attended yesterday's game in goodly numbers."
7/29/1921	Oates Park, Asheville	Y.M.I. stars	???	first of two games
7/30/1921	Oates Park, Asheville	Y.M.I. Stars	???	second of two games
7/4/1922	Spartanburg	Greenville Black Spinners	???	first game of a two-city double-header
7/4/1922	Greenville, League Park on Perry Avenue	Greenville Black Spinners	???	second of a double-header
7/22/1922	Wofford Park, Spartanburg	The Johnston Jints	???	two games; Lefty Chambers and R. Salters the Sluggers battery
7/23/1922	Wofford Park, Spartanburg	The Johnston Jints	???	
8/9/1922	???	The Black Spinners	5-5	No decision—game called b/c of darkness after 15 innings. P: Lefty Chambers; fanned 15
8/17/1922	Wofford Park, Spartanburg	Greenwood Giants	W: 3-1	An excursion from Greenwood, w/500 Greenwood fans. The day also included "the Kid Thomas Review Company, featuring the Creole Jazz Band."
8/21/1922	Wofford Park, Spartanburg	Johnston Jints		Lefty Chambers and R. Salters the battery; white spectators likely allowed
8/22/1922	Wofford Park, Spartanburg	Johnston Jints		

9/4/1922	Greer	Greenville Black Spinners	???	Excursion train from Greenville; large numbers. of White and colored fans expected
5/21/1923		Greenville Black Spinners	L: 7-12	"a whale of a game is expected;" excursion train from Spartanburg; losing pitcher: Chambers
6/4/1923	Wofford Park, Spartanburg	Greenville Black Spinners	???	
6/14/1923	Wofford Park?	Greenwood	???	"A large crowd will be present, as keen rivalry is always shown at the negro contests."
7/4/1923	Wofford Park, Spartanburg	Greenville Black Spinners	???	
6/2/1924	Wofford Park, Spartanburg	"the Greenville negro team"	???	
6/20/1924	Wofford Park, Spartanburg	Anderson White Sox	???	P: Lefty Chambers
7/16/1924	Wofford Park, Spartanburg	Greenville Black Spinners	???	doubleheader
7/22/1924	Fairfield Park (Anderson?)	Anderson Stars	???	Warren Golightly, captain of the Sluggers
sometime during the week prior to 07/10/1925	Asheville	the Giants?	???	
7/13/1925	Wofford Park, Spartanburg	Greenville Black Spinners	???	P: John Sanders, "the best negro pitcher in the Piedmont section;" C: Ligon Maine, "one of the few left-handed catchers in the game"
10/8/1925	Johnson City, TN	Johnson City White Socks	???	Clinchfield RR excursion train ($3.50 round trip)
"a few days" before 06/21/1926	Columbia, SC	???	3-2	

6/21/1926	Wofford Park, Spartanburg	Greenville Black Spinners	???	"among the best colored teams of the piedmont Section"
7/26/1926	Wofford Park, Spartanburg	Anderson Hard Hitters	???	Piedmont & Northern RR excursion train from Anderson
8/30/1926	Sptbg, BDP	Greenville Black Spinners	???	Piedmont & Northern RR excursion train
5/12/1927	McCormick Field, A'ville	Asheville Giants	???	"Special Reservations" for White fans
5/16/1927	Graham Field, Greenville	Greenville Black Spinners	???	
7/18/1927	Sptbg, BDP	Knoxville Giants	W: 1-0	P: "Steel Armed John" (one-hitter)
7/19/1927	Sptbg, BDP	Knoxville Giants	???	P: "Red" Thompson
7/25/1927	Sptbg, BDP	Concord Royal Giants	???	
6/4/1928	Sptbg, BDP	Asheville Black Tourists	???	"The colored churches of the city will be privileged to sell at the game." "Music will be furnished by an Asheville orchestra..."
6/25/1928	Sptbg, BDP	Newberry All Stars	???	
7/4/1928	Sptbg, BDP	Asheville Black Tourists	???	
7/23/1928	Sptbg, BDP	Greenville Black Spinners	???	P: "Lefty" Wilburn; C: Ligon Maine
6/17/1929	Sptbg, BDP	Anderson Hard Hitters	W: 1-0	P: "Wilburn"
7/4/1929	Sptbg, Wofford Park	Asheville Black Tourists	W: 7-3	
7/4/1929	Sptbg, Wofford Park	Charlotte Hard Hitters	W: 5-2	"Rosebud" on 1B! "The crowd was reported as the largest ever assembled here at a ball game."

6/23/1930	Sptbg, BDP	Greensboro Tigers	???	Manager John Styles
7/4/1930	Sptbg, BDP	Asheville Black Tourists	???	Excursion trains from Winston-Salem & Salisbury; P: Whitmire; also hit a HR
7/4/1931	Sptbg, BDP	Winston-Salem All Stars	???	
7/31/1931	Graham Field, G'ville	Greenville Black Spinners	???	
8/3/1931	Graham Field, G'ville	Greenville Black Spinners	???	
8/9/1931	Sptbg, BDP	Bessemer City White Sox	???	
8/25/1931	Sptbg, BDP	Greensboro Togers	???	
7/4/1932	Charlotte	Charlotte Black Hornetts	???	Doubleheader. "Sluggers have lost only two games, and they are anxious to meet Charlotte, so they will be ready for Gainesville Tigers."
6/5/1933	Sptbg, BDP	Asheville Black Tourists	???	"The Tourists are composed of the best players in North Carolina, along with several eastern states. The Spartanburg Sluggers boast a number of southern college players."
6/17/1933	McCormick Field, A'ville	Asheville Black Tourists	L: 3-9	P: Bird & Austiin
6/17/1933	McCormick Field, A'ville	Asheville Black Tourists	L: 8-11	P: Sullivan & Austin
8/2/1933	Pacolet	Pacolet Tigers	???	P: Eddie Tucker
7/4/1934	Pacolet	Pacolet Tigers	???	
7/23/1934	Sptbg, BDP	"a team from Lyman"	???	Benefit game for Camp Friendship and the TB Association

Date	Location	Team	Result	Notes
8/5/1934	McCormick Field, A'ville	Asheville Black Tourists	???	double-header; teams tied 1-1 the week before
9/14/1934	McCormick Field, A'ville	Asheville Black Tourists	L: 5-6	rain-shortened seven-inning game; "First in a series to decide the negro championship of the Carolinas;" P: H. Smith & R. Smith
5/12/1935	McCormick Field, Asheville	Asheville Black Tourists	L: 4-7	P: Smith & Whitmore
5/12/1935	McCormick Field, A'ville	Asheville Black Tourists	L: 4-8	P: Hall & Whitmire
9/2/1935	Baptist assembly grounds, East Flat Rock, NC	Tryon Giants	???	part of a Labor Day festival featuring "special music by the Southern railway and Pullman porter's band, spirituals by well known negro quartets, bicycle and foot races, the address by Dr. [C.F.] Gandy at 1:30 o'clock and a baseball game between the Spartanburg Sluggers and the Tryon Giants." Winner of this game would play the Saluda Tigers.
9/14/1936	Sptbg, BDP	Greenville Stars	???	"for the South Carolina championship"
4/18/1938	Sptbg, BDP	Greenville Stars	???	
6/13/1938	Sptbg, BDP	Anderson Stars	???	opening night of the Sluggers season
6/20/1938	Sptbg, BDP	Asheville Black Tourists	L: 0-1	P: Howard
6/21/1938	Sptbg, BDP	Asheville Black Tourists	???	
7/7/1938	Sptbg, BDP	Laurens	W: 19-3!	P: Morgan; Dover & Russell had three hits each
7/11/1938	Sptbg, BDP	Newberry Stars	W: 16-7	P: Brooks; Morris & Dover had three hits each

8/1/1938	Sptbg, BDP	Charlotte Ramblers	W: 5-3	
8/15/1938	Sptbg, BDP	Gastonia Tigers	W: 11-7	17 Sluggers hits
8/18/1938	Sptbg, BDP	Gastonia Tigers	W: 4-0	Pee Wee Williams had three hits; opposing P: Branson (Bob maybe?)
08/22/1938 (?)	Sptbg, BDP	Charleston Tigers	W: 15-0	P: Brannon [?], fanned 10
08/23/1938 (?)	Sptbg, BDP	Charleston Tigers	W: 18-6	CF Kelly was 4-5
8/29/1938	Charleston	Charleston Tigers	???	
8/30/1938	Charleston	Charleston Tigers	???	
9/11/1938	McCormick Field, A'ville	Asheville Black Tourists	L: 3-5	P: Jones & Rainford
9/11/1938	McCormick Field, A'ville	Asheville Black Tourists	L: 1-2	P: Long & S. Whitmire
5/15/1939	Sptbg, BDP	Morganton, NC, Bears	???	
6/7/1939	Sptbg, BDP	Anderson Red Socks	W: 2-1 [?]	P: Lefty Bob Branson
6/26/1939	Sptbg, BDP	Gastonia All-Stars	W: 18-0	P: Wilburn & Morris; C Winfield went 5-6
7/4/1939	Cambria Park, G'ville	Greenville Black Spinners	???	first game of a double-header completed the same evening
7/4/1939	Sptbg, BDP	Greenville Black Spinners	???	8:30 2nd game of the double-header which began w/the game above in G'ville at 3:30: P: Pat Wilburn
7/10/1939	Sptbg, BDP	Asheville Black Tourists	???	
7/17/1939	Sptbg, BDP	Atlanta White Sox	???	
7/18/1939	Sptbg, BDP	Atlanta White Sox	???	

8/1/1939	Sptbg, BDP	Asheville Black Tourists	???	
8/15/1939	Sptbg, BDP	Greensboro Red Wings	L: 2-7	P: Pat Wilburn
8/29/1939	Sptbg, BDP	Norfolk Black Tars	???	P: Pat Wilburn
9/4/1939	Sptbg, BDP???	Greenville Black Spinners	???	first game of double-header
9/4/1939	Cambria Park, G'ville	Greenville Black Spinners	???	
9/11/1939	McCormick Field, A'ville	Asheville Black Tourists	???	1st game of a double-header; "There will be a reserved seat section for White spectators."
5/19/1940	McCormick Field, A'ville	Asheville Black Tourists	W: 8-2	Tourists' "first opening game defeat in eight years;" 600 fans attended; P: Winford and Williams
5/19/1940	McCormick Field, A'ville	Asheville Black Tourists	L: 2-4	P: Stafford & Garner
5/20/1940	Sptbg, BDP	Augusta Giants	???	
5/21/1940	Sptbg, BDP	Augusta Giants	???	
5/27/1940	Sptbg, BDP	Anderson Sluggers	W: 6-5	
6/3/1940	Sptbg, BDP	House of David	W: 18-8	
6/8/1940	Harper Field, Atlanta	Atlanta All-Stars	L: 5-9	first game of double-header
6/8/1940	Harper field, Atlanta	Atlanta All-Stars	W: 6-2	Sack Morgan, LHP from Atlanta who formerly played for the Scripto Athletics, won for the Sluggers. Former Atlanta players who also played w/Sluggers in the game, were James Brown and Red DeWitt.
6/10/1940	Sptbg, BDP	Greenville Black Spinners	W: 9-3	

6/12/1940	Sptbg, BDP		W: 28-0!	Part of state Black Elks convention
6/14/1940	Sptbg, BDP	Lyman	???	
6/17/1940	Sptbg, BDP	Asheville	???	
7/1/1940	Sptbg, BDP	Lyman Black Cats	W: 16-3	
7/4/1940	Sptbg, BDP	Greenville Black Spinners	W: 15-3	P: Benson [?]
7/4/1940	Cambria Park, G'ville	Greenville Black Spinners	???	
7/22/1940	Sprbg, BDP	Asheville Black Tourists	W: 12-1	21 Slugger hits
8/5/1940	Sptbg, BDP	Charlotte Black Hornets	W: 12-2	Jitterbug contest before the game! P: "Bronson"
9/2/1940	Sptbg, BDP	Gastonia Bears		
4/30/1941	Sptbg, BDP	Ethiopian Clowns	L: 3-16	Sluggers were "Smothered!" "The Sluggers are primed to entertain this combination of baseball and pantomime experts who have been praised by newspapermen of both races as absolute tops." "Among the Clowns are such celebrities as Showboat Thomas, 'Khora' Haywood and 'Peanut' Nyasses, the clown prince of baseball." Sptbg P: Miller; C: Glenn
5/12/1941	Sptbg, BDP	New York Mohawk Giants		"Spartanburg's top-notch diamond game of the season between negroe players;" Giants were five times champs of the Eastern NY state baseball championship; Sluggers owner is N. H. Whitmire, the manager C.W. Whitmire
5/19/1941	Sptbg, BDP	West Indian Royals	W: 13-1	13 Sluggers hits; P: "Bronson"

5/26/1941	Sptbg, BDP	Greenville Black Spinners	W: 7-6	Attendance 1,100; P: "Bronson" and Glenn
6/5/1941	McCormick Field, A'ville	Asheville Black Tourists	L: 5-13	"The first night game ever played at McCormick field between negro teams... "A special section will be reserved for White fans and a big crowd is anticipated. The Black Tourists will sport new uniforms."
6/9/1941	Sptbg, BDP	Asheville Black Tourists		
6/15/1941	Sptbg, BDP	Charleston (?)	W: 11-5	
6/16/1941	Sptbg, BDP	Newberry All-Stars	W: 13-3	P: Glenn
6/24/1941	Sptbg, BDP	New York Royal Reds	???	
7/4/1941	Sptbg, BDP	Camp Croft (military team)	???	
7/7/1941	Sptbg, BDP	Charlotte Black Hornets	???	

7/13/1941	Ponce De Leon Park, Atlanta	Scripto Black Cats from "Scripto College" ("pencil factory to you"); Scripto players included George "Zulu Cannibal" Humphrey (RF), Snake Terrell (3B), William "Gorilla" Riley or "Sweet" Fudge at SS; Sluggers unnamed	???	first game of a doubleheader played that day. Sluggers the 1940 state semi-pro champions of SC. Sluggers had "two crack pitching aces, one a southpaw and one a right-handed [sic] who has a smoking fast one, baffling curve, and also goes in for that ancient 'crossfire' stuff."
7/17/1941	Sptbg, BDP	Tampa, FL. Pepsi-Cola Giants	???	Also a promotional appearance by Jesse Owens "in an exhibition race"
7/21/1941	Sptbg, BDP	Charlotte Black Hornets	???	
7/27/1941	McCormick Field, A'ville	Asheville Black Tourists	W: 6-5	P: Smith & Glenn
7/27/1941	McCormick Field, A'ville	Asheville Black Tourists	W: 10-5	P: Bronson & Glenn [Bronson here is likely Bob Branson]
8/11/1941	Sptbg, BDP	Asheville Black Tourists	???	
8/18/1941	Sptbg, BDP	Greenville Black Spinners	???	
4/13/1942	Sptbg, BDP	Greenville Black Spinners	W: 5-1	P: E. Grey

4/20/1942	Sptbg, BDP	New York Cuban Giants	L: 12-16	
4/21/1942	Sptbg, BDP	Cuban All-Stars	???	
4/27/1942	Sptbg, BDP	Charlotte Black Travelers	W: 2-1	Attendance 500; Slugger battery of Blue and Bus Glenn
5/4/1942	Sptbg, BDP	Camp Croft 10th Regimental All-Stars	W: 14-13	700 spectators; P: Ross; C: Glenn
6/1/1942	Sptbg, BDP	Camp Croft 10th Regimental All-Stars	W: 13-7	900 spectators; P: Smith
6/15/1942	Sptbg, BDP	Laurens Tigers	W: 9-4	P: "Ranson;" 700 spectators
7/4/1942	Greenville	Greenville Black Spinners	W: 4-1	
7/4/1942	Sptbg, BDP	Greenville Black Spinners	L: 1-4	
7/5/1942	McCormick Field, A'ville	Asheville Black Tourists	W: 7-4	P: Grady & Rhinehart; special section of the stands reserved for White fans
7/5/1942	McCormick Field, A'ville	Asheville Black Tourists	W: 5-3	P: Humphrey & Rhinehardt
7/6/1942	McCormick Field, A'ville	Asheville Black Tourists	???	"It will be the Black Tourists' first night game at McCormick field." BUT SEE ABOVE, 06/05/1941!
7/13/1942	Sptbg, BDP	Asheville Black Tourists	W: 17-1	P: "Ransom"
7/20/1942	Sptbg, BDP	Charlotte Black Travelers/ Red Sox	L: 4-6	P: Branson
8/3/1942	Sptbg, BDP	Charlotte Red Sox	W: 5-3	P: Branson, struck out 10; 1,000 spectators

8/9/1942	Columbia	Columbia White Sox	W: 10-2	
8/10/1942	Meadowbrook Park, G'ville	G'ville Black Spinners	W: 11-9	"A grandstand section will be reserved for White patrons."
8/11/1942	Sptbg, BDP	Atlanta Black Crackers	W: 9-2	1,000+ fans; P: Branson, 14 strikeouts
8/12/1942	Sptbg, BDP	Atlanta Black Crackers	L: 3-7	P: Alexander
8/30/1942	Ponce De Leon Park, Atlanta	Atlanta All-Stars	L: 16-1 and L: 5-0	A doubleheader "Atlanta diamond fans are being 'built up' for a gander at probably the fastest man in baseball Sunday afternoon when a deer footed centerfielder by the label of Kelly, colorfully nicknamed 'Ghost,' comes to town with the Spartanburg Sluggers to play the Atlanta All-Stars…" Sluggers first game pitcher was Bob Brinson [sic], "a six-foot, 180-pound southpaw fast ball pitcher," also called "a sensational stake-out king on the mound;" good paragraph w/additional quotable comments about both Branson and "the whole team"—Gabby Giles in RF, Howdy Man Holland in LF; Bull Humphrey at 1B, Monk Wilson at 2B, Blue Glenn at SS, Jelly Jackson at 3B, and "T" Bird Tracy at C. One of three articles includes a paragraph about Nish Williams and Red Moore.
9/7/1942	Greenville	Greenville Black Spinners	W: 7-0	P: Tracy
9/7/1942	Sptbg, BDP	Greenville Black Spinners	W: 8-2	1,000 spectators; P: Branson
9/14/1942	Sptbg, BDP	Asheville Black Tourists	???	Proceeds to be split between the players and the defense program
4/26/1943	Sptbg, BDP	Greenville Black Sox	???	

5/1/1943	Meadowbrook Park, Greenville	Greenville Black Sox	???	special section reserved for White spectators
5/10/1943	Sptbg, BDP	Asheville Black Tourists	L: 8-9	P: Gray
5/17/1943	Sptbg, BDP	Columbia Black Caps	W: 9-2	600 spectators
5/18/1943	Sptbg, BDP	Atlanta Black Crackers	???	
6/7/1943	Sptbg, BDP	Charlotte Black Sox	W: 12-7	
6/8/1943	Sptbg, BDP	Atlanta Black Crackers	???	
6/30/1943	Sptbg, BDP	Asheville Black Tourists	???	
07/05/1943 ?	Sptbg, BDP	Greenville Black Spinners	???	
07/06/1943 ?	Sptbg, BDP	Greenville Black Spinners	???	
8/6/1943	Sptbg, BDP	Gastonia All-Stars	L: 3-5	
8/9/1943	Sptbg, BDP	Charlotte Red Sox	???	
8/24/1943	Sptbg, BDP	Greenville Black Spinners	W: 2-1	
8/30/1943	Sptbg, BDP	Lenoir, NC, Indians	???	
9/6/1943	Sptbg, BDP	Greenville Black Spinners	W: 2-1	
9/13/1943	Sptbg, BDP	Asheville Black Tourists	???	
7/10/1944	Sptbg, BDP	North Charlotte	W: 10-0	P: Brantzel
7/17/1944	Sptbg, BDP	Union [?]	W: 6-2	

8/20/1944	Memorial Stadium, Greensboro, NC	U.S. Marine outfit vs. the South in the All-Star Classic	???	"Fifth annual south's original All-Star game." James Dunn, Spartanburg Sluggers 2B, will play for the South; some other players from the best black teams of the era, including the Atlanta Black Crackers and the Birmingham Black Barons
9/24/1944	Yankee Stadium, NYC		NA	"The Negro National League's four-team doubleheader at the Yankee Stadium, New York City, this Sunday, September 24th, has been aptly named 'Carolina Day,' seeing that the chief attraction itself is being furnished by those 2 great sister States, North and South Carolina. In fact, it could be almost regarded as the transferring of their famous north-south classic to the Metropolitan area." First game: NC All-Stars vs. New York Black Yankees; second game: South Carolina All-Stars vs. Philadelphia Stars. NC team: stars from the Durham Black Sox, Charlotte Red Sox, Charlotte Black Hornets, Winston-Salem Pond Giants, Asheville Blues, Greensboro Red Wings, Raleigh All-Stars, & Gastonia Spinners. SC team: Florence Red Sox, Spartanburg Sluggers Columbia All-Stars, Fort Jackson Red Caps, Greenville Black Spinners, Anderson Sluggers, Charleston Crusaders, Union Giants, & Rock Hill Rockets. Sluggers' rep was "Al" Cunningham. "...one of the season's greatest crowds is anticipated to sit in and see the Tarheels and Palmettos give those stuck-up Northerners a thorough shellacking."
4/1/1945	Sptbg, BDP	Union Giants	???	Spartanburg Manager is Earl Whitmire

4/8/1945	McCormick Field, A'ville	Asheville Blues	W: 9-7	New box seats will be installed at McC Field, also "additional seats for White fans. Service men turned out in good numbers last Wednesday night when the world's champion Homestead Grays ran over the Blues 21-1." An indication of the relative strength of the A'ville team?
4/8/1945	McCormick Field, A'ville	Asheville Blues	L: 3-12	Second game of a double-header
4/28/1945	Sptbg, BDP	Atlanta Black Crackers	???	"one of the hottest negro games of the season"
7/4/1945	McCormick Field, A'ville	Asheville Blues	L: 4-14	a game the Blues were to have played against the New Orleans Black Pelicans, who wired they couldn't get there in time, so Sluggers were substituted
5/6/1946	Columbia	Columbia Blues	???	
5/13/1946	Sptbg, BDP	Augusta Giants	W: 10-9	P: Clarence Norris; only 300 fans in rainy weather
5/20/1946	Elm Street Park, Gaffney	Gaffney Black Tigers	???	
5/25/1946	Sptbg, BDP	Clinton [?]	W: 6-2 [or 6-4?]	
6/7/1946	Sptbg, BDP	Columbia Sluggers	W: 7-1	
6/8/1946	McCormick Field, A'ville	Asheville Blues	L: 2-12	First appearance of the year by the Sluggers against the Blues; an exhibition game; Sptbg P: Evans, gave up 15 hits
6/9/1946	Columbia	Columbia All-Stars	W	
6/10/1946	Sptbg, BDP	Atlanta Scripto Giants	???	
6/14/1946	Orangeburg	Orangeburg Tigers	???	

7/1/1946	Sptbg, BDP	Atlanta Black Crackers	???	[Some accounts record the date of this game to be July 4; on the other hand, other accounts record games against the St. Anthony Braves on July 4.]
7/4/1946	Greenville	St. Anthony Braves	???	
7/4/1946	Sptbg, BDP	St. Anthony Braves	???	
7/15/1946	Lyman, SC	Lyman Tigers	???	
7/16/1946	Sptbg, BDP	Greenville [?]	W: 5-3	P: Crosby, struck out 11 and hit two RBIs in 9th
7/31/1946	Sptbg, BDP	Charlotte Red Sox	???	
8/2/1946	Lyman, SC	Lyman Tigers	???	
8/4/1946	Augusta, GA	Augusta Champions	W: 6-5	
8/4/1946	Augusta, GA	Augusta Champions	W: 7-0	
8/6/1946	Sptbg, BDP	Lakeland, Fla., All-Stars	W: 11-2	320 paying spectators
8/7/1946	Sptbg, BDP	Lakeland, FL, All-Stars	???	
8/26/1946	Sptbg, BDP	Charlotte Red Sox	W: 7-6	
8/27/1946	Sptbg, BDP	Baltimore Panthers		
8/28/1946	Sptbg, BDP	Columbia All-Stars	W: 13-0	P: Russ Evans, four-hitter; ss Blue Glenn went 4-5
9/9/1946	Sptbg, BDP	Athens, GA, Red Sox		W: 13-2; P: Russ Evans
9/11/1946	Sptbg, BDP	Greenville Giants		W: 13-1; P: Lefty Bob Branson struck out 22!

3/30/1947	McCormick Field, A'ville	Asheville Blues	L: 5-6	P: Crausby, Branson and Glenn; Foster, Tracy, and Glenn were all 2 for 4 at the plate. Blues were 1946 champions of the Negro Southern League. In 1947 they also played exhibition games against the Homestead Grays, The Cleveland Buckeyes, the Baltimore Elite Giants and the NY Black Yankees.
3/31/1947	Sptbg, BDP	Asheville Blues	???	
4/7/1947	Sptbg, BDP	Orangeburg Tigers	W: 9-7	P: Bob Branson
4/8/1947	Shelby, NC	Shelby [?]	???	
4/13/1947	A'ville	Asheville Blues	???	
4/15/1947	Shelby, NC	Shelby [?]	???	
4/18/1947	Lyman, SC	Lyman Tigers	???	
4/19/1947	Orangeburg, SC	Orangeburg Tigers	???	
4/21/1947	Sptbg, BDP	Atlanta Black Crackers	???	Lefty Bob Branson
5/5/1947	Sptbg, BDP	Columbia All Stars	W: 14-6	"a large number of spectators;" P: Russ Evans
5/9/1947	Sptbg, BDP	Asheville Blues	???	
5/19/1947	Sptbg, BDP	Durham Eagles	???	
5/22/1947	A'ville	Durham Eagles	???	
5/28/1947	Sptbg, BDP	Athens Red Sox	W: 7-6	P: "Lefty Branson twirled a six-hitter for the Sluggers."
7/4/1947	Orangeburg, SC	Orangeburg Tigers	L: 1-3	P: Evans. "The game with Spartanburg will be played for the mythical state championship. Lefty Bob Brunson [Branson] will pitch for the visitors."

7/4/1947	Stbg, BDP	Orangeburg Tigers	W: 4-0	Teams traveled to Spartanburg immediately after a 2 o'clock game in Orangeburg! "...behind the five-hit pitching of Lefty Bob Branson, rated as one of the best left-handers in the South"
7/16/1947	Rock Hill Stadium, Rock Hill, SC	York Grays	W: 6-5	"The first annual semi-pro baseball tournament open to all colored teams in South Carolina and sanctioned by the National Baseball Congress," played in Orangeburg, Whitmire, Cheraw, and Rock Hill. Teams: Orangeburg Tigers, Charleston Eagles, Arthurtown Sluggers, Whitmire, Sumter All Stars, Cheraw Red Sox, York Grays, Spartanburg Sluggers. Four-day tournament. "Representatives from all over the state met in Columbia with Commissioner W. L. Laval, Harry Laval, assistant to the commissioner; and Paul S.C. Weber Jr., tournament manager, to draw up plans for the tourney."
7/17/1947	Spartanburg High School	Spartan Mills	W: 5-4	P: Hudson; an exhibition SOFTBALL game!
7/20/1947	Sptbg, BDP	Winston-Salem Pond's Giants	W: 11-3	
7/22/1947	Florence, SC	Florence [?]	???	
7/23/1947	Sptbg, BDP	Florence [?]	???	

7/27/1947	Harper Field, Atlanta	Atlanta All-Stars	a dou-ble-header sched-uled, but Sluggers arrived late—only one game W: 6-4	"near-capacity crowd" expected; "...the Sluggers have made a great record against some of the tough-est teams in the country and will be out to give the Atlanta Stars a busy afternoon." P: Bob "Bronson;" BOB BRANSON, SLUGGERS MANAGER, FORMER ACE OF THE ATLANTA BLACK CRACKERS; good paragraph about Branson in the third article!!! Fourth article—other Slugger players in the game included Johnnie James, June Beckman, "Nat" Kelly, and "Blue" Glenn; Branson hit a HR and had 12 strikeouts; Kelly had three singles, "Blue" Glenn two
8/18/1947	Sptbg, BDP	NC State All-Stars	???	
9/3/1947	McCormick Field, A'ville	Asheville Blues	L: 5-15	P: Branson and Foster
10/6/1947	Sptbg, BDP	Asheville Blues	???	
3/21/1948	Raleigh, NC	Raleigh Tigers	L: 3-7	
3/27/1948	Sptbg, BDP	Homestead Grays	L: 4-9	Louis Marques, the Grays' Puerto Rican regular center fielder, pitched for Homestead. Bob Boston, "big Ohio star," played 3B. "Buck Leonard, in great shape, held down first base, gathering thirteen putouts and showing the rest of the Greys' veterans and rookies just why he is rated as one of the best Negro first sackers in the business." P for Sluggers: Crosby & Branson

3/28/1948	Columbia, SC	Richmond Giants	???	
3/29/1948	Sptbg, BDP	Richmond Giants	???	
3/30/1948	Sptbg, BDP	Richmond Giants	W: 7-3	P: Crosby & Branson
3/31/1948	Union, SC	Richmond Giants	???	
4/2/1948	Lyman, SC	Richmond Giants	L: 1-2	P: Russ Evans.
4/4/1948	Athens, GA	Richmond Giants	???	
4/5/1948	Athens, GA	Richmond Giants	L: 4-8	Bob Branson hit two triples
4/6/1948	Savannah, GA	Baltimore Panthers	???	
4/7/1948	Savannah, GA	Baltimore Panthers	???	
4/8/1948	Lakeland, FL	Lakeland [?]	???	
4/10/1948	Stewart, FL	Stewart [?]	W: 5-3	P: F. G. Crosby. Sluggers John Parker, Wilson Glenn, and Johnny James Johnson had two hits each; 3B Harry Russell hit a solo homer in the 8th to win the game.
4/11/1948	West Palm Beach, FL	West Palm Beach[?] Yankees	W: 8-5	"The Sluggers were negro champions of South Carolina last year." P: Lefty Bob Branson, struck out 10.
4/12/1948	Miami, FL	Miami Red Sox	W: 17-7	
4/13/1948	Miami, FL	Miami Giants	W: 6-5	
4/18/1948	Macon, GA	Pepsi-Cola Giants	???	
4/19/1948	Macon, GA	Pepsi-Cola Giants	W: 17-1	P: Lefty Branson struck out 12.
4/29/1948	Valdosta, GA	Valdosta [?]	W: 15-0	Bob Branson pitched a NO-HITTER in this game; Blue Glenn hit two HRs, Branson hit three triples, and both players had two other hits in the game.

5/2/1948	Miami, FL	Miami Giants	W: 6-4	P: Lefty Branson struck out 10.
5/5/1948	Lincoln Park, Tampa, FL	(West Palm Beach?) Rockets	L: 1-2	Second of a doubleheader?
5/7/1948	Sptbg, BDP	Nashville, TN, Cubs	???	
5/16/1948	Nashville, TN	Nashville Cubs	W: 4-1	P: Lefty Branson; Southern Negro Baseball League game
5/17/1948	Mills Park, Pacolet, SC	Pacolet Black Trojans	???	Black Trojans played in the Carolina Colored League.
5/22/1948	Mirmow Field, Orangeburg, SC	Orangeburg Tigers	???	P: Bob Branson, "Their sensational southpaw pitcher," in a game celebrating the third anniversary of the Tigers
6/9/1948	Columbia, SC	Columbia All-Stars	???	
6/16/1948	Sptbg, BDP		???	Negro Southern League game; "Felix Manning, former Manager of the Birmingham Black Barons, has been named skipper of the Sluggers..." Organizational meeting of Sluggers was held at Newt's Place on 06/07.
6/17/1948	Mirmow Field, Orangeburg, SC	Orangeburg Tigers	W: 4-1	P: Bob Branson, "their sensational southpaw hurler ... in an effort to become the first team in the state to stop the Tigers." Branson struck out 10.
6/26/1948	Mills Park, Pacolet, SC	Pacolet Black Trojans	L: 6-9	P: Bob Branson
7/3/1948	Mirmow Field, Orangeburg (?)	Orangeburg Tigers	W: 2-1	a 12-inning game in which Bob Branson struck out 21 men and gave up seven hits. Spartanburg batters incl. Russell and Shelton.

7/12/1948	Sptbg, BDP	Orangeburg Tigers	???	"Lefty Branson Night;" Negro American Association umpire "Conyers" will call the game behind the plate.
7/14/1948	Florence, SC	Florence Tigers	L: 1-2	Bob Branson vs. the Tigers' Jafers Parler
7/15/1948	Florence, SC	Florence Tigers	???	
7/18/1948	Miami, FL	Miami Giants	W: 7-5	P: Culbreth, struck out 15! "Pud" Shelton hit grand slam for the Sluggers.
7/19/1948	Miami, FL	Miami Giants	???	
7/26/1948	Sptbg, BDP?	Charleston Red Sox	???	
8/9/1948	Sptbg, BDP	Greenville Giants	W: 3-0	P: Bob Branson
8/25/1948	Sptbg, BDP	Greenville Giants	W: 4-2	P: Lefty Branson; 15 strike outs; Johnny James Johnson hit two triples.
8/28/1948	Mirmow Field, Orangeburg, SC	Orangeburg Tigers	???	a rematch between Branson and Parler
9/6/1948	Sptbg, BDP	Charlotte All-Stars	???	P: Lefty Branson; C: Buss Glenn
9/20/1948	Sptbg, BDP	Taylor All-Stars	???	P: Lefty Bob Branson; the All-Stars were a WHITE semi-pro team from Gastonia, NC! Season finale. BUT: game was canceled on order of City Manager T. Edward Temple; "The Sluggers played another Negro team instead."
4/16/1949	Mirmow Field, Orangeburg, SC	Orangeburg Tigers	???	"...their arch rivals, the Spartanburg Sluggers, who are sparked by 'Lefty Bob' Branson, sensational pitcher, who will renew his duel with the Tigers ace hurler, Jafers Parler." Tigers actually pitched Dumpson, who in 1949 defeated the NY Cubans in a game at Mirmow Field.

4/21/1949	Sptbg, BDP	Charlotte Red Sox	???	P: Lefty Branson; C: "Hog" Foster
4/24/1949	Meadowbrook Park, Greenville, SC	Greenville Giants	W: 6-2	P: Jeep Crosby; ss G. Wannamaker had 2 hits
5/6/1949	Lyman, SC	Lyman Red Sox	W: 12-1	P: Lefty Norris; C: Hog Foster; Branson hits a grand slam.
5/7/1949	Riley Park, Sumter, SC	Orangeburg Tigers	W: 5-3	P: Jeep Crosby and Lefty Branson
5/12/1949	Mirmow Field, Orangeburg, SC	Orangeburg Tigers	L: 5-8	Pitchers again will be WILLIAM Dumpson and "the colorful left-hander Bob Branson." The Tigers will play the NY Black Yankees on 05/21 in O'burg!
5/23/1949	Sptbg, BDP	Orangeburg Tigers	W: 6-3	P: "Crossfire" Crosby; C: Glenn
5/24/1949	Sptbg, BDP ?	Orangeburg Tigers	W: 5-3 [?]	
5/29/1949	High Point, NC	Winston-Salem, NC Pond Giants	8-8	Game called because of curfew rule
5/30/1949	Sptbg, BDP	Winston-Salem, NC Pond Giants	???	P: Jeep Crosby; C: Buss Glenn
6/4/1949	Sptbg, BDP	Asheville Blues	L: 8-9	
6/12/1949	High Point, NC	Winston-Salem, NC Giants	6-6	P: "Jeep" Crosby; C: Buss Glenn; Dave Bailey was 3-4. including a triple and a double. Game called because of curfew rule.
6/19/1949	Meadowbrook Park, Greenville, SC	Orangeburg Tigers	L: 0-2	
6/20/1949	Meadowbrook Park, Greenville, SC	Greenville Giants	W: 3-2	P: Crosby; C: Glenn; Wannamaker scored winning run.
6/30/1949	Erwin Memorial Stadium, Gastonia, NC	Asheville Blues	???	

7/3/1949	Meadowbrook Park, Greenville, SC	Greenville Giants	W: 8-1	P: Lefty "Bronson;" C: Buss Glenn. First game of a doubleheader
7/3/1949	Meadowbrook Park, Greenville, SC	Greenville Giants	L: 2-5	P: Jeep Crosby; C: Buss Glenn
7/4/1949	Greensboro, NC	???	???	
7/14/1949	Sptbg, BDP	Asheville Blues	L: 1-2	P: Lefty Branson; struck out nine, tripled home only Slugger run
7/20/1949	Riley Park, Sumter, SC	Orangeburg Tigers	???	
7/21/1949	Mirmow Field, Orangeburg, SC	Orangeburg Tigers	???	
8/8/1949	Sptbg, BDP	Greenville Giants	W: 10-2	P: "Brunson," struck out 10: C: Glenn
8/28/1949	Charlotte, NC	Charlotte Black Hornets	???	P: Jeep Crosby; C: Buss Glenn
8/29/1949	Sptbg, BDP	NC All-Stars	W: 4-0	P: Lefty "Brunson," struck out 22, gave up but two hits! C: Harry Russell
10/15/1949	Charlotte, NC	Jackie Robinson's All-Stars	???	Spartanburg starters, acc. to Charles Whitmire: P: Lefty Branson; 2b George Wannamaker; cj James Heffner; 3b Willie Bailey; 1b George Collins; lf David Bailey; rf J. L. Chipper; ss Raymond Glenn; c Wilson Glenn. Reserves incl ps James F. Crosby, Odell Murphy and of James Johnson
4/10/1950	Lyman Park, Lyman, SC	Baltimore Elite Giants	L: 8-14	Sluggers play in the Negro Southern American Baseball Association; Branson hits three-run HR.
4/14/1950	Erwin Memorial Stadium, Gastonia, NC	Asheville Blues	???	"two strong Negro semi-pro teams;" the next night the Baltimore Elite Giants played the Belmont Blues!

4/19/1950	Sptbg, BDP	Brooklyn Cuban Giants	L: 4-8	P: Crosby. George Wannamaker had a single and double, Dave Bailey and Buss Glenn had two hits each.
4/24/1950	Sptbg, BDP	Asheville Blues	W: 3-1	P: Lefty Branson, struck out 16; George Wannamaker, Monk Humphrey, and Walt Bailey had two hits each.
5/1/1950	Sptbg, BDP	Greensboro Red Birds	???	P: Lefty "Brunson;" C: Lonnie Tracy
5/14/1950	Greensboro, NC	Greensboro Red Birds		A Southern Negro American Baseball League game
5/23/1950	Hendersonville, NC	Asheville Blues	???	
5/24/1950	McCormick Field, A'ville	Asheville Blues	???	"The South Carolina team is made up of veteran players. Some of the outstanding among these players are Tracy, catcher, Russ Evans, pitcher, Willie Bailey, third baseman all former members of the Blues. In Lefty Branson, the Sluggers have the league's outstanding pitcher."
5/25/1950	Meadowbrook Park, Greenville, SC	Greenville Black Spinners	???	Spinners are "members of the Negro American Association League." Spinners are "one of the top teams in the league." Special section for White spectators.
5/26/1950	A'ville	Asheville Blues	???	
5/28/1950	Raleigh, NC	Raleigh Tigers	???	
5/29/1950	Sptbg, BDP	Asheville Blues	W: 9-2	P: Lefty Branson; C: Tracey. George Wannamaker hit a double and triple. Negro American Association game.
6/2/1950	Greensboro, NC	Greensboro Red Birds	???	
6/5/1950	Sptbg, BDP	Raleigh Tigers	???	

6/7/1950	Sptbg, BDP	Greenville Black Spinners	???	
6/11/1950	Greenville, SC	Greenville Black Spinners	???	
6/12/1950	Sptbg, BDP	Greenville Black Spinners	???	
6/15/1950	A'ville	Asheville Bues	???	
6/16/1950	Sptbg, BDP	Asheville Blues	???	
6/18/1950	Raleigh, NC	Raleigh Tigers	???	
6/25/1950	Greenville, SC	Greenville Black Spinners	???	
7/4/1950	Sptbg, BDP	All-Star team from Allen University and Benedict College	???	First game of a doubleheader
7/4/1950	Sptbg, BDP	All-Star team from Allen University and Benedict College	???	Second game of a doubleheader
8/30/1950	Sptbg, BDP	Greensboro Red Wings	W: 11-7	P: Crosby; C: Glenn; Willie Bailey was 4-5.
10/23/1951	Sptbg, BDP	Jackie Robinson's All-Stars vs the Indianapolis Clowns		Scheduled as a game with the Sluggers, "a former Negro semi-pro team here … made up of outstanding players from all over the county." BUT that game was canceled and it became the All-Stars vs. the Indianapolis Clowns. The All-Stars would include Sam Jethroe, Luke Easter, and SC native Larry Doby; the Clowns would feature Honey Lott, Sherwood Brewer, and Len Preacher Williams

4/12/1952	Arkwright Mill Park, Spartanburg		???	
4/14/1952	Rock Hill, SC	Rock Hill	???	
4/19/1952	Drayton, SC	Drayton Black Dragons	W: 8-6	A Textile League game perhaps?
4/20/1952	Tryon, NC	Tryon Red Sox	W: 16-3	
4/27/1952	Greensboro, NC	Greensboro Red Sox	???	
5/1/1952	Sptbg, BDP		L: 1-8	"The Stars whipped an inexperienced, but hustling Spartan team." Stars 1b James Parker is a former Slugger. P: likely Lewis Booker or Lewis Duckett, but maybe 16-year-old Wes Cheek. Sluggers lineup: 2b Wallace Humphries, 3b Cecil Murray, ss Raymond Glenn, rf Harry Russell, c Wilson Glenn, 1b Walter Sanders, cf Dave Bailey, lf Tom Smith
5/3/1952	Mills Park, Woodruff, SC	Woodruff Grays	???	
5/4/1952	Greensboro, NC	Greensboro Red Sox	W: 13-5	P: Lewis Duckett; Raymond Glenn went 3-5, Wilson Glenn had a bases loaded triple. A rescheduled game.
5/16/1952	Whitmire, NC	Greensboro Red Birds	L: 2-3	P: Lewis Glenn; C: Glenn
5/26/1952	Sptbg, BDP	Greensboro Red Birds	W: 5-4	P: Lewis Booker; C. Buss Glenn Ray. Glenn was 3-5; Buss Glenn 2-5
5/29/1952	McCormick Field, A'ville	A'ville Blues	???	P: Lewis Booker; C: Bus Glenn
6/1/1952	Tryon, NC	Tryon All Stars	W: 7-2	P: Salters; C: Glenn; Ray "Glen," "Bus Glen," and Thomas Smith each had two hits
6/2/1952	Sptbg, BDP	Charlotte ABC's	16-16	P: Lefty Branson, "the Satchel Paige of the South"!
6/5/1952	McCormick Field, A'ville	A'ville Blues	???	P: Lewis Booker or 17-year-old Bobby Anderson; C: "Bus" Glenn; Sluggers coming off two straight wins against the Greensboro Red Birds (but no dates or scores given).

6/6/1952	Pacolet Mill	Pacolet Mill Black Trojans	???	P: Lewis Booker; C: "Bus" Glenn
6/8/1952	Charlotte, NC	Charlotte ABC's	W: 8-6	P: Harry Russell, also hit a HR
6/10/1952	Lancaster, SC	Lancaster Tigers	???	
6/13/1952	Pacolet Mills	Pacolet Mills	L: 6-11	
6/23/1952	Sptbg, BDP	Greensboro Red Wings	???	
6/24/1952	Sptbg, BDP	Greenville Black Spinners	1-1, called after 12 innings	P: 17-year-old Bobby Anderson; C: 17-year-old Cecil Murray
6/25/1952	Drayton, SC	Drayton Black Dragons	???	
7/4/1952	Tryon, NC	Tryon Red Sox	???	P: Bobby Anderson, O'Neil Edwards
7/4/1952	Sptbg, BDP	Greenville Black Spinners	???	P: Lefty Bill Bennett, J. W. Alexander
7/6/1952	Columbia, SC	Columbia Red Caps	???	
7/13/1952	Greensboro, NC	Greensboro Red Birds	???	
7/17/1952	McCormick Field, A'ville	Asheville Stars	W: 18-3	P: O'Neill Edwards; C: J.W. Alexander. This game was part of the culmination of a week-long Market Street branch YMCA day camp. Campers were guests of Blues manager Rufus Hatten for the game. The two teams were tied for second in the Negro American Association and trailed first place Greensboro by 1/2 game with 4-1 records.
8/25/1952	Meadowbrook Park, G'ville, SC	Greenville Black Spinners	???	"The Sluggers is one of the top teams in the upper part of South Carolina…;" special section for White spectators; final game of the year for the Spinners.

2/23/1953	Sptbg, BDP	Jackie Robinson's All Stars vs. Negro American League All-Stars			Robinson's lineup: Sherwood Brewer ss, Sam Jethroe lf, Minnie Minoso 3b, Robinson 2b, Larry Doby cf, Luke Easter 1b, Henry "Speed" Merchant rf, Sam "Piggy" Sands c; NAL team to include Milton Smith 2b, Edwin Ford lf, Nat Peeples cf, Ben "Honey" Lott 3b, Ben Littles rf, Wesley Dennis 1b, Joe Spencer ss, Leonard "Fatso" Pigg c. Earlier in the week the two teams played in Asheville. Admission: $2 gen adm, $2.50 box seats, $1 children
4/5/1953	Meadowbrook Park, Greenville, SC	Greenville Black Spinners	???		reserve section for White spectators
8/9/1953	Capital City Park, Columbia, SC	Columbia Red Caps	???		"A girl first-baseman is expected to be in the lineup for the Spartanburg Sluggers when they meet the Columbia Red Caps in Capital City Park Sunday." First meeting of the year between the two teams after a car accident involving Spartanburg players postponed an earlier game.
07/05/19??	Riley Park, Sumter, SC	Orangeburg Tigers	???		
07/06/19??	Mirmow Field, Orangeburg, SC	Orangeburg [?]	???		
6/17/1961	Sptbg, BDP???	Atlanta Stars	???		"The Atlanta All-Stars are composed of the area's best college and high school performers." Luther Norman confirms that the Sluggers did indeed play games at least as late as 1961. The team did not belong to an organized league at this time; rather they played promotional or exhibition games on a more or less ad hoc basis, as did similar teams in other cities after the collapse of official Negro Leagues baseball.

Sources include newspapers indexed in newspapers.com and NewsBank.com databases and elsewhere, also clipped articles pasted into city of Spartanburg scrapbooks without a stated source. Specific newspapers include the local Daily Herald; *The Spartanburg Journal* and the Carolina Spartan; Spartanburg Herald-Journal; local newspapers in nearby towns in South Carolina, North Carolina, Georgia, and Florida; and occasionally others.

APPENDIX II

· ·

The Spartanburg Peaches Residency

This chart outlines the barebones administrative record of the team's stay at Duncan Park stadium. Details about Peaches players in Major League Baseball follow in Appendix III.

Year	Team Owners	Manager	Record	League Standing/ Playoffs
1946	G. Leo Hughes & R.E. Littlejohn, Jr.	Ed Doncisak	52-87	6th
1947	G. Leo Hughes & R.E. Littlejohn, Jr.	Kerby Farrell	88-51	8th
1948	G. Leo Hughes & R.E. Littlejohn, Jr.	Kerby Farrell	68-77	1st; lost in first round
1949	G. Leo Hughes & R.E. Littlejohn, Jr.	Kerby Farrell	81-60	2nd; lost in League finals
1950	G. Leo Hughes & R.E. Littlejohn, Jr.	Kerby Farrell	80-63	3rd; lost in first round
1951	G. Leo Hughes & R.E. Littlejohn, Jr.	Harry Griswold	73-67	4th; League Champions
1952	G. Leo Hughes & R.E. Littlejohn, Jr.	Pinky May	83-55	3rd; lost in League finals
1953	G. Leo Hughes & R.E. Littlejohn, Jr.	Jimmy Bloodworth	96-54	1st; lost in first round
1954	G. Leo Hughes & R.E. Littlejohn, Jr.	Jimmy Bloodworth	66-72	4th; lost in first round
1955	G. Leo Hughes & R.E. Littlejohn, Jr.	Spud Chandler	74-44	1st; League Champions

APPENDIX III

· ·

Spartanburg Peaches Who Made The Show

During their 10 years in Spartanburg the Peaches fielded 19 players who were to make it to the Majors. Details of their careers appear below.

Player	Year(s) with Peaches	Year(s) in MLB	MLB teams	Position and notes
Jerome Edward "Jerry" Lynn	1946	1937	Washington Senators	Played one game only; batted 2 for 3
Frank "Frankie" Pack	1946	1949	St. Louis Browns	Played one game; no hits
Frederick Lee "Ted" Petoskey	1946	1934-5	Cincinnati Reds	CF; batted .167 in 12 ABs
Kenneth Lanier "Ken" Wood	1946	1948-9	St. Louis Browns	OF; batted .224 in 995 ABs
Major Kerby Farrell	1947-50	1943, 1945	Boston Braves, Chicago White Sox	Pitcher (0-1, 4.30 ERA), 1B; batted .262. Farrell played for a total of 19 years in the Minors, compiling a .291 BA and a 21-10 record as a pitcher.
William James "Pete" Milne	1947	1948-50 (parts only of each season)	New York Giants	1B; batted .233. Milne also played a dozen years in the Minors.
Al "Lefty" Aber	1948-49	1950, 1953-57	Cleveland Indians, Detroit Tigers, Kansas City Athletics	Pitcher (24-25, 4.18 ERA)

George Zuverink	1948	1951-52, 1954-59	Cleveland Indians, Detroit Tigers, Cincinnati Redlegs, Baltimore Orioles	Pitcher (32-36, 3.54 ERA); interestingly, Zuverink's stats were better in the Majors than the Minors
James Riley "Big Jim" Fridley	1949	1952, 1954, 1958	Cleveland Indians, Baltimore Orioles, Cincinnati Redlegs	RF; batted .248 in the Majors. Fridley also played 14 years in MiLB for as many teams.
Stanley "Stan" Pitula	1951	1957	Cleveland Indians	Pitcher (2-2; 4.98 ERA), also nine years in the Minors with 11 different teams, including 1954, when he went 20-9 for the Keokuk, IA, Kernels
Rocco Domenico "Rocky" Colavito	1952	1955-68	Cleveland Indians, Detroit Tigers, Kansas City Athletics, Chicago White Sox, Los Angeles Dodgers, New York Yankees	RF; batted .266 in MLB. Colavito also pitched in two games, in which he was 1-0 with a 0.00 ERA. Colavito was clearly the best player the Peaches ever had; more about him will be found in Chapter Four.
William Ray "Bill" Upton	1952	1954	Philadelphia Athletics	Pitcher (0-0; 1.80 ERA); like Kerby Farrell, Upton was mainly a journeyman Minor Leaguer, playing on 13 different teams and winning almost twice as many games (60) as he lost (34).
James Henry "Jimmy" Bloodworth	1953-54	1937, 1939-43, 1946-47, 1949-51	Washington Senators, Detroit Tigers, Pittsburgh Pirates, Cincinnati Reds, Philadelphia Phillies	2B, 3B, RF; batted .248 in the Majors and played 11 seasons in the Minors and 11 in the Majors

William Nelson "Billy" Moran	1953	1958-59, 1961-65	Cleveland Indians, Los Angeles Angels	2B, SS, 3B; batted .263. Moran beat out Bobby Richardson for the starting job at 2B in the two 1962 All-Star games.
Dolan Levon Nichols	1953	1958	Chicago Cubs	Pitcher (0-4; 5.01 ERA); played on 11 MiLB teams in nine years
Richard Ernest "Dick" Brown	1954	1957-65	Cleveland Indians, Chicago White Sox, Detroit Tigers, Baltimore Orioles	C (.244 BA in the Majors, .273 in the Minors)
Gordon Calvin "Gordy" Coleman	1954	1959-67	Cleveland Indians, Cincinnati Reds	1B (.273 in the Majors, .320 in the Minors); member of the Cincinnati Reds Hall of Fame and former broadcaster for Reds television
Spurgeon Ferdinand "Spud" Chandler	1955	1937-47	New York Yankees	Pitcher (109-43; 2.84 ERA); Chandler managed and pitched in two games for Spartanburg in 1955, with a 0-0 record. Chandler was Major League Player of the Year in 1943, when he had a 20-4 record with a 1.64 ERA; he pitched for six World Series Champion teams. In 1946, when he was playing for the Bob Feller All-Stars, he hit a home run against Satchel Paige, who was pitching for his own barnstorming All-Stars.
Daniel "Dan" Osinksi	1955	1962-70	Kansas City Athletics, Los Angeles Angels, Milwaukee Braves, Boston Red Sox, Chicago White Sox, Houston Astros	Relief pitcher (29-28; 3.34 ERA); 108-81 in 11 seasons in the Minors and called "The Silencer" as a bear-down fastball pitcher during a time when relief pitchers were first coming into their own.

APPENDIX IV

· ·

A Timeline of the Spartanburg Phillies, 1963-1994

Year	Record	Finish	Manager	Future MLB Players on the Team	Notes
1963	66-58	3rd	Lou Kahn	Jackie Brown, Dave Roberts, Gene Stone, Dick Thoenen	R.E. Littlejohn and Leo Hughes, who had owned the Peaches in 1946-1955, led the effort to bring baseball back to the city of Spartanburg; in 2007 the two were inducted into the South Atlantic League Hall of Fame.
1964	47-80	8th	Dick Teed	Mike Jackson	
1965	54-68	7th	Moose Johnson	Barry Lersch, Manny Muniz, Gene Rounsaville	Pat Williams, in his first year as GM, told Greenville Mets GM Art Perkins that he and Mayor Bob Stoddard would usher at the May 8 game in Greenville if the Phillies lost one of their two opening games. In addition, the losing team in each game in '65 would house the goat "Greenburg" for the next game. The 1965 season was also John Gordon's first as Phillies broadcaster.

1966	91-35	1st, Western Carolina League Champs	Bob Wellman	Ron Allen, Larry Bowa, Denny Doyle, Barry Lersch, Lowell Palmer, Mike Strahler	MiLB.com named the '66 Phillies as no. 78 in its list of the Top 100 Minor League teams all-time. Paved parking was added above the left field side of Duncan Park, and GM Pat Williams asked City Council to consider additional upgrades to allow the transition from A to AA ball. After Larry Bowa struck out four times during his first game, Bob Wellman told him that "this guy [the pitcher]'s gonna be something special." It was Nolan Ryan.
1967	80-43	1st	Dick Teed	Larry Cox, Manny Muniz, Scott Reid, Ken Reynolds, Mike Strahler, John Vukovich	City and the Phillies split the cost of $38,000 in improvements to the park; 1,000 new seats were installed in the box seats area.
1968	71-54	2nd	Bobby Malkmus	George Banks, Larry Cox, Buck Martinez, Bob Terlecki, John Vukovich	
1969	58-65	5th	Bobby Malkmus	Andre Thornton, Manny Trillo	
1970	64-64	3rd	Howie Bedell	Billy Bryan, Jim Essian, Juan Jimenez, Dave Wallace, Mike Wallace	After the closure of Connie Mack Stadium (formerly Shibe Park) in October, the MLB Phillies gave 587 wooden seats to the Spartanburg team. Many have been restored and are reinstalled at Duncan Park.
1971	78-47	2nd	Bob Wellman	Fred Andrews, Dave Downs, Jesus Hernaiz, Juan Jimenez, Erskine . Thomason	The city was excited to welcome Bob Wellman back to the manager's spot on the bench.

1972	89-43	1st	Bob Wellman	Fred Andrews, Jerry Martin, Roy Thomas	Jerry Martin, who had been a star basketball player at Furman University and MVP in the Southern Conference Tournament, was undersized for pro ball so opted for baseball and joined the Phillies; a journeyman MLB player, he was also one of the first disciplined for use of prohibited substances.
1973	67-61	3rd	Howie Bedell	Rick Bosetti, Tom Underwood	City Council approved an amount up to $25,000 for mercury vapor stadium lights to bring the ballpark lighting up to MLB standards to ensure that the Phillies remained in Spartanburg. Neither the MLB team nor the City is making any money on the team. (The low bid for the lighting came in at $10,000 more than council approved.)
1974	49-84	6th	Howie Bedell	Dan Boitano, Warren Brusstar, Willie Hernandez, Jim Morrison	
1975	81-59	1st	Lee Elia	Don McCormack, Keith Moreland, Lonnie Smith, Kevin Saucier, Jim Wright	
1976	59-80	4th	Lee Elia	Luis Aguayo, Joe Charboneau, Orlando Isales, Jose Moreno, Orlando Sanchez, Derek Botelho, Dave Downs, Dickie Noles	

1977	67-73	4th	Mike Compton	Jay Loviglio, Ozzie Virgil, Marty Bystrom, Bob Walk	The Phillies approach City Council about the need to spend $25,000 to repair the roof of the stadium, fragments of which are falling onto the seats below; Council wants to find funds elsewhere than the city budget.
1978	73-67	4th	Ron Clark	Bob Dernier, Greg Walker, Scott Munninghoff, Jerry Reed	The Phillies hire Mel Roberts, who was to become an extremely popular manager, as a coach this year; Roberts had coached with former Phillies manager Lee Elia in Reading, PA , in 1975-76. In March the City received only one bid for the destruction of the rightfield bleachers and NO bids for the renovation of the central grandstand and repairs to the left side. Also in March future Braves Manager Brian Snitker threw out two Phillies in a row attempting to steal second, and city natives the Marshall Tucker Band briefly considered buying the Phillies; Toy Caldwell said that he had attended almost all games the summer before.

1979	73-66	3rd	Bill Dancy	George Bell, Dan Carman, Will Culmer, Mark Davis, Ryne Sandberg	Last year as a member of the Western Carolinas League; future MLB star Sandberg played 138 games, more than any other Phillies player, this summer, batted .247, and stole 21 bases. Total cost of repairs to the stadium, shared by the team and the City, exceed $70,000. Dr. Frank Weir agrees to buy the club from an Oklahoma City group headed by Patty Cox that had owned the team for less than a year. Weir and his family set an ambitious 1980 attendance goal of 70,000, compared to only 22,000 in 1979.
1980	73-65	2nd in the Division	Tom Harmon	Ed Hearn, Steve Jeltz, Alejandro Sanchez, Jay Baller, Kelly Downs, Nino Espinoso	The Phillies' first year as members of the South Division of the South Atlantic League.
1981	71-70	3rd in the North Division	Tom Harmon	Darren Daulton, Ken Dowell, Mike LaValliere, Francisco Melendez, Juan Samuel, Jeff Stone, Tony Ghelfi, Kevin Gross, Bill Johnson, Ed Wojna	

1982	69-71	3rd	P. J. Carey and Tony Taylor	Jim Olander, Rick Schu, Rocky Childress, Jose Segura, Rich Surhoff	This year the Phillies became the Spartanburg Traders, a renaming resulting from a contest intended to stimulate new interest in the team. Team owner Dr. Frank Weir is increasingly interested in selling the team, perhaps to a partnership consisting of Robert Anderson of NYC, Clyde Wilmeth of Charlotte, and Dennis Bastien.
1983	72-71	3rd	Rollie De Armas	Keith Hughes, Ken Jackson, Chris James, Greg Jelks, Johnny Paredes, Wilfredo Tejada, Mike Maddux, Lance McCullers, Jose Segura	In 1983 the team became known as the Spinners. The City and the team dicker over the terms of who would pay for needed repairs to Duncan Park stadium, who would pay how much, the need for twice yearly inspections of the ballpark, etc. Team management also argues with Post 28 over use of the field. In October Lou Eliopolus buys the team from Bob Anderson and his two partners. S-Phils pitcher Mike Maddux is the brother of future HOFer Greg Maddux.
1984	70-70	3rd	Jay Ward	Michael Jackson, Ricky Jordan, Tom Magrann, Tony Ghelfi	Now the team is the Suns.
1985	66-70	4th	Rollie De Armas	Julio Machado, Tom Newell, Bob Scanlan	Still the Suns. In May minority owner Jeff Kirkus proposes upgrading the seating capacity of the stadium to 10,000 from 3,700. Ray Wilson, Spartanburg County School District Seven athletic director, and Mark Richardson oppose the idea, which fails.

1986	40-95	5th	Rollie De Armas	Julio Machado, Rick Parker, Scott Service	The name finally reverts to the Phillies.
1987	66-74	3rd	Ramon Aviles	Andy Ashby, Cliff Brantley, Jason Grimsley, Jeff Grotewold, Garland Kiser, Chuck McElroy	
1988	69-69	2nd	Mel Roberts	Kim Batiste, Doug Lindsey, Jim Vatcher, Andy Ashby, Andy Carter, Tim Mauser, Greg McCarthy	Attendance is up 61 percent over 1987, a fact that prevents team owner Brad Shover from moving the team to Augusta. New Manager Mel Roberts is a community favorite, gives back in many ways, and becomes a close friend of Mayor James Talley, Spartanburg's first Black mayor.
1989	62-79	5th	Mel Roberts	Doug Lindsey, Tom Marsh, Joe Millette, Mickey Morandini, Andy Ashby, Toby Borland, Andy Carter, Donnie Elliott, Greg McCarthy	
1990	63-78	5th	Mel Roberts	Tom Marsh, Donnie Elliott, Paul Fletcher, Bob Wells	Phillies money problems continue. SALLY League rejects sale of team by Brad Shover to a NY partnership led by Jim Pickles and Pete Wyso. Attendance is down and the City has not received full rent on the stadium for three years.

| 1991 | 70-70 | 3rd | Mel Roberts | Steve Bieser, Mike Farmer, Mike Lieberthal, Kevin Stocker, Joel Adamson, Ricky Bottalico, Brad Brink, Donnie Elliott, Mike Grace, Jeff Patterson | Former MLB pitcher Buzz Capra becomes pitching coach; Phillies unveil new clubhouse (offices, weight room, training room, players' lounge). Owner Jim Pickles sings praises of new facilities. Rosie Putnam, one of four women GMs in MiLB, begins her second year at the helm. New employee Rookie, team's mascot black lab, arrives as facilities guardian. After this year, popular Manager Mel Roberts moves up to Philadelphia, where he will become the parent club's first base coach. |
| 1992 | 70-68 | 6th | Roy Majtyka | Gene Schall, Jon Zuber, Ron Blazier, Ricky Bottalico, Mike Grace, Matt Whisenant | City and the Phillies agree on additional renovations and repairs, including paint, better field drainage, and connecting the water fountains. Still, in September the Phillies announce that due to continuing poor attendance and promotions, the team might have to leave. In spite of $44,000 in ticket sales by the Chamber of Commerce AND unprecedented spending on stadium improvements by the City, financial viability still proves elusive. Rumors of an impending sale to a Wilmington group are rife; GM Rosie Putnam says that to make money, attendance needs to average 1,000-1,200 fans per game; in '92 it was 750. |

| 1993 | 62-80 | 5th | Roy Majtyka | Gary Bennett, David Dosser, Larry Mitchell | On Easter Sunday, two days after opening day, attendance is only 263 fans. Average attendance in '93 is only 850 fans per game. Rumors emerge of a move to Kannapolis, NC. |
| 1994 | 67-72 | 4th | Roy Majtyka | Bobby Estalella, Scott Rolen, Matt Beech, Tony Fiore, Mike Grace | The Phillies are sold to Larry Hedrick of Statesville, NC, and will move to Kannapolis. Purchase price: $1.5 million, an increase of more than $1.25 million over the price owner Brad Shover had paid. Fred Palmerino, who had conspicuous success and won an award for promotions and marketing as GM for the El Paso Diablos, will be the new GM. Attendance in Spartanburg in 1994 is the worst in the SALLY League. There is a two-hour rain delay before the Phillies final game. |

APPENDIX V

· ·

Ninety Years of American Legion Baseball

The information which follows was gleaned from Post 28 archives, old registration forms, newspaper accounts, and communications with Post members and former players. Some of these sources of information occasionally contradicted others. As a result, although the chart is generally accurate, at times a listed name or date is based upon a best guess estimate of the most likely reliable source of two or more which disagree

YEAR	POST 28 BASEBALL OFFICIALS	COACHES	
	ATHLETIC DIRECTOR (In some earlier years this position is identi-fied as "Team Manager" or "Athletic Officer" or "Chairman of the Athletic Committee.")	SENIORS COACH(ES) (Players ages 18-19 from 2013 on)	JUNIORS COACH(ES) (Players ages 13-17 from 2013 on)
2022	John J. Barron	Blake Burress	Tray Young
2021	John J. Barron	Blake Burress	Nick Turner
		Steve Burress (Asst.)	Tray Young (Asst.)
		David Burress (Asst.)	
2020	[There was no official Legion base-ball in 2020 because of COVID-19 restrictions; therefore coaches and parents organized the independent "Dixie" League program so that players could continue to compete.]	(Dixie Majors)	(Dixie Pre-Majors)
		Blake Burress	Mark Woody
	John J. Barron	Steve Burress (Asst.)	Nick Turner (Asst.)
		David Burress (Asst.)	
		Russell Parry (Asst.)	
2019	John J. Barron	Blake Burress	Mark Woody
		Steve Burress (Asst.)	Nick Turner (Asst.)
		Jacob Roper (Asst.)	

2018	John J. Barron	Micah Stancil	Blake Burress
		Jacob Roper (Asst.)	Steve Burress (Asst.)
2017	John J. Barron	Micah Stancil	Blake Burress
		Justin Bloom (Asst.)	Steve Burress (Asst.)
		Jacob Roper (Asst.)	
2016	John J. Barron	Micah Stancil	Blake Burress
		Justin Bloom (Asst.)	Steve Burress (Asst.)
2015	John J. Barron	Micah Stancil	Blake Burress
		Blake Burress (Asst.)	
		Justin Bloom (Asst.)	
2014	John J. Barron	Barry Keith	Blake Burress
		Craig Burnette (Asst.)	
		Kyle Heppeard (Asst.)	
2013	John J. Barron	Barry Keith	Blake Burress
		Blake Burress (Asst.)	
		Craig Burnette (Asst.)	
		Kyle Heppeard (Asst.)	
	Prior to 2005 American Legion Baseball offered only one level of competition. Beginning in 2005, the national Legion program began to offer "Juniors" competition for ages 13-17, and "Seniors" competition for ages 18-19. Locally Post 28 did not field both Juniors and Seniors teams until 2013. In 2024/2025 American Legion Baseball will offer an additional age division.		

2012	John J. Barron		Ken Hanna
			Blake Burress (Asst.)
			Barry Keith (Asst.)
2011	Jesse E. Campbell		Matthew H. West
2010	Jesse E. Campbell		Matthew H. West
2009	Jesse E. Campbell		Matthew H. West
2008	Jesse E. Campbell		Matthew H. West (?)
2007	Jesse E. Campbell		Adam Newberry
2006	Jesse E. Campbell		Matthew H. West (?)
2005	Jesse E. Campbell		Timothy W. Wallace
2004	Jesse E. Campbell		Timothy W. Wallace
2003	Jesse E. Campbell		Timothy W. Wallace
2002	Jesse E. Campbell		Brandon McKillop
2001	Jesse E. Campbell		Brandon McKillop
2000	Jesse E. Campbell		Brandon McKillop
1999	Jesse E. Campbell		Brandon McKillop
1998	Jesse E. Campbell		Brandon McKillop
1997	Jesse E. Campbell		Bubba Dorman
1996	Jesse E. Campbell		Bubba Dorman
1995	Jesse E. Campbell		Bubba Dorman
1994	Jesse E. Campbell		Bubba Dorman
1993	Jesse E. Campbell		Bubba Dorman
1992	Jesse E. Campbell		Bubba Dorman
1991	Jesse E. Campbell		John Daurity
1990	Jesse E. Campbell		Bubba Dorman
1989	Jesse E. Campbell		John Daurity
1988	Jesse E. Campbell		Mike Tolleson

1987	Jesse E. Campbell		Mike Tolleson and Charles H. Dorman
1986	Jesse E. Campbell		Mike Tolleson
1985	Jesse E. Campbell		Mike Tolleson and Mike Campbell
1984	Jesse E. Campbell		Michael E. Campbell
1983	Jesse E. Campbell		William A. Wilkins
1982	Jesse E. Campbell		William A. Wilkins
1981	Jesse E. Campbell		Jimmy Tolleson
1980	Jesse E. Campbell		Jimmy Tolleson
1979	Jesse E. Campbell		Terry Floyd
1978	Jesse E. Campbell		Terry Floyd
1977	Robert L. Tallant		Eddie Cole
1976	Jesse E. Campbell		Eddie Cole
1975	Jesse E. Campbell		Tommy Owens
1974	Bob Tallant		Tommy Owens
1973	Bob Tallant		Tommy Owens
1972			
1971	NO LEGION TEAMS 1970-1972: Combined Dorman and Spartanburg High School enrollments were too high to meet Legion regulations, and there were not two venues suitable to enable splitting into two teams. Apparently some games were played in 1970 but perhaps [?] not a whole season.		
1970			Bill Blanton
1969			Bob Tallant
1968			Bob Tallant
1967			Bob Tallant
1966			Bob Tallant
1965	Sam P. Manning		Curtis Powell
1964	Sam P. Manning		E. George Floyd (?)
1963	Sam P. Manning		E. George Floyd

1962	Sam P. Manning		Enoch George Floyd Sr.
1961	Sam P. Manning		Bud Teaster
1960	Sam P. Manning		James "Pee Wee" Lambert
1959	Sam P. Manning		James "Pee Wee" Lambert
1958	Doug Loveday		J. Paul Edwards [Ernie White coached the first game of the season, then left to coach MiLB in Midland, TX.]
1957			Ty Wood
	[In 1957 The Post 28 team played at the Spartanburg Junior College field because the Duncan Park field had been altered for softball.]		
1956	Ty Wood		Ty Wood
1955	Walter F. Marks		Ty Wood
1954	J.L. "Tuck" McConnell		Ty Wood
1953			NO team in '53; unknown reason
1952			Roy Brannon
1951			Roy Brannon
1950			W.P. "Sarge" Hughes
1949			W.P. "Sarge" Hughes
	[In 1949 and 1950 the Legion had to play its games at the Piedmont Interstate Fairgrounds because Duncan Park was under lease to the Spartanburg Baseball Club (the Spartanburg Peaches).]		
1948			W.P. "Sarge" Hughes
1947			W.P. "Sarge" Hughes
1946			W.P. "Sarge" Hughes

1945	R.H. Ashmore		Frank Helderman
1944	R.H. Ashmore		Frank Helderman
1943	R.H. Ashmore		Frank Helderman
1942	W. Paul Williams		Frank Helderman
1941	W. Paul Williams		Lonnie Dunlap
1940	G.L. Hughes		Carlisle Bagwell
1939	W. Paul Williams		E. R. "Tuck" McConnell
1938	Sam R. Bagwell		W.P. "Sarge" Hughes
1937	Sam R. Bagwell?		W.P. "Sarge" Hughes
1936	Sam R. Bagwell		W.P. "Sarge" Hughes
1935	[? W.P. Hughes]		W.P. "Sarge" Hughes
1934	[? M. W. Burgin]		W.P. "Sarge" Hughes
1933	Mike Burgin		W.P. "Sarge" Hughes

APPENDIX VI

. . . .

Recipients of the American Legion Post 28 Brian Peahuff Scholarships

Year	Recipient	College
1993	Demetrius Turner	University of South Carolina
1994	Thomas Martin	The Citadel
1995	David Pless	Gardner Webb University
1996	Jason Queen	USC Spartanburg
1997	Gary Lee	Lander University
1998	Tack Hill	Spartanburg Methodist College
1999	Brian Casey	Wofford College
2000	Kevin White	Presbyterian College
2001	Ryan Parry	Brigham Young University
2002	Jordy Snyder	Coastal Carolina University
2003	Jordy Snyder	Spartanburg Methodist College
2004	Will Dozier	USC Upstate
2005	Ryan Wilkins	Spartanburg Methodist College
2006	Ryan Wilkins	Spartanburg Methodist College
2007	Kyle Worthy	Clemson University
2008	Andrew Patterson	University of South Carolina
2009	Brian Poteat	The Citadel
2010	Dominick Aiken	USC Salkehatchie
2011	Dillon Bonner	Spartanburg Methodist College
2012	William Edward Schüler II	USC Sumter
2013	Ian Riley Metts	USC Sumter
2014	Luke Chandler Graves	Presbyterian College
2015	Chase Brown Harper	University of South Carolina
2016	Davis William Keller	Wofford College
2017	Zachary Harold Lee	USC Upstate
2018	Lee Jordan Cavendish	Clemson University

2019	Robert Eli Ewing	Wofford College
2020	Carter Ryan Peeler	Lander University
2021	Michael Shane Blackwood	Spartanburg Methodist College

APPENDIX VII

. . . .

Teams at Duncan Park 1995-2021

Dates	Team	League	Notes
1995-2003	University of South Carolina Spartanburg (later Upstate) Rifles (later Spartans)	Big South Conference, NCAA Division II	The USC Upstate team played at Duncan Park stadium before they built a modern stadium of their own, a situation common to other teams whose institutional home was located physically elsewhere than at the Park. The Rifles also played at DP from 1991-1993.
1995	The Spartanburg Alley Cats	Atlantic Coast League (an independent league of unaffiliated teams)	The ACL was composed of only four teams and folded after a total of only 32 games.
1996-2003	The Wofford Terriers	Southern Conference	Wofford fans reinvigorated the stadium for a while until the construction of their own Russell C. King Field.
2001-2005	The Spartanburg Crickets	Southern Collegiate Baseball League	The Crickets were owned by local businessman Steve Cunningham, whose untimely death was a blow to both the team and the Spartanburg community.
2003-2006	The Spartanburg Stingers	Coastal Plain League	One more attempt to save Duncan Park stadium by attracting yet another wooden bat league team to entertain diehard fans. The Stingers had to leave Duncan Park after 2006 when the City, unwilling to spend the money necessary to restore and renovate the stadium, closed it.

Dates	Team	League	Notes
2008-current	Spartanburg High School Vikings	Class AAAAA, Region II, South Carolina High School League	Spartanburg County School District Seven and the City of Spartanburg jointly operate and financially support Duncan Park stadium today under a letter of intent signed by the District Seven School Board and Spartanburg City Council.
2021	The Spartan-burgers	Coastal Plain League	The Spartanburgers were owned by an out-of-state partnership composed of individuals mostly in the Northeast of the United States; the team leased the stadium from the City and District Seven and contributed to repairs and renovations as necessary and as agreed by the three parties.

ACKNOWLEDGMENTS

. . . .

LIKE BASEBALL ITSELF, writing a book like *Duncan Park: Stories of a Classic American Ballpark* is largely a team sport. The number of players on this team is substantial, and my indebtedness to each of them is as well.

To begin with, I must acknowledge the contributions of Myles Wilson, former athletic director for Spartanburg High School and director of athletic facilities for Spartanburg County School District Seven. Myles became one of Spartanburg's early victims of the COVID virus in August 2020, and he was beloved by hundreds whose lives he had touched. For this book he conducted me on several tours of Duncan Park stadium during its restoration and renovation and answered many telephone and email queries, reminding me often that it was School District Seven's agreement with the City of Spartanburg that saved the stadium from demolition. In addition Myles introduced me to many others whom I interviewed for this project, and he met many of my interviewees and sources at the ballpark to unlock the stadium and show them around as well. Thanks, Milo.

I owe a similarly large indebtedness to Luther Norman, who was married to Lorraine Whitmire Norman, the daughter of Little Newt Whitmire, the owner of the Spartanburg Sluggers and son of the team's founder, Big Newt Whitmire. Luther is a former college and Minor League player himself and the director of the Youth Sports Bureau, which sponsors baseball clinics and tournaments for area youth and serves the city of Spartanburg in too many ways to list here. Luther owns a huge store of Spartanburg Sluggers memorabilia, photographs, and documents, and his generosity in sharing these and his personal knowledge of the Sluggers and Negro Leagues Baseball with me was and continues to be beyond my wildest expectations. This book contains more information about Black baseball in Spartanburg, South Carolina, than can be found in all other sources combined, and the reason for that is Luther Norman.

I interviewed a large and diverse group of people for my research on Beautiful Duncan Park, and they were all gracious and helpful beyond my expectations. Among these was Pat Williams, former senior vice president of the Orlando Magic, whose sports management career began in the mid-1960s when he became the general manager of the Spartanburg Phillies. Pat still has many friends in Spartanburg and was kind enough to give me a couple of hours out of his busy schedule for an interview in Orlando in 2017. One of the owners of the Spartanburg Phillies when Pat was their GM was R.E. Littlejohn, and I was fortunate enough to interview Littlejohn's son-in-law Bobby Pinson both in person and on the telephone. I also enjoyed a productive interview with attorneys Wesley A. and Robert L. Stoddard Jr., whose father Robert L. Stoddard Sr., was a longtime mayor of Spartanburg and threw out the first pitch for both the first and last Spartanburg Phillies games played 31 years apart at Duncan Park. Another local attorney, Terry Haselden, one of the founding members of the Friends of Duncan Park, answered my questions in person, on the telephone, and via email.

Spartanburg American Legion Post 28 has been the longest-serving home team at Duncan Park stadium, and several Legionnaires provided me with un-equaled access. Among these, prime of place goes, of course, to the legendary Jesse "Geno" Campbell, long-serving athletic director of the Post. Historian of the Post's baseball team John Barron, another athletic director, provided much information unavailable anywhere else; and Jim Harbison, former ad-jutant of Post 28, shared connections between Duncan Park, the Spartanburg Sluggers, and Sluggers owner Newt Whitmire. Another source with personal connections to Duncan Park was Susan Wood Pope, whose father, Ty Wood, was bat boy for the 1936 Post 28 Little World Series Champions, a player for the 1938 Legion team, a veteran Textile Leagues player, founder of the fondly re-membered Textile League reunions, and player for the Cleveland Indians farm team the Spartanburg Peaches. Susan possesses much of Ty Wood's Legion and Peaches memorabilia, and a number of images of those are to be found in these pages.

Among others who shared their knowledge and memories with me were four of my former colleagues in Spartanburg County School District Seven: Principal Chip Rivers, Director of Adult Education Morgan King, and math teacher extraordinaire Dan Smith, all of whom worked at Duncan Park sta-dium during their summers off; the fourth was teacher of economics Randy Foster, who also taught my son the guitar and shared his memories of the Hefty bag full of vintage baseball cards his mom made him throw out and the fistful of some 40 of those cards that he grabbed, saved from the garbage, and still cherishes today. Former district superintendents Dr. Thomas White and Dr. Russell Booker and current Superintendent Jeff Stevens also contributed in important ways to my understanding of District Seven's relationship with the City of Spartanburg and the preservation of the stadium. Eula Williams, my former colleague in the language arts department of McCracken Junior High School, shared her memories of children's birthday parties at the ballpark and an unexpected encounter with a baseball great. Former Spartanburg High School baseball coach Wes Brown, who was also coach of the Spartanburgers in the summer of 2021, was another of my informants.

Others who shared their information with me were Lenny Mathis, the founder and original president of the Friends of Duncan Park; architectural historian Donnie Love, who prepared the application that resulted in Duncan Park stadium's recognition on the National Register of Historic Places; Clemson University baseball coach Monte Lee; former Spartanburg Phillies broadcaster Mack Amick; Suzanne Brooks, the executive director of the Spartanburg County Historical Association; Spartanburg County Librarian Todd Stephens, the library's director of local history Charity Rouse, Assistant Director Brad Steinecke, and the Kennedy Room staff; longtime Spartanburg residents and baseball fans Vernon Beatty (also board secretary for Spartanburg County School District Seven), Don Bramblett, and Don Camby; Ed Dickerson, public address voice of both the Spartanburg Phillies and the Spartanburg High School Vikings; Mandy Merck, former City of Spartanburg special events manager and former keeper of the city's encyclopedic scrapbooks of newspaper clippings and other documents related to events in the city; Kenn Blankenship, Spartanburg sports radio personality and son of former Spartanburg Phillies General Manager Herbert E. "Hub" Blankenship; Terry Floyd, who played and coached at Duncan Park; Wayne Tolleson, player for Spartanburg High School and the New York Yankees; Marie "Rie" Boniface Duncan, wife of local attorney Michael Nelson Duncan, whose family sold the land for Duncan Park to the City of Spartanburg for a nominal amount; Danielle Eisner, former proprietor of The Duncan Estate, a property originally owned by the Duncan family; Katie DiPietro, current proprietor of The Duncan Estate; Tommy J. Ordoyne, professor at USC Upstate and member of the Friends of Duncan Park; George Taylor, proud dad of two sons who played at Duncan Park; John Featherstone, music promoter and proprietor of the Music Camp just outside Spartanburg; Billy Byars, whose archive of the Drayton community of Spartanburg is unequalled; Eric Shuffler, a minority owner of the Spartanburgers baseball team;

Joe Clarke, former Spartanburg High School principal and LA Dodgers collector extraordinaire; Jimmy Tobias, former Spartanburg Phillies bat boy and owner of Cedar Springs Pawn Shop; the Honorable Max Hyde, representing Spartanburg District 32 in the South Carolina General Assembly, also the nephew of Spartanburg Phillies broadcaster Warner Fusselle; Jerry Martin, who played in the outfield for the S-Phils in 1972 and then for 11 years in MLB for the Philadelphia Phillies, the Chicago Cubs, and others; and Dr. Frank Pickens, team physician for the Georgia Tech baseball team, who remembered watching Rocky Colavito play for the Peaches when he was a boy growing up in Spartanburg.

The national community of baseball researchers and public and institutional librarians have been invaluable to me in providing answers to my queries, suggesting resources, and guiding me to primary sources unknown to me as I undertook this journey. These experienced and graceful helpers include Fritz Hamer, the chief curator of history at the South Carolina State Museum; Dr. Pellom McDaniels III, Curator of African American Collections at the Stuart A. Rose Manuscript, Archives, & Rare Book Library at Emory University; Courtney E. Chartier and Randall K. Burkett, also of the Woodruff Library at Emory; Gayle Martinson, reference librarian for Library, Archives, and Museum Collections at the Wisconsin Historical Society; Mike Berry, archivist at South Carolina Political Collections, University of South Carolina Libraries; Dr. Raymond Doswell, vice president of Curatorial Services at the Negro Leagues Baseball Museum Inc. in Kansas City, Missouri; Larry Lester, author and chairman of the Negro League Committee of the Society for American Baseball Research (SABR); Wayne Stivers, Negro Leagues researcher, author, and collector; Dr. Layton Revel, founder and executive director of the Center for Negro League Baseball Research (CNLBR) in Carrollton, Texas; Cam Perron, Negro Leagues researcher, historian, and collector; SABR members Mark Aubrey, Bob Barrier, Patrick Gallagher, and Chuck McGIll; Cassidy Lent, reference librarian for the National Baseball Hall of Fame and Museum in Cooperstown, New York; and Terry Pluto, sports columnist for the Cleveland, Ohio, *Plain Dealer*. Linda Conley, staff writer for the *Spartanburg Herald-Journal* and goupstate.com, has written knowledgeably about Duncan Park stadium and the teams that played there many times; her pieces on Lefty Bob Branson and the Spartanburg Sluggers were especially helpful to me. Greenville author Mike Chibbaro alerted me in several instances to information about South Carolina athletes and coaches that I was not aware of and also graciously provided me with some pretty cool memorabilia.

The work of two filmmakers has been instructive to me, and I profited from becoming friends with both. Tim Farrell and his wife, Robyn Hussa Farrell, are co-directors and principals of White Elephant Enterprises, a production company based in South Carolina and California. White Elephant produced the 18-minute *Duncan Park Ball Field History* for The Balmer Foundation during the late stages of my work on this book, and we talked a number of times and collaborated on an interview featured in the film. Lauren Meyer in Hoboken, New Jersey, is executive producer of Tumbleweed Productions and the director of *The Other Boys of Summer*, a 42-minute documentary based upon the experiences of more than a dozen former Negro Leagues ballplayers and narrated by Cicely Tyson. Lauren brought her film to Spartanburg for five screenings in the community in February 2020, and I both learned from it and was inspired to interview one of Lauren's subjects, Robert "Bob" Scott, who lived in Macon, Georgia. Scott, who played in Spartanburg and for the New York Black Yankees and other well-known Negro Leagues teams, passed away not long after we talked. I also interviewed former Negro Leagues player Russell "Crazy Legs" Patterson, who now lives in South Carolina.

Finally I owe a huge debt to Executive Director Meg Reid, Managing Editor Kate McMullen, Sales and Marketing Assistant Julie Jarema, the staff of Hub City Press and a dream team if ever there was one. Hub City Press is the premier independent literary press in the South and now has published more than a hundred titles in the past quarter century, many of which are solidly place-based and written by authors from across the American South. Hub City Writers Project is a model of the many exemplary ways a visionary nonprofit can enrich its home community.

NOTES

• •

CHAPTER ONE:

Richard Irby, *History of Randolph-Macon College*, Virginia (Richmond: Whittet & Shepperson, n.d.), 65.

Major David R. Duncan, *Cyclopedia of Eminent and Representative Men of the Carolinas of the Nineteenth Century, I* (Madison, WI: Brant & Fuller, 1892), 256. Details of the Major's life are from this source unless otherwise noted.

"Park Commission and City Council Take Duncan Park," *The Spartanburg Herald*, 7 February 1923, 1.

The discussions with the Governor are provided in the article "City Park Commission Act Repealed When Governor Signs Bill; Arguments Made" by P. H. Fike in *The Spartanburg Herald*, 16 February 1923, 1-2.

"Cannot Develop Duncan Park; Deed Is Returned," *The Spartanburg Herald*, 17 February 1923, 3.

"The Delegation and Duncan Park," 8 March 1923, 4.

"Duncan Park Said to Have Been Accepted," 21 March 1923, 9.

Photocopy of deed provided by Marie Duncan.

"Bids on Stadium to Be Advertised." *Daily Herald*, 12 January 1926, 10.

CHAPTER TWO:

Microfilm accounts of the progress of construction on the stadium from January through June 1926, *Spartanburg Daily Herald* and *The Spartanburg Journal*, The Kennedy Room, Spartanburg County Public Libraries.

"Grandstand Seats Bought by Council," *The Spartanburg Herald*, 11 February 1926, 7.

"Huge Crowd Will Attend Opening of Duncan Stadium," *The Spartanburg Journal* and *The Carolina Spartan*, 8 July 1926, 6.

"Landis Expected to Attend Sally Opening in City," 16 February 1926, 1.

"Judge Landis Says Park Is Fine," *The Spartanburg Journal*, 28 July 1926, 1.

"1919 Spartanburg Pioneers," Baseball Reference, https://www.baseball-reference.com/register/team.cgi?id=745effef, accessed 25 July 2021.

"Doc Bass," Baseball Reference, https://www.baseballreference.com/register/player.fc-gi?id=bass--002wil, accessed 25 July 2021.

"Will Konigsmark," Baseball Reference, https://www.baseball-reference.com/register/player.fcgi?id=koenig002wil, accessed 25 July 2021.

All teams and players listed for these early years were confirmed via Baseball Reference web pages.

"Huge Crowd Will Attend Opening of Duncan Stadium," 6.

Bill Nowlin, "Hal Wagner," SABR Baseball Biography Project, http://sabr.org/bioproj/person/ac639ef9. Wagner's yearly totals are tallied at Baseball-Reference.com.

Bill Nowlin, "George Murray," SABR Baseball Biography Project, https://sabr.org/bioproj/person/george-murray.

Gregory H. Wolf, "Les Sweetland," SABR Baseball Biography Project, https://sabr.org/bioproj/person/les-sweetland.

Marshall D. Wright, *The South Atlantic League, 1904-1963: A Year-by-Year Statistical History* (Jefferson, NC, and London: McFarland & Company, Inc., Publishers, 2009). Baseball-Reference.com notes that Garms played in Spartanburg but does not list his stats for 1929.

Greg Erion, "Debs Garms," SABR Baseball Biography Project, https://sabr/bioproj/person/debs-garms. An especially well written and engaging example of the SABR Biography Project's important work.

CHAPTER THREE:

"On the circuit Spartanburg was part of the tour for nation's top black entertainers," GoUpstate.com, 20 February 2000, https://www.goupstate.com/news/20000220/on-the-circuit-spartanburg-was-part-of-the-tour-for-nation39s-top-black-entertainers; and "Baseball legend remembers the sluggers: 85-year-old still evokes memories," GoUpstate.com, 11 February 2001, https://www.goupstate.com/article/NC/20010211/News/605177568/SJ.

"Introducing the New Negro Leagues Database," The Baseball Gauge, 5 December 2016, https://thebaseballgauge.com/blog/index.php/2016/12/05/the-negro-leagues-database/

"Introduction," *The Biographical Encyclopedia of the Negro Baseball Leagues* (New York: Carroll & Graf Publishers, Inc., 1994), xix.

"Blue Ridge Colored Baseball League, 1921," Agate Type: Reconstructing Negro League and Latin American Baseball History, 9 March 2011, http://agatetype.typepad.com/agate_type/2011/03/blue-ridge-colored-baseball-league-1921.html.

Bill Ballew, *A History of Professional Baseball in Asheville* (Charleston and London: History Press, 2007); and Bob A. Nestor, *Baseball in Greenville and Spartanburg* (Charleston, Chicago, Portsmouth NH, and San Francisco: Arcadia Publishing, 2003).

"Sports," *The Hub City Observer*, 22 June 1929, 9.

"Sports," *The Hub City Observer*, 13 July 1929, 7.

I have interviewed Luther Norman, both formally and informally, many times. Although most of these interviews have taken place at The Episcopal Church of the Epiphany, some have occurred elsewhere, including at The Skillet on South Pine Street in Spartanburg, at Duncan Park stadium, at the new Spartanburg High School on East Main Street, and at the Spartanburg County Headquarters Library. Luther knows more about the Spartanburg Sluggers than anyone else now living and has a wealth of photos, documents, and memorabilia related to the team and the Whitmires who owned it.

Palmetto Conservation Foundation, Historical and Architectural Survey of Newberry County, South Carolina: Final Report (Columbia, SC: Palmetto Conservation Foundation, 2003), 52-54.

"Jesse Owens To Race Thursday at Duncan Park," *Daily Herald*, 13 July 1941, 21.

Pvt. Hiland Clay, "Week in Sports at Croft," *The Spartanburg Journal* and *The Carolina Spartan*, 20 July 1941, 26.

"Baseball and Boxing Feature 'Field Day' at New Duncan Park," *The Spartanburg Journal* and *The Carolina Spartan*, 31 August 1926, 6.

Jim Harbison, personal interview with Luther Norman, 13 May 2021.

"Negroes will commemorate their emancipation with elaborate program next Tuesday," *The Greenville News*, 22 August 1911, 6.

January and February 1948 *Daily Herald*.

"Spartanburg Sluggers Tangle With Chattanooga Here," *Daily Herald*, 7 June 1948, 7.

Layton Revel, private telephone communication, 25 April 2018.

"Preserving Negro League History Has Never Been Easier, or Harder, Depending on Who You Ask," *Smithsonian Magazine* (23 October 1918), https://www.smithsonianmag.com/history/preserving-negro-league-history-has-never-been-easier-or-harder-depending-who-you-ask-180970614/.

John Hammond Moore, *South Carolina Newspapers,* (Columbia: University of South Carolina Press in Cooperation with the South Caroliniana Library, 1988).

"Bids on Stadium To Be Advertised," *The Spartanburg Herald*, 12 January 1926, 10.

Edwin C. Epps, "In Search of the Greatest Baseball Player in the World," in *Stars Fell on Spartanburg: Hub City's Celebrity Encounters*, ed. Jeremy L. C. Jones and Betsy Wakefield Teter (Spartanburg: Hub City Writers Project, 2008), 26-29.

"Stage 'Carolina Day' at Yankee Stadium," *The Pittsburgh Courier*, 23 September 1944, 12.

"Semi-Pro Tourney Starts Tomorrow For Colored 9," *The [Orangeburg] Times and Democrat*, 15 July 1947, p. 9.

Bijan C. Bayne, "Early Black Baseball in North Carolina," *Tar Heel Junior Historian* 51, no. 1 (Fall 2011), 5—7.

"Atlanta All-Stars Engage Spartanburg At Poncey," *Atlanta Daily World*, 30 August 1942, 8.

For information about Wannamaker, Clifford, and Free, I am indebted to Luther Norman. For a heads-up on Alexander, I am grateful to Latria Graham, a Spartanburg writer who is also a cultural historian and baseball fan.

Another source of my information for Wanamaker, Free, Layton, and Carl Long was Negro Leagues researcher extraordinaire Wayne Stivers, personal email correspondence, 18 July 2020.

"Spartan Signs Milwaukee Contract," *Daily Herald*, 20 February 1955, 10.

Chick Jacobs, "Clifford Layton," The Fayetteville Observer, 28 February 2016, https://www.fayobserver.con/article/20160228/NEWS/302289843.

Adam Thompson, "Baseball: Playing with Pride," *New Bern Sun Journal*, 13 April 2013, https://newbernsj.com/article/20130413/Sports/304139874.

"Ken Free," Baseball Reference, https://www.baseball-reference.com/register/player.fcgi?id=free--001ken

Luther Norman, personal interview, 21 June 2019.

Rob Neyer, "Ted Alexander," Society for American Baseball Research, https://sabr.org/bioproj/person/ted-alexander/.

CHAPTER FOUR:

The most useful account of Kerby Farrell's career as both a player and manager is Andrew Sharp, "Kerby Farrell," Society for American Baseball Research, https://sabr.org/bioproj/person/kerby-farrell/, accessed November 10, 2020. Team and league statistics are available at baseball-reference.com.

"Light Failure Costs Spartanburg Victory," *The Gastonia Gazette*, 12 July 12 1946, 9. See also Tim Hagerty, "This Day in History: Prankster Shuts Off Stadium Lights in the Ninth Inning," *The Sporting News*, 20 July 2015, https://www.sportingnews.com/us/mlb/news/this-day-in-history-prankster-shuts-off-stadium-lights-spartanburg-duncan-park-knoxville/1gmlstkuwurp116hmda7xmpbxt. Accessed November 10, 2020.

Thomas K. Perry, *Textile League Baseball: South Carolina's Mill Teams, 1880-1955* (Jefferson, NC, and London: McFarland & Company, Inc., 1993), 99.

Susan W. Pope, personal email correspondence, 6 December 2020. Mrs. Pope is the daughter of Ty Wood. Both of her sons, Will and Adam, played baseball at Duncan Park for Spartanburg High School and American Legion Post 28.

Joseph Wancho, "Rocky Colavito," SABR BioProject, Society for American Baseball Research, https://sabr.org/bioproj/person/rocky-colavito/, accessed 18 November 2020. Wancho's biography of Colavito is well researched, comprehensive, and engaging. A more detailed, fuller account is *The Curse of Rocky Colavito* by Cleveland Plain Dealer journalist Terry Pluto (New York: Simon Simon & Schuster, 1994), a longtime friend of the ballplayer.

Kirk H. Neely, "My Introduction to Rocky Road Ice Cream," *Stars Fell on Spartanburg: Hub City's Celebrity Encounters*, ed. Jeremy L. C. Jones and Betsy Wakefield Teter

(Spartanburg: Hub City Writers Project, 208), 36-39.

Scott Ferkovich, "Lane Field (San Diego)," SABR BioProject, https://sabr.org/bioproj/park/lane-field-san-diego/, accessed 19 November 2020.

"Rocky Colavito," SABR BR Bullpen, https://www.baseball-reference.com/bullpen/Rocky_Colavito, accessed 19 November 2020.

According to "Tri-State League Threatens to Fold Over Negro Player," *The Media [Texas] Daily News*, 2 August 1954, 4. Other papers reported that Salvent played the whole game; see, for example, "Spartanburg Pulls Out Of League In Protest," *The Brownsville [Texas] Herald*, 2 August 1954, 8.

"Tri-State Caim [sic] Again As Spartanburg Back," *The [Sumter, SC] Item*, 4 August 1954, 7.

"Negro Player Banished; Tri-State Loop Continues," *Hartford Courant*, 4 August 1954, 9.

Atlanta Daily World, 12 August 1954, 5

"Peaches' Prexy Just Tired, Quits Baseball." *The Charlotte News*, 12 June 1952, 15.

"Spartanburg Trying to Save Ball Franchise," *The Greenville News*, 17 June 1952, 11.

"Spartanburg May Fall From Tri-State Loop," *Johnson City Press*, 15 September 1955, 19.

"Peaches Plan for '55 Season," *The Knoxville News-Sentinel*, 1 September 1954, 26.

CHAPTER FIVE:

For more on promotions and other attractions at Duncan Park stadium, see Chapter 8 below.

Jim Foster, "Council Votes 'Yes' On Pro Baseball Team," *The Spartanburg Herald*, 11 January 1963, 1.

Quoted in a discussion in the "Sparkle City Storyteller," Facebook, https://www.facebook.com/groups/sparklecitystoryteller/permalink/520601612285119/, accessed 19 May 2021.

John Lombardo, "Magic Man: Pat Williams, the NBA's Consummate Showman," *Sports Business Journal* (11 February 2013), https://www.sportsbusinessjournal.com/Journal/Issues/2013/02/11/Champions/Pat-Williams.aspx, accessed 5 July 2022, is a very good introduction to Pat Williams as both a major league sports executive and a man. A better one, especially about Williams's relationship with the Carpenters and his time as General manager of the Spartanburg Phillies, is the one by Williams himself in his memoir *Ahead of the Game: The Pat Williams Story*, with James D. Denny (Grand Rapids: Fleming H. Revel, A Division of Baker Book House, 1999), especially in chapters 1-3.

Steve Potter and Larry Shenk, "Class A Affiliates," typescript chapter of *Life in the Minors: 5th Annual Phillies Minor League Digest*, Foreword by Tom McCarthy, ed. Jim Peyton (Independently published, 5 February 2021).

Pat Williams, personal interview with the author, 10 November 2015.

Pat Williams, telephone interview with the author, 21 December 2022.

A good overview of Gordon's career is that by Steve Thornley for the SABR Biography

Project, https://sabr.org/bioproj/person/john-gordon, accessed 11 December 2020.

John Gordon, personal interview with the author, 17 August 2022.

Legends Start in Spartanburg: 25th Anniversary Issue Official Magazine of the 1988 Spartanburg Phillies, 25.

Tim Herlich, "Ryne Sandberg," SABR Biography Project, 10 September 2019, https://sabr. org/bioproj/person/ryne-sandberg/, accessed July 22, 2021.

"Warner Fusselle (2002) on His Career and Baseball," YouTube (4 January 2019), https://www. youtube.com/watch?v=loGq6__N4cw&list=PLm3MTzB9i2v_OmMYrvhJzGtKo_1-w_ dVo&index=2, accessed 21 July 2021.

Kenn Blankenship, personal interview, 3 November 2015.

Ed Dickerson, personal interview, 21 May 2018.

SMC News (2021), https://www.smcsc.edu/category/smc-news/, accessed July 21, 2021.

Mack Amick, personal interview, 14 November 2016.

Ken McMillan, "Meet the GM: Rosie Putnam fills non-traditional role," 1991 Spartanburg Phillies Souvenir Program, 9. This is the best account of Putnam and her time with the Phillies that I have been able to locate.

"$38,000 Ball Park Work OK'd," *The Spartanburg Herald*, 10 January 1967, 9.

1974 Spartanburg Phillies Souvenir Program.

Tom Miller, "As Bid to Keep Phils, Council OKs New Lights," *The Spartanburg Herald*, 18 September 1973, B1.

Jim Fair, "Marshall Tucker Band Wants To Buy S-Phils," *The Spartanburg Herald-Journal*, 16 April 1978; John Gwinn, "City, Phillies At Odds Again Over Park," *The Spartanburg Herald-Journal*, 21 June 1978, 21.

Ultimately the City, the Philadelphia Phillies, and the Spartanburg Phillies combined to spend more than $70,000 on improvements. Jim Fair, "Ballpark Renovation Passes $70,000," *The Spartanburg Herald*, 30 May 1979, D2.

Leslie Timms, Sports Editor, *The Spartanburg Journal and The Carolina Spartan*, 13 September 1979, 25.

"New Owners Set to Go," *The Spartanburg Journal and The Carolina Spartan*, 4 January 1979, 14.

Three sources here: an otherwise unidentified newspaper clipping, "Weir to Buy S-Phils from Oklahoma City Group" by Jim Fair, *The Spartanburg Herald*, 6 November 1979, 12, and another entitled simply "Phillies" from the Metro, both pasted into the city of Spartanburg local features scrapbook for August 1979—May 1951; also Terry Hamilton, "Traders Plan 'Family Fun' Season, *The Spartanburg Herald-Journal*, 14 January 1980, 9.

Attendance figures are those recorded in "Spartanburg Phillies Franchise History (1963-1994)," Stats Crew, www. statscrew.com/minorbaseball/t-sp14649, accessed July 24, 2021.

Tim Wheatley, "City May Lose Minor League Franchise," *The Spartanburg Herald-Journal*,

28 January 1983, C1.

Tim Wheatley, "Spartanburg Team Gets a New Nickname, Logo," *The Spartanburg Herald-Journal*, 22 February 1983, B2.

Tim Wheatley, "Spinners' Bastien Pleads Innocent to Car Caper," *The Spartanburg Herald-Journal*, 16 July 1983, 12.

Tim Wheatley, "Eliopulos 'Assumes' He Owns Spinners," *The Spartanburg Herald-Journal*, 2B.

Jim Fair, "Spartanburg Gets New Nickname, GM," *The Spartanburg Herald-Journal*, 2B.

Scott Fowler, "Suns Are For Sale, Little Interest Shown," *The Spartanburg Herald-Journal*, 19 December 1985, C1.

Steve Sanders, "S-Phillies Ownership Gets National Flavor," *The Spartanburg Herald-Journal*, 17 February 1986, B1.

Dan Smith, personal interview with the author, 5 August 2004.

Debra Lester, "Minor League Team Has Two Owners?" *The Spartanburg Herald-Journal*, 27 March 1986, D1; and Jim Fair, "Wright Uses Her Money To Pay S-Phil Players," *The Spartanburg Herald-Journal*, 16 April 1986, A1.

Steve Sanders, "Frustrated Phils Finally Get to Play Ball, *The Spartanburg Herald-Journal*, 12 April 1986, 15; and Jim Fair, "Phillies Ready to Leave Town, Official Says," *The Spartanburg Herald-Journal*, 12 April 1986, A1.

"S-Phillies Robbed," *The Spartanburg Herald-Journal*, 24 May 1986, B1.

"Erdman, Wilhite Given Jail Terms," *The Spartanburg Herald-Journal*, 19 July 1986, C1.

Randy Beard, "Clean, But Still Empty, Are the Seats at Duncan Park," *The Spartanburg Herald-Journal*, 3 May 1987, C1. The other facts in this paragraph are also from Beard's piece.

"City Council Agrees to Lease for Phillies," GoUpstate.com, 9 October 1990, https://www.goupstate.com/article/NC/19901009/News/605197709/SJ, accessed July 24, 2021.

"N. C. Group Bidding for S-Phillies," GoUpstate.com, 20 October 20, 1992, www.goupstate.com/article/NC/19921020/News/605198170/SJ, accessed July 24, 2021.

Andy Friedlander, "Decision Day for Duncan?" *The Spartanburg Herald-Journal*, 11 July 1994, City of Spartanburg local news scrapbook, April 1994—February 1997.

Jim Fair, "S-Phillies Say They'll Be Back," *The Spartanburg Herald-Journal*, 15 October 1992, D1.

"S-Phillies Management Upset at Lack of Fan Support," *The Spartanburg Herald-Journal*, 12 July 1992, D5.

Andy Friedlander, "Phillies Trying to Fill Seats," *The Spartanburg Herald-Journal*, 22 June 1993, D1, D4.27 October 1993, D1.

Andy Friedlander, "Hedrick Anxious to Own S-Phillies," *The Spartanburg Herald-Journal*, 23 November 1993, A1.

Andy Friedlander, "Phillies Went Out with a Bang," *The Spartanburg Herald-Journal*, 2

September 1994, B7.

CHAPTER SIX:

Brian L. Robson, "American Legion Building," United States Department of the Interior/National Park Service National Register of Historic Places Registration Form ([Washington, DC], 18 April 2003).

John J. Barron, "A Rich and Exciting 80 Year History," Spartanburg American Legion Post 28 2013 Program [Spartanburg: American Legion Post 28, 2013]. Barron, the Post 28 Athletic Director at the time this book was being written, continued the story of Post 28 baseball in the team's Programs for 2014 and 2015, and was of invaluable assistance to the author, providing information via interviews, email correspondence, and numerous telephone conversations.

Another unique source of information, cited below, was Jesse "Gene-O" Campbell, Post 28's "Mr. Baseball."

Ms. Pope was helpful far beyond what I expected when I visited her in her home to see her dad's memorabilia and to chat with her about her dad's playing days—and her two sons' as well—at Duncan Park stadium. Many of the original photos and items of memorabilia photographed for this chapter and in the one about the Spartanburg Peaches belong to her. I am indebted to her for her assistance with this project.

"History of American Legion Baseball," American Legion, www.legion.org/baseball/history, 2022, accessed 21 October 2022

The State newspaper in Columbia, SC, celebrated the importance of the occasion with an inning by inning account of the game, and it devoted substantial space to the accounts of games two through five as well. A collection of clippings of these accounts, discovered by Wofford graduate W. N. Bennett of Hemingway and given to B. G. Stephens, was photocopied by Don Camby for the author. Among these clippings is a photo of part of the crowd that attended the final game, some 20,000 fans who watched "from every available hillock, pine tree, auto top, and soap box in South Spartanburg."

Gary Henderson, "Glory Days Still Fresh for Reunited Players," *The Spartanburg Herald-Journal*, 2 September 1997, A1.

"Baseball," Chapter IX of *The American Legion in South Carolina: The First Thirty Years*, edited by Robert T. Fairey (N. p.: The American Legion Department of South Carolina, 195?), 109-121.

John Barron, Piedmont Historical Association presentation. Spartanburg County Public Libraries, 13 April 2017.

Collection of Susan Wood Pope; also the collection of the Spartanburg County Regional Museum of History. Often reprinted.

Jesse E. "Gene-O" Campbell, personal interview, American Legion Post 28 Headquarters,

28 October 2015.

Wayne Tolleson, personal telephone interview, 24 March 2022.

Jesse E. "Gene" Campbell, personal interview, American Legion Post 28 Headquarters, 4 November 2015.

Campbell, personal interview, 28 October 2015.

Campbell, personal interview, 4 November 2015.

Spartanburg American Legion Post 28 2014 Program, [4].

Todd Shanesy, "Spartanburg Rips Greer in American Legion Opener," GoUpstate.com, 25 May 2010, https://www.goupstate.com/article/NC/20100525/Sports/605154252/SJ, accessed 16 June 2021.

"Brian Peahuff," Spartanburg American Legion Post 28 Program.

Rory Costello, "Terry Hughes," SABR Biography Project, 2015, https://sabr.org/bioproj/person/terry-hughes/, accessed 17 June 2021.

Wayne Tolleson, personal telephone interview, 24 March 2022.

"Wayne Tolleson," Baseball Reference, 17 March 2019, https://www.baseball-reference.com/bullpen/Wayne_Tolleson, accessed 26 June 2021; Keith Jarrett, "Catching Up with… Wayne Tolleson," *Citizen-Times*, 17 August 2014, https://www.citizen-times.com/story/sports/2014/08/17/catching-wayne-tolleson/14210307/, accessed 21 June 2021.

CHAPTER SEVEN:

When Nobody Knows Your Name: Life in the Minor Leagues of Baseball (New York: Doubleday, 2014), 2.

Pat Williams with James D. Denney, *Ahead of the Game: The Pat Williams Story* (Grand Rapids: Fleming H. Revel, 1999), 76.

Pat Williams, personal interview, Orlando, FL, 10 November 2015.

Bill Veeck with Ed Linn, *Veeck as in Wreck* (1962; Chicago: The University of Chicago Press, 2001).

Morgan King, personal interview, 3 August 2004.

Ed Dickerson, personal interview.

There are lots of accounts of the legendary Bandit. One good one is Sue Anne Pressley, "Kissing Bandit Steals Back to Her Baltimore Roots," *The Washington Post*, 20 June 1988, https://www.washingtonpost.com/archive/local/1988/06/20/kissing-bandit-steals-back-to-her-baltimore-roots/be26c894-0dbc-4032-93d1-55192ff2d49d/. Another, with a surprising connection to the Atlanta Braves is "Braves Throwback Thursday: Clete Boyer 'Victimized' by Morganna the Kissing Bandit, 50 years ago this month," Battery Power, 22 August 2019, https://www.batterypower.com/2019/8/22/20827757/atlanta-braves-throwback-thursday-clete-boyer-victimized-by-morganna-the-kissing-bandit, accessed 9 June

2022.

A good profile of this "artist" can be found at "Henri LaMothe," Flatiron 23rd Street Partnership, 1 April 2009, https://www.flatirondistrict.nyc/discover-flatiron/flatiron-history/henri-lamothe.

Murray Cook, telephone interview with the author, 18 August 2022.

The King and His Court Official Souvenir, [Ramona, CA, 1987?].

Jose Franco, "Visit from 'Pretty Woman' Once Stirred Up Upstate," GoUpstate.com, 25 March 2001, https://www.goupstate.com/article/NC/20010325/News/605179374/SJ, accessed 2 July 2021.

"The Ultimate Fan: Libby's Heart Belongs to the Phillies," GoUpstate.com, 21 June 1992, https://www.goupstate.com/article/NC/19920621/News/605194461/SJ", accessed 3 July 2021. The games that Libby missed during that span were all because of the deaths of friends.

Jerry Martin, personal interview, 2 April 2017.

Bull Durham, IMDb, https://www.imdb.com/title/tt0094812/, accessed 3 July 2021.

Jimmy Tobias, personal interview, 27 October 2015.

Eula Williams, email correspondence, 29 October 2015.

"Spartanburg Phillies Franchise History," Stats Crew, www.statscrew.com/minorbaseball/t-sp14649, accessed 24 July 2021.

"1988 Spartanburg Phillies Promotional Schedule," *Legends Start in Spartanburg*: *Official Magazine of the 1988 Spartanburg Phillies*, 52.

"1993 Spartanburg Phillies Promotional Schedule," Spartanburg Phillies: Real Grass, Real Dirt, Real Family Fun [1993 Souvenir Program], 4-5. Stats Crew.

Chris Thomasson, "Phillies Make Their Final Pitch," *The Spartanburg Herald-Journal*, 1 September 1994, D1, D9.

CHAPTER EIGHT:

https://Upstatespartans.com/sports/baseball, accessed 30 July 2021

Codie Kunstmann, USC Upstate Associate Athletic Communications Director, personal correspondence, 2 August 2021.

"1995 Atlantic Coast League," Baseball Reference, https://www.baseball-reference.com/register/league.cgi?id=fc27b646, accessed 31 July 2021.

"Buzz Capra," Baseball Reference, https://www.baseball-reference.com/register/player.fcgi?id=capra-001lee, accessed 31 July 2021.

"1995 Spartanburg Alley Cats," Baseball Reference, https://www.baseball-reference.com/register/team.cgi?id=5b18b370, accessed 31 July 2021.

"Russell C. King Field," https://woffordterriers.com/facilities/russell-c-king-field/3, accessed 3 August 2021.

"Team Season Records," 2021 Wofford Baseball Media Guide, 47.

"2001 Schedule," Spartanburg Crickets program insert.

Lou Parris, "Missing Support," GoUpstate.com, www.goupstate.com/article/NC/20010731/News/605184142/SJ, accessed 3 August 2021.

"Spartanburg Crickets 2002," Welcome to Cricket Baseball Southern Division Tournament 2002.

Welcome to Cricket Baseball 2004, [Spartanburg Crickets 2004 roster handout].

Brian Peahuff, "Crickets Eager to get Season Under Way," GoUpstate.com, www.goupstate.com/article/NC/20050601/News/605169266/SJ, accessed 3 August 2021.

"2003 Spartanburg Stingers Roster," Spartanburg Stingers Souvenir Scorecard insert.

"Spartanburg Stingers Baseball Have Opening Game at Historic Duncan Park," spartanburg.com Community News, www.spartanburg.com/news/stingershost.html, accessed 5 August 2021.

"Spartanburg Stingers," Baseball Reference, www.baseball-reference.com/bullpen/Spartanburg_Stingers, accessed 5 August 2021.

Details of actual and projected expenditures for maintenance, repairs, and potential renovations and expansion of the ballpark which follow come primarily from the pages of *The Spartanburg Herald*, *The Spartanburg Journal*, and *The Spartanburg Herald-Journal* from 1966 through 2020.

Contract between the Spartanburg Crickets and the city of Spartanburg, [illegible month and day], 2002, for the summers of 2003 and 2004 with an option for 2005; also, contract between Coastal Plain League, LLC, and the City of Spartanburg, 14 January 2003, for summers 2003 and 2004. city of Spartanburg archives.

Shelly Haskins, "Duncan Park Wall Comes Tumbling Down," *The Spartanburg Herald-Journal*, 18 May 1995, 15.

Minutes, Spartanburg City Council meeting, 28 October 1996. City archives.

Gary Henderson, "Spartanburg Considers Fate of Duncan Park Baseball Stadium, *The Spartanburg Herald-Journal*, 31 October 1998, https://www.goupstate.com/news/19981031/spartanburg-considers-fate-of-duncan-park-baseball-stadium, accessed 5 August 2021. All details in this paragraph come from this source.

Letter from Michael N. Duncan to Steve Cunningham, 18 September 2002. Office of City Clerk, Connie Littlejohn.

CHAPTER NINE:

Lenny Mathis, personal email communication, 27 August 2021.

Unless indicated to the contrary, information about the Friends, their communications, and their meetings in this section comes from email messages sent out by Lenny Mathis or the hotmail Friends account. Later communications from these Friends accounts were labeled "editions" of the Friends Newsletter.

Edwin C. Epps, Notes, Friends of Duncan Park Meeting, 24 September 2005.

Lane Filler, "Some City Money Available for Duncan Park stadium," *The Spartanburg Herald-Journal*, 24 July 2006, A11.

Robert W. Dalton, "Too Little, Too Late?" *The Spartanburg Herald-Journal*, 6 August 2006, A1, A14.

Lane Filler, "Sports vs. Culture: It's No Contest," *The Spartanburg Herald-Journal*, 6 August 2006, A1, A9.

Lynne P. Shackleford and Ashlei N. Stevens, "District 7 Might Revive Duncan Park stadium," Goupstate.com, www.goupstate.com/article/NC/20070803/News/605209992/SJ, accessed 8 August 2021.

Myles Wilson and Thomas White, personal interview, 13 February 2017.

Ed Epps, "A Glimmer at the End of the Tunnel: Updating the Drive to Save Duncan Park," *Spartanburg Today*, 1 August 2007.

Lynne P. Shackleford, "Deal to Share Historic Duncan Park Sealed," GoUpstate.com, 13 May 2008, https://www.goupstate.com/article/NC/20080513/News/605172461/SJ, accessed 1 September 2021.

Memo of Understanding between Spartanburg County School District No. 7 and city of Spartanburg, 7 January 2013.

Adam Orr, "Latest Duncan Park stadium Upgrades Nearing Completion," GoUpstate.com, 8 February 2019, https://www.goupstate.com/news/20190208/latest-duncan-park-stadium-upgrades-nearing-completion, accessed 2 September 2021.

Thomas White, personal email correspondence, 2 September 2021.

National Sports Services (www.nsssports.com), the principals in the South Carolina Family Entertainment partnership which owned the Spartanburgers, were highly experienced and already owned other teams in the region. Their no-nonsense business smarts as well as their appreciation for baseball history and one-of-a-kind historic facilities like Duncan Park stadium were promising for the future of the stadium.

"Spartanburgers to Honor Negro League Sluggers During Weekend Games at Duncan Park," GoUpstate.com, 15 July 2021, https://www.goupstate.com/story/news/local/2021/07/15/spartanburgers-honor-negro-league-sluggers-duncan-park-baseball-history-south-carolina/7963682002/, accessed 1 August 2021.

Lenny Mathis, email correspondence, 27 August 2021.

BIBLIOGRAPHY

· ·

In addition to the citations for sources of specific information included in the Notes, these additional sources were valuable in providing necessary general background information. Of particular help were the personal interviews.

INTERVIEWS AND PERSONAL COMMUNICATIONS

Beatty, Vernon. Personal interview, 30 September 2017.

Booker, Dr. Russell, and Luther Norman. Personal interview, 14 January 2020.

Byars, Billy Joe and Johnie. Personal interview, 8 June 2018.

Camby, Don. Personal interview, 2 February 2016.

Clarke, Joe. Personal Interview, 20 April 2017.

Duncan, Marie. Personal interview, 31 May 2018.

Featherstone, John. Personal interview, 12 July 2018.

Floyd, Terry. Personal interview, 22 March 2017.

Foster, Randy. Personal interview, 30 June 2022.

Haselden, Terry. Personal interview, 3 February 2017.

Lawrence, Jack. Personal telephone interview, 3 January 2023.

Lee, Monte. Personal interview via FaceTime, 9 January 2018.

Lester, Larry. Personal email communication, 16 July 2020

Love, Donnie. Personal email communication, 27 August 2021; personal interview, 18 December 2018.

Meyer, Lauren. Personal telephone interview, 20 April 2018.

Personal email communications, 2 July 2019; 5 September 2019; 15 September 2019; 2 March 2020; 20 March 2020; 6 July 2020; 28 March 2021; 18 December 2021

Personal interview, 17 February 2020 and additional dates 2021-2022.

Ordoyne, Tommy. Telephone interview, 14 September 2005.

Patterson, Russell "Crazy Legs," and Luther Norman. Personal interview, 26 August 2020.

Pickens, Frank M. Personal email communication, 21 August 2017.

Pinson, Bobby. Telephone interview with the author, 28 February 2022.

Pope, Susan Wood. Personal interview with the author, 5 November 2015.

Rivers, Chip. Personal interview with the author, August 2004.

Scott, Robert "Bob." Personal interview, 28 March 2019.

Shaw, James. Telephone interview with the author, 10 January 2023.

Shenk, Larry. Telephone interview with the author, 15 September 2022.

Shuffler, Eric. Personal interview, 28 July 2021; telephone interview, 4 September 2021.

Stoddard, Wesley and Robert. Personal interview, 8 January 2016.

Thornton, Andre. Telephone interview with the author, 17 August 2022.

Wilson, Myles. Personal interview with the author, 20 October 2015.

Wilson, Myles, and Dr. Thomas White, personal interview with the author, 13 February 2017.

BOOKS

Potter, Steve, and Larry Shenk. *Life in the Minors: 5th annual Phillies Minor League Digest.* Foreword by Tom McCarthy. Ed. Jim Peyton. Privately published, 5 February 2021.

PERIODICALS

"American Legion Baseball." *American Legion*, 2022. https://www.legion.org/baseball. Accessed 21 October 2022.

Ashwill, Gary. "Blue Ridge Colored Baseball League, 1921." *Agate Type: Reconstructing Negro League and Latin American Baseball History,* 9 March 2011. http://agatetype.typepad.com/agate_type/2011/03/blue-ridge-colored-baseball-league-1921.html. Accessed 5 June 2022.

Beard, Randy. "The 'Phillies' Return Again." *Spartanburg Herald-Journal*, 4 February 1986, p. B2.

and Steve Sanders. "The Success of '60s is Gone." *Spartanburg Herald-Journal*, 4 May 1986, pp. A1, A13.

"Brian Peahuff," Spartanburg American Legion Post 28 Program. [Spartanburg: American Legion Post 28, 2019].

Caldwell, Jud. "Eliopulos Seeks Full Accounting." *Spartanburg Herald-Journal*, 1 July 1986, p. B3.

Contract between Coastal Plain League, LLC, and the City of Spartanburg, 14 January 2003, for summers 2003 and 2004. City of Spartanburg archives.

Contract between the Harrisburg Baseball Club and the City of Spartanburg, 21 September 1987, City of Spartanburg archives.

Contract between Peake Construction Co. and the City of Spartanburg, 24 September 1990, for "Concrete Rehabilitation at Duncan Park Grandstand." City of Spartanburg archives.

Contract between Southeastern Roofing Company and the City of Spartanburg for "Roofing Duncan Park Stadium." City of Spartanburg archives.

Cooper, Rick. "Roberts Starts New Chapter." *Spartanburg Herald-Journal*, 13 February 1992, p. D4.

"Roberts Takes Calm Manner to Big Leagues." *Spartanburg Herald-Journal*, 4 June 1992, p. D1.

"Duncan Estate Will Be Developed Into Park," *Spartanburg Herald*, 22 March 1923, p. 9.

Fair, Jim. "City Wants Phillies to Make Up Their Minds." Spartanburg Herald-Journal, 7 October 1992, p. D1.

"Eliopolus [sic] Retains Control of Suns," *Spartanburg Herald-Journal*, 24 April 1986, p. A1.

"It Might Be Time to Say Goodbye to S-Phils." *Spartanburg Herald-Journal*, 10 September 1992, p. D1.

"More Than One Battle Set for Duncan Park," *Spartanburg Herald-Journal*, 22 April 1986, p. 2B.

Greg, Erion "Debs Garms." *SABR Baseball Biography Project*, https:sabr.org/bioproj/debs-garms. Accessed 2 June 2022.

Jackson, Marion E. "Sports of the World." *Atlanta Daily World*, 12 August 1954, p. 5.

Lester, Debra. "Lawsuit Is Filed Over Suns' Sale." *Spartanburg Herald-Journal*, 11 March 1986, p. 2B.

Mathis, Lenny. Newsletter communications issued by The Friends of Duncan Park, various dates, 2005-2006.

Mooty, Melinda. "Team Assets: Recognition, Entertainment." *Spartanburg Herald-Journal*, 13 September 1992, p. B1.

"New Park Drives Almost Finished." *Spartanburg Herald*, 17 March 1924, p. 3.

"Opening Night Activities Slated at Renovated Duncan Park." *Spartanburg Herald-Journal*, 8 April 1979, p. 21.

"Parks Are Taken Over by City Commission." *Spartanburg Herald,* 21 February 1923, p. 10.

"Phillies to Hold News Conference." *Spartanburg Herald-Journal*, 14 October 1992, p. B1.

Pickles, Jim. Open letter to the people of Spartanburg. *Spartanburg Herald-Journal*, 12 July 1992, p. D5.

Robson, Brian L. "American Legion Building," United States Department of the Interior/ National Park Service National Register of Historic Places Registration Form, [Washington, DC:],18 April 2003.

Roper, Wayne. "Two Pennsylvania Businessmen Buy S-Phils." The Greenville News, 16 July 1986, p. 2D.

Salsameda, Chloe. "City, Fans React to Spartanburgers Suspending Season." WSPA-TV, 4 March 2022.

Sanders, Steve. "S-Phils Fanfare Takes Backseat to Problems." *Spartanburg Herald-Journal*, ^ 1 June 1986, C1.

Sauer, Patrick. "Preserving Negro League History Has Never Been Easier, or Harder, Depending on Who You Ask." Smithsonian Magazine, 23 October 2018, https://www.smithsonianmag.com/history/preserving-negro-league-history-has-never-been-easier-or-harder-depending-who-you-ask-180970614/. Accessed 5 June 2022.

Smith, Eileen. "Local Ownership of S-Phils Nears Formal Approval." *Spartanburg Herald*, 20 November 1979, p. B2.

SMC News, 2021, https://www.smcsc.edu/category/smc-news/. Accessed 21 July 2021.

Stanley, Jeff. "Suns' Sale Imminent." *Spartanburg Herald-Journal*, 24 January 1986, p. B1.

"Suns' Case Dismissed." *Spartanburg Herald-Journal*, 4 June 1986, p. C1.

The State. Series of newspaper clippings of articles from The State in the summer of 1936 during the American Legion Little World Series played in Spartanburg. These accounts, discovered by Wofford graduate W. N. Bennett of Hemingway and given to B. G. Stephens, were copied by Don Camby for the author.

Thomasson, Chris. "Time for Phillies to Change Name." *Spartanburg Herald-Journal*, 5 August 1993, p. D1.

"2003 Spartanburg Stingers Roster." [Spartanburg Stingers Souvenir Scorecard insert.] [Spartanburg Stingers, 2003.]

Wheatley, Tim. "Eliopulos 'Assumes' He Owns Spinners." *Spartanburg Herald-Journal*, 25 October 1983, p. 2B.

"Spinners Begin Home Season." *Spartanburg Herald-Journal,* 11 April 1983, p. 11.

Whisnant, Gabe. "Spartanburgers to Honor Negro League Sluggers During Weekend Games at Duncan Park." *Go Upstate*, 15 July 2021, https://www.goupstate.com/story/news/local/2021/07/15/spartanburgers-honor-negro-league-sluggers-duncan-park-baseball-history-south-carolina/7963682002/. Accessed 1 August 2021.

MEDIA

Duncan Park Ball Field History. A White Elephant Enterprises Film. Co-Directed by Tim Farrell and Robyn Hussa Farrell. Executive Producer: The Balmer Foundation. San Diego and Spartanburg, SC: White Elephant Enterprises, n.d. whiteelephantenterprises.com.

Duncan Park Stadium: 85 Years of Baseball Memories. Script and narration: Dr. Albert Bolognese. Photography and editing: Mark S. Nortz. [Rock Hill, SC:] Albert Bolognese and Mark S. Nortz, Winthrop University, 2011. DVD video, also available on YouTube.

ABOUT THE AUTHOR

. . . .

DR. EDWIN C. EPPS is a retired educator with more than forty years' experience in public school classrooms, as an instructor in graduate classes for teachers, and as Lead Instructor in South Carolina's Program for Alternative Certification of Educators (PACE) for teachers entering the classroom from the worlds of business and industry. He has published widely in the education press, as an occasional poet, and as a freelancer. He is the author of Literary South Carolina (Hub City Press, 2004) and a proud member of Phi Beta Kappa who believes in the value of the humanities in a rapidly changing world.

HUB CITY WRITERS PROJECT is an imprint of Hub City Press focused on highlighting Spartanburg voices. Founded in Spartanburg, South Carolina in 1995, Hub City Press has emerged as the South's premier independent literary press. Focused on finding and spotlighting new and extraordinary voices from the American South, the press has published over one-hundred high-caliber literary works, including novels, short stories, poetry, memoir, and books emphasizing the region's culture and history. Hub City is interested in books with a strong sense of place and is committed to introducing a diverse roster of lesser-heard Southern voices including: people of color, members of LGBTQ and gender diverse communities, people with disabilities, neurodivergent people, as well as ethnic, cultural, and religious minorities.